Most CelebrityPress® titles are available at special quantity discounts for bulk purchases for sales promotions, premiums, fundraising, and educational use. Special versions or book excerpts can also be created to fit specific needs.

For more information, please write:
CelebrityPress®
520 N. Orlando Ave, #2
Winter Park, FL 32789
or call 1.877.261.4930

Visit us online at: www.CelebrityPressPublishing.com

CRACKING
THE CODE TO
SUCCESS

CelebrityPress®
Winter Park, Florida

CONTENTS

CHAPTER 1

SELL YOUR WAY TO SUCCESS

BY BRIAN TRACY

This is a great time to be alive. As of 2016, there are 10,600,000 millionaires and 2,473 billionaires in the world, fully 87% of whom started with nothing and then got into business of some kind and became wealthy. Your goal should be to do the same. This chapter will help you to achieve all the riches you desire.

No matter what kind of business you are in, you are in the sales and marketing business. Your financial success will depend upon your ability to find qualified prospects and then convert them into paying customers. Fortunately, selling is a skill. In fact, you could be only one skill away from doubling your income and putting yourself onto the high road to riches.

Millions of dollars have been spent on research with thousands of customers to discover exactly how and why they buy. When you learn and practice these ideas, you will make more sales, faster, than ever before.

MASTER THE ART

Selling is an art as well as a science. The effective sales process has several moving parts. Your ability to identify and then master each of the key result areas of selling is essential for you to earn the maximum income that is possible for you.

When Vince Lombardi took over the Green Bay Packers some years ago, he was asked what he was going to change. The players? The plays? The training process? How was he going to turn this team around after a string of failures and several bad years?

BRILLIANT ON THE BASICS

Lombardi is reported to have replied, "I am not going to change anything. We will use the same players, the same plays and the same training system. But we will concentrate on becoming *brilliant on the basics*. Before I am finished, we will be the best team in the National Football League in kicking, passing, blocking, running and catching. We will run our plays with such precision that the other side will know what we are going to do, but will be unable to stop us. We will be brilliant on the basics."

This principle applies to you as well. Your job is to become brilliant on the basics of selling. This begins by your identifying the seven essential parts of the professional selling process and then by developing a plan to upgrade your skills in each area.

Fortunately, all sales skills are *learnable.* It does not matter how well you have performed in different areas in the past. You can learn any sales skill that you need to learn to achieve any sales goal that you can set for yourself.

JOIN THE TOP 10%

Everyone in the top 10% of your field started in the bottom 10%. Everyone who is doing well today was once doing poorly. The top people in your industry were at one time not even in your industry and did not know that it existed. But once they began, they committed themselves to becoming excellent in each of the key result areas that make up the successful sale.

Here is an important discovery. Your *weakest* key skill sets the height of your income. Just as a chain breaks at the weakest link, the skill at which you perform the worst determines how many sales and how much money you will earn. By improving a single skill, the one skill that can help you the most, you can increase your sales and your income faster than in any other way.

Here is the key question: *"What one skill, if you were absolutely excellent at it, would help you the most to double your sales and your income?"*

This is one of the most important questions you will ever ask and answer. When you ask yourself this question, the answer will usually jump into your mind. If you are not sure of the answer, it is essential that you find out, and find out quickly. Ask your manager. Ask your best customers. Ask your colleagues. You must know your weakest skill if you are going to improve in that area and unlock your full potential for higher income.

BE THE BEST AT WHAT YOU DO

In the pages ahead, I will give you the seven key result areas of selling and show you how to improve your performance and your ability in each one.

Give yourself a grade of 1 to 10 in each of the key result areas of selling. A 1 means that you are low in that area and 10 means you are highly skilled in that area. Be honest with yourself. If you are not sure about the accuracy of your answers, review your personal scores with your sales manager, or someone else who knows the truth about your sales ability. The starting point of personal improvement is when you become absolutely honest with yourself and others about the areas in which improvement can have the greatest impact on your sales.

1. Talk to More People

The first key result area of selling is *prospecting*. This is defined as your ability to get face-to-face or ear-to-ear with qualified prospects who can and will buy your product or service within a reasonable period of time.

Please note that this does not mean that you talk to lots of interesting people who may or may not buy your product sometime in the future. Prospecting requires that you spend more and more time with people who can buy and pay for what you are selling in the very near future.

A score of 10 means that you are fully occupied talking to qualified prospects, every hour of every day, and you have so many prospects that you cannot take on any more. You may even have an appointments secretary who keeps track of people who are eager to talk to you and to buy from you. If this is your situation today, you would give yourself a 10.

A score of 1 means that you are a lonely person. You sit around the office like the Maytag repairman. You don't phone anyone and no one calls you. You probably drink a lot of coffee, read the newspaper, play on the Internet, and chat with your friends much of the time.

It is easy to give yourself a grade on the subject of prospecting. Just calculate what percentage of your time is spent each day with prearranged prospects. If it is 50%, give yourself a 5. If it is 70%, give yourself a 7. Your goal is to get to 80%.

2. They Have to Like You

The second key result area of selling is *establishing rapport, trust and credibility.* People will not buy from you until they like you, trust you and are convinced that you are their friend and acting in their best interests.

A score of 10 in this area means that you are a positive, cheerful, high energy individual with a warm, empathetic personality and you get along wonderfully with almost everyone you meet. A score of 1 means that you may get to see or talk to people for the first time, but after that, they never want to talk to you or see you again.

3. Ask Lots of Questions

The third key result area of selling is *identifying needs accurately.* The biggest mistake that you can make when you meet or talk to a new prospect is to assume that you already know what this prospect needs, wants and is willing to pay for. Each prospect is unique, special and different from all other prospects. He or she has special wants, needs, hopes, fears and desires.

In the initial stage of your conversation with the prospect, your single focus is to ask questions and listen carefully to ascertain whether or not a genuine need for what you sell exists in the mind and heart of the person you are talking to.

Preparation Is the Mark of the Professional.

A score of 10 in identifying needs would mean that you have a predetermined series of questions, from the general to the particular, which you go through one-by-one with the prospect, to clearly ascertain that the prospect needs the product or service you are selling. At the end of your questioning process, it becomes abundantly clear to both the prospect and yourself that the prospect can use, benefit and pay for what you are selling.

If you scored a 1 in identifying needs, this would mean that your approach to each prospect is random. You ask whatever questions pop into your mind and say whatever falls out of your mouth. For you, every sales call is a new adventure. You have no idea what is going to happen, or how it is going to turn out.

The mark of the professional is *preparation*. He has thought through and prepared every part of the sales conversation. He leaves nothing to chance.

4. Where the Sale Is Made

The fourth key result area of selling is the *presentation*. In reality, the presentation is where the sale is made to a qualified prospect. Every part of your presentation must be thought though and planned in advance. Nothing must be left to chance. You must make every effort to make sure that your presentation is effective, believable and persuasive.

A score of 10 in presenting skills means that you have carefully thought through and prepared and practiced your presentation. You move smoothly from one step to the other, asking questions, showing how your product or service works, and how the prospect can most benefit from owning and enjoying what you sell. At the end of your presentation, if you are a good salesperson, the prospect will be completely convinced and ready to buy, even without asking the price.

At the other end of this scale, a 1 in presentation skills means that you walk into sales meetings unprepared and say whatever occurs to you. You do little or no preparation and are more concerned with talking faster and louder in a vain attempt to convince the prospect that he should buy than you are with following a professional sales process. At the end of your conversation, the prospect looks at you with some confusion, shakes his head and says, "Well, it sounds very interesting. Let me think it over."

However, the fact is that nobody thinks it over. Nobody thinks about your product after you leave. The words, "I want to think it over" is a polite way of asking you to leave. As soon as you are out of sight, the prospect forgets that you ever lived. The first thing he does after you leave his presence is to throw your sales materials in his wastebasket.

5. Objections Are Good

The fifth key result in selling is *answering objections effectively*. As it happens, there are no sales without objections. Objections indicate interest. All top salespeople have carefully thought though every objection that a qualified prospect is likely to give them as reasons for not buying at this time. They have then developed a powerful, practical and persuasive answer to that objection.

On a scale from 1 to 10, you would earn a 10 in answering objections if your pre-prepared answers were so clear and focused that as soon as you gave your answer, the prospect immediately dropped his opposition and was open to buying.

A score of 1 in this area would mean that you have given little or no thought to the objections you might receive, and whatever the prospect says, as part of natural sales resistance, causes you to become angry and defensive. Sometimes you get red-faced and argue with the prospect. Sometimes you start to question your own skills and ability and wonder whether your product or service is any good in the first place. If you get too many objections, you would probably think about quitting. The feelings of rejection triggered by objections are the primary reason why people drop out of the selling profession each year.

6. Ask for the Order

The sixth key result area of selling is *closing the sale*. In golf, they say that "You drive for show, but you putt for dough." In selling, you present for show, but you close for dough.

A score of 10 in closing the sale means that you have carefully thought through how to ask for the order in a variety of different ways. You know how to assure that the prospect knows you and likes you, that the prospect wants, needs and can afford your product or service, that the prospect has no further objections and you know how to ask the proper question at the correct time.

A score of 1 in closing the sale means that when you reach the end of the sale, you start to go into a state of semi-panic. Your heart rate increases. You begin to perspire. You feel nervous and uneasy. You feel like a trapped rat in a tunnel, unable to go forward or backward.

The customer senses your level of stress and unease, and begins to wonder if something terrible is about to happen. As a result, the customer tenses up as well, folds his arms, and goes into a defensive position. He is ready to protect his wallet against your request, whenever it comes. Finally, you say something like, "Well, what would you like to do now?" and the customer says, "Well, let me think about it."

7. Get Them Coming Back

The seventh key result area of selling is *getting resales and referrals*. For you to move into the top 10% of your field, you must develop the skill of generating resales and eliciting referrals to a high level. Fortunately, this is a learnable skill as well. All the highest paid sales people, in every field, have become artists at getting their customers to buy from them again and again, and getting qualified referrals from satisfied customers.

A score of 10 in getting resales and referrals means that you have what is called a "Golden Chain" of referrals from happy customers. Because you take such good care of your customers, and continually ask them for the names of other people that may be interested in what you sell, people are opening doors, making telephone calls and introducing you to prospective customers day after day.

If you have a score of 10, this means that you are so busy calling on referrals that you no longer have any time to prospect. You have so many referrals that you probably need a sales assistant to keep your appointment book straight. You have a waiting list of customers who want to buy from you, if you have an opening. From morning to night, you are calling on qualified people who are eager to buy and are just waiting for you to give them the number to fill in on the check. That's a ten.

A score of 1 in this area means that you seldom get a resale or a referral. Once you have sold to someone, you quickly forget about them, throw their name over your shoulder to the company, and go on finding new customers.

Don't Be Afraid to Ask

You don't know how to ask for referrals, and you are terrified of rejection so at the very most, you will say, "Do you know anyone else who may be interested in my product?" Because of this phrasing, the prospect or customer says, "No, not right now, let me think about it."

Wherever you have given yourself the *lowest* score is also your greatest opportunity for rapid improvement in your sales results. No matter how nervous you are, no matter how much fear you have of failure or rejection in this particular skill area, remember that it is *learnable*. As you learn and master this skill, all your fears will go away, and be replaced by confidence, courage and a feeling of personal power.

Resolve today to make the next year the very best and highest paid year of your life. Resolve today to fulfill your potential in selling, and become all that you are capable of becoming. Resolve today that you are going to become "Brilliant on the basics" and never stop improving.

About Brian

Brian Tracy is one of the top sales experts and trainers in the world. He has taught more than 2,000,000 sales people in 80 countries. He is the President of Brian Tracy International, committed to teaching ambitious individuals how to rapidly increase their sales and personal incomes.

CHAPTER 2

BUILDING YOUR VERY OWN SUPER-TEAM!

BY BEVERLY A. WHITE

Ask yourself this question: "What could you do that would enable you to create a very special team, a team with almost unbelievable capability, flexibility and drive, in other words, a super team that would ensure you the success you seek and more?"

I am known as Super-Team Lady and I have almost forty years' experience in creating one Super-Team after another for my own companies and for others. You may well ask how I came to know the amazing techniques that took my career farther and faster than I dreamt possible. As for Super-Team Lady, you'll understand that one by the end of this chapter.

Right up front, I am a nerd. With a talent for all mechanical things I would eventually become an excellent engineer. Yet, I was socially inept and awkward with people. I didn't even like people. When I was a child I used to spend most of my time in the basement of our small home, hoping to avoid whatever was going on above me.

When I was just five, I found an old bicycle in that basement behind some boxes. It had belonged to my Godfather who had been a Golden Gloves boxer in his youth and it was immense. It didn't help that I was small for my age. I fixed the tires and a jumped chain and then taught myself to ride by positioning one pedal horizontal to the ground, standing on a little curb to help me reach the handle bars, jumping on the pedal and using my weight to propel me across our little patio. I am that kind of nerd.

That was why I found it so hard to work with other people. It didn't matter much to me until, as a natural result of being a good engineer, I was eventually assigned my own team.

To say my first attempt at running a team was a disaster would be a gross understatement. After just two months, my manager literally had me thrown out of the building and mailed my belongings home. This was excruciatingly painful because I had a young son to support and suddenly no income. It was far more than an embarrassment to me, and I vowed this wouldn't, and couldn't, happen again. I also knew I needed help.

I thought back in time and remembered some very special leaders who were part of my life. I reached out and they agreed to help me. What they shared with me changed my life. Today, when I speak to team managers and business owners, I often say, "I know people, people who know people" – then assure them I have no intention to sing. That is how I started my path to becoming Super-Team Lady.

What I share with others interested in building teams that outperform their resumes are the techniques I learned from these amazing and generous people. Of course, because I am an engineer, I was compelled to codify them into a set of concepts and techniques that anyone, even I, could use. These techniques have earned me a valuable reputation. I was once even introduced as a Pillar of the Company by a VP – all thanks to my team-building skills. As you will see soon, I have had some amazing, touching and powerfully humbling moments in my life and path to becoming Super-Team Lady.

If you had a team whose members could say they were "dedicated" to each other what would that mean? We would gain insight into how that team works, especially since it is not something you find most teams expressing. Let's take a look at a real-life example:

In 2013, the Seattle Seahawks, who on paper should have been a sub-average football team, managed to fight their way to the Super Bowl, and in February 2014 won the very first championship ever for Seattle. "How,"

I asked, "could a team of mostly undistinguished players outperform such giants in the sport as… well, for example the San Francisco Giants, or Denver Broncos?"

They were clearly a Super-Team, yet it wasn't until the 2015 season that I spotted one of the signs of a super-team. The "Hawks" had struggled through many games that year, and in one game they took a terrible beating in the first half, letting the opposing team build up a huge lead. In the second half they rallied, and not only closed the lead in some dramatic and exciting plays, but took the lead and won with seconds on the clock. In a telling post-game interview one player was asked, "What happened in the locker room at half time to make such a difference?" His reply was, "We went into the locker room and re-dedicated ourselves to each other." That said it all!

If your team members are not dedicated to each other, you are leaving team performance on the table. By understanding and applying some simple but powerful concepts to your own team dynamics you can take a good or even great team to much higher levels of performance and competiveness. A super-team in business is a rare combination of luck and timing. The pay-off for you is that almost no one realizes how this can be done on demand.

For most, team building is simple. Either a team is hired or it is selected from a group of existing people. They have the skills needed and there they are. Most management training will tell you that you need to communicate well, offer positive evaluation and set clear goals and timelines. That is what most managers or business owners do.

What drives team members in that model is often their need for an income; some may like what they do, or other individual reasons. In teams of professionals there is also the desire to be regarded personally as a professional. Often managers are tempted to pit members against each other in hopes that competition will hone the team's performance.

The problems of this type of model are multiple. To drive productivity, they often artificially shorten schedules or create unattainable goals and then demand constant reports on progress. All of this is work that produces nothing. It also alienates the team members. You are about to be empowered to surpass all of them with very own Super-Team.

THE PATH TO A SUPER-TEAM

- Increase personal dedication (there is that word again) and performance.
- Increase Team cohesion and dedication to each other.

Since dedication is directed toward something or someone, you will need to create a set of relationships between yourself and the people of the team. These are specifically working relationships. Here is how you will do it.

1. **Establish a trust relationship with the individuals on your team.** This can be expedited if you make a show of your trustworthiness in front of, or within notice of, the team. When you defend or stand up for one team member you gain the trust of the others. After you have done this a few times, everyone should be on board. Continue building trust anyway. It is the foundation upon which you will build your Super-Team.

2. **Challenge and reward the individual.** You do this by assigning them a task that is a stretch for their abilities, offering some small reward and then you make sure they triumph (by working with them or as we will see later in the Team section... assign an expert to guide them) and when they succeed, deliver the reward. A common reward is public praise. The rest of the team will feel rewarded as well. Be careful that you do not overwhelm or "break" them as it will only make them reluctant to participate next time plus it makes the whole team wary.

3. **Repeat this for every member of the team.** Give them a challenge, work with them to make sure they succeed and then reward them in front of the group. It doesn't take long for everyone to get the idea. Keep this up too.

A brief note about rewards: As you go from the basics, of which this is but one, to more advanced techniques you will find more and more powerful free or low-cost rewards to offer, such as certificates, titles, new responsibilities that give them a sense of rising in the ranks and so on. The willingness to stretch and to surpass their old limits grows each time this cycle is completed. Their dedication to you will also grow as well, because it is natural to admire anyone who shows you that you are more than you thought you were. If you can afford a raise for a job particularly well done, that is great but it isn't always necessary. *Just don't promise anything you can't deliver.*

Their dedication grows as you proactively create opportunities for each member to grow. Senior members can mentor junior members; you reward both for the success. Make sure you are involved in the process. As a pattern emerges, they will let you step away and you'll get the credit for making them winners. Everyone wants to be a winner and will be grateful to whoever makes them feel that way. Enough said.

For the team, create two- or three-person mini-teams and guide them to success and you will build a relationship between all of those members (dedication). Any rivalry or dislike for each other will fall apart as they see that the other team members are the key to their own success. You will notice that the work you are doing is going better than before in a very short order. My shortest time frame for conversion of a team is two hours, but if you take a month to begin with, you are doing great. You will be seeing the benefits of a better team during this transformation and you win as well with team members helping and supporting each other. The best part is that there is no cost to this process other than your proactive planning, and the results that are generated soon become contagious.

LOCKING IT IN!

Never, ever, allow competition within the team... all competition (and isn't there plenty of that?) should be from the outside. Create a sense of identity for the team. Make it an exclusive club... members are inside, everyone else isn't. They will soon gain a sense of pride and almost invincibility that will astound you. Better yet, they will be fun to work with, be more focused and inventive. Since they are not threatened by those inside the team, it is natural to open up about ideas... but you have to lead on this to get it started. Attendance and inter-personal issues will become non-issues for this team. I have had teams that refuse to be beaten and who stepped in for a sick or missing member to make sure we hit deadlines and goals. A typical sign that all is going as planned is when the team starts to demand its own holiday party or a team lunch or ultimately when they literally create a name for themselves.

Keep in mind that this is a bit of a rough and dirty outline, but it is sufficient to make a very real and very significant difference to your team. They will dedicate themselves to you and each other, even if they do not say so directly.

Here are some keys to your success and a Super-Team of your own:

1. **Be subtle.** This is just a working environment to them, to you it is a deliberate and purposeful move to connect the dots in the team relationship puzzle.
2. **Be consistent.** You can't be a super-team builder one day and a micromanager or worse the next.
3. **Look for opportunities to make them winners but don't give the rewards easily.** You are training them to reach, to exceed and to strive as much as to complete. Use the work to drive the building process.
4. **Never take personal advantage of them.** Keep this all about work. Make them keep it that way too.
5. **Absolutely no competition within the team.** Leaders will naturally emerge but the team will naturally acknowledge and accept that leadership. All competition is to be against the outside competitors.

Stick with this and you will quickly see a new dynamic emerge within your team. All the effort you put in will pay off quickly. I offer this quick story to illustrate my point:

Remember my original disastrous beginning? As I had anticipated, the time finally came when I was given another chance. Yes, in a different company. I applied the techniques and concepts that had been given to me, admittedly nervous that they would work for me, and they worked… boy, did they ever work. The team I built overcame the loss of the industry the company served; they triumphed as we took on new industries and customers, new projects and new skills. Everything this team touched turned to new opportunity. We outpaced, out-did and out-earned our competition, over and over again. What was the best side effect of all? We had more fun and energy, harmony and collaboration at work, than I had ever experienced.

In the end, our parent company decided to consolidate a number of smaller subsidiaries, of which we were one, and our team was going to be broken up. After we found out what was going to happen, my core team, six people, appeared at my door. They shuffled around a bit and out popped Donna.

"We all talked it over, and we all agree," she stated in a serious and measured tone, making extra sure I understood, "if you start a company we will work for you… **for free** to make that happen."

I was stunned, flattered and humbled. They hadn't offered to work for a while and let me catch up with the pay later. They hadn't given a time limit. What they offered they offered because they wanted to be a part of the same team they had come to love. They were dedicated to each other and to me. This after years of working harder than any of our competition, stretching their skill levels beyond each of their own personal limits and then doing it again and again. They also fully believed we would succeed, they believed in me but they also believed in themselves. I started the company; but I couldn't make them work for free. I wouldn't risk breaking their trust in me.

Today they own that company. You now have a powerful technique and all the evidence of what it can do for you. Now ask yourself this question, "What could you do with a very special team, a team with almost unbelievable capability, flexibility and drive, in other words a Super-Team that would ensure you the success you seek and more?"

Isn't it time to start building your Super-Team?

About Beverly

Beverly A. White helps small businesses and large corporations alike to become more competitive by providing them with a set of tools and methods that create ultra-performing teams which she calls Super-Teams. With a long career in engineering – mechanical, electrical, process & control and software engineering – Beverly has a proven technical background. Yet it is what she provides on 'human performance tuning' that is most unique and valuable about what she does and what she can offer to others.

Beverly found early on in her career that her technical skills were not enough to make her even a passably decent manager, a lesson that she learned the hard and painful way. Through the generosity of some incredible people in her own life, she was able to come away with some deep truths and techniques that would ultimately lead her to becoming a master of team building and a highly sought-after leader. She often says, "The team building methods I share not only build a great team, but turn the user into a potentially great leader." She adds, "Just add Vision!"

Beverly has applied her methods to teams in the United States and in the Netherlands, even Saudi Arabia. She has worked with engineers and day laborers, professionals and volunteers, people on multi-national projects, teams of people within a company and teams made of people from multiple companies all with the same powerful results. She has improved the working relationships of companies and their vendors and partners, customers and relationships up the corporate management chain. All of those teams out-performed their competition all while having the high energy and morale of a team that truly has fun at what it does.

While many team builders offer a day off-site doing a team building exercise, Beverly shares techniques that work during the normal course of business. Using everyday work and work situations in clever ways, you not so slowly build a team that exceeds their apparent capabilities. Beverly certainly encourages you to treat your fabulous Super-Team to a day of "play" to deepen their relationships, but only after you have built the team around the work they do.

Beverly is an amazing speaker, an author and a Team Building expert with a unique message and someone who is dedicated to making better teams wherever and whenever she can.

You can reach Beverly at:
- Beverly@BeverlyAnnWhite.com
- https://twitter.com/BevAnnWhite
- https://www.facebook.com/beverly.a.white.5

CHAPTER 3

WORK ETHICS AND OUTCOMES
FINDING LIFE'S GREATEST JOYS THROUGH DISCIPLINE AND HARD WORK

BY RICHARD YADA, CPA

*Regardless of what life brings you, there is a path
to a better place that you can take.*

My parents' every action and move was very notable to me from a very young age, a driving force for who I have grown into today. From a very young age onwards, I always took note of the stellar example that my parents set forth on how to always carry yourself—no excuses allowed—in both a disciplined and accomplished manner. To do anything less than this was a deprivation of dignity. How they did this was through exuding humbleness, accentuated by a willingness to work hard.

Unlike many children born to American citizen parents in the US, I was not born in a hospital or a cozy home under the care of a midwife. I was born in an internment camp for Japanese-Americans that were rounded up after the devastating attack on Pearl Harbor on December 7, 1941. These people were forced to report to assembly centers where their freedoms were temporarily taken away. They were termed as "enemy non-aliens". During this period of America's history, there was such madness everywhere, a lack of clarity that was a result of the unprecedented event that took place. It was hard for everyone to grasp—including the

Japanese-Americans, who were proud and patriotic in every sense of the word. They wanted to serve, and offered to serve, but instead, they were ordered to report to internment camps. Today, this is history, just as much as it is the foundation of what has moved my entire life forward.

WITNESSING RESILIENCE IN MOTION

No matter what others did, my parents always stood strong in the face of it, never allowing it to dictate their efforts.

My parents were farmers in California. My father's parents had legally come to Hawaii before he was born and my mother's parents were legal immigrant farmers that had landed in California. Married in 1935, my parents worked hard until a life-changing message came: they had to get rid of their belongings, evacuate their home, and report to assembly centers for Japanese-Americans with no more than what they could carry. Then they would wait for further instructions.

For my parents, this meant selling farm equipment and getting rid of the things they had worked many hard, long days to purchase. No more living at home, instead they lived in a horse stable for nearly six months; something that even the most avid horse enthusiast can agree would be less than ideal.

Although I wasn't born yet, from the way they carried themselves throughout my life, I am certain they maintained a dignified air about them during that time, likely even through some cruel moments. Those moments were never shared with me, as it would have served no purpose to dwell on what was tough in the past over the lessons to be learned from those tough times.

Somewhere in there, both my brother and I were born and we were transferred to the internment camp in Rohwer, Arkansas, along with approximately 17,000 other Japanese-Americans. Despite being so young, I recalled how much work my parents did, day in and day out in that camp. That was 1942, and then three years later, in 1945, the camps were closed and my parents were released, each receiving $25 and a bus ticket to wherever they'd like to go.

Most people returned to where they had lived before to try and pick up their lives again. Many were professionals such as doctors, college professors, attorneys, etc. However, my parents decided to remain in Arkansas, along with a handful of other families from the camp. They became sharecroppers and worked endlessly for a very small financial return.

However, my forty-year-old father wasn't deterred, because he found a way to take that little bit of return and grow it through:

- Working hard
- Always saving something—no matter how small the amount

Fast-forward until my parents were around seventy. They managed to save seven figures and achieve the purposes they desired:
    1). to have their children go to college; and
    2). instill their values in their children.

These are the aspirations of many parents, and they had done it despite their tumultuous younger years. They were always steadfast and resilient, and those are personal attributes that I appreciate in others, as well as try to show through what I do today.

THE ACTIONS THAT DEFINED ME

As soon as I could walk, I was taught to work.

Development and growth are constantly evolving in our lives, and for me, instilling a strong work ethic was a part of my life from the time I took my first steps. There was something age appropriate that I could do, even if it was picking up small rocks in a field.

As days went on and I grew into a young man, my parents still remained hard-working individuals, only their efforts paid off because their financial return harvested more and they were able to achieve their goals of paying for my brother's and my college, and also retire comfortably. The sharecroppers had become the owners of the largest greenhouse in Arkansas at the time.

When I went to college, I decided to go for accounting, finding that I enjoyed numbers and it was interesting to be on that side of helping people such as my parents who worked hard their entire lives to earn those funds. I graduated and got married, ready for what came next. What I didn't anticipate was that it would be the Vietnam War. Like many men my age, I was drafted. Since I'd graduated from college and participated in the Air Force ROTC program, I got to enlist as an Officer. How quickly things had changed—just two decades later, Japanese-Americans were required to serve, not turned away.

Not one to avoid challenges and always eager to learn, I decided that I wanted to be a pilot so I entered the Air Force to fly B52s. What I didn't know was how going to flight school did not count toward my four years of service that I had to serve. Ultimately, I ended up being a navigator for the B52 Bomber, and participated in 59 combat missions, from which I obviously survived.

> *What revealed itself in the reflections of an older me some years later was that my role in the Air Force had also been a role that caused great agony for my family during World War II. When the atomic bomb was dropped on Hiroshima, I had a cousin in Japan who was killed by it, and my mother's parents also lived there. Strangely enough, her parents happened to be on the other side of the hill. The story has it that my grandmother's skirt blew up from the wind of it, but they survived with no ill effects. It reiterates the point that we just never know what will happen, so we need to give every moment our best.*

After my five years of service, I left the Air Force as a Captain, and went back home to my family, which had grown. I now had three children, which meant I had to get busy and focus on the future. The ingrained work ethic I'd grown up in kicked back in, and I decided to get my CPA certificate.

Then life's moments to learn, achieve, and grow in the civilian world began. I worked in the corporate world for a time and then opened up a CPA firm with a partner, only to leave three years later to become a financial advisor. Once I arrived there, I knew without a doubt that I was where I'd been meant to arrive—in a career that could help others in a profound way.

GUIDING PRINCIPLES IN LIFE AND FINANCE

*I love helping people with their futures, not just attempting
to minimize what has already been done.*

When I was a CPA, they mainly did tax returns and dabbled a bit in planning and strategy. By switching to a financial advisory role, I was able to help people make the decision that would move them ahead. Two things that are consistent through all generations are:

- that people want their children to have opportunities and a better life than they had.
- people want to retire in a position where they don't have to worry about their finances.

When I first worked as a financial advisor I decided to join one of the larger firms out there so I could gain the training and certifications I needed to be the best financial advisor I could. Every person that I had an opportunity to help deserved nothing less than that. It was through this that the perfect immersion of discipline, hard work, and a desire to help others surfaced. They have become guiding principles in life and lessons that I personally and professionally strive to live by, whether I'm helping clients, people in my community, or causes that I am passionate about.

1. **It's important to strategize from a position of how I can help others maximize their ideas, plans, and goals.**
   When you are connected to peoples' aspirations, you'd best take that seriously and recognize that it's through your efforts and diligence that they have the best chance of achieving their plan. I recall my father's first steps toward achieving this for his life. He'd decided to get a jump start on growing the plants for farming season. He'd created a greenhouse to begin during off-season. Before long, other farmers were interested and a new idea took off. He began selling plants and produce to farmer's markets, Wal-Mart, and grocery stores. This is an amazing example of maximizing an idea!

2. **Recognize that hard work is never done.**
   In a world that never stops, things are constantly changing, including both financial goals and personal ambitions. What this means is that

every action we choose to take in a day is an important one, having an impact of some level in our lives. For me, acknowledging this helps guide me in how I serve my clients. I am always aware.

3. Caring for people.

The appreciation and warmth that I receive from witnessing how others enjoy the fruits of their labor is a constant source of inspiration. Heading in the right direction is where we all want to go, after all. On a personal level, I am very motivated by this through the work that I do with the Japanese-American National Museum in LA. This museum is devoted to educating and remembering a dark period in American history. My hope and desire is to ensure that what happened to Japanese-Americans after World War II does not happen again.

4. Giving back.

Through giving back we are reminded of our responsibility in this world to be mindful of others' struggles and needs. I receive great joy from my involvement on the Board of Directors for my regional Ronald McDonald House. For over 35 years, I've met so many wonderful people and grown in a profound way from helping the parents of ill children know that the House is there to support them during their toughest times.

5. Always embrace learning, transitioning, and growing in your world.

For a financial planner, trends and research on all things financial is imperative. This is how you remain an effective advocate for your clients' best interests and it is a wonderful reminder of how important your decisions can be in another's life.

Life's best lessons are simple to understand, but harder to live by. Not fearing having the discipline to work hard when you need to is important; so also is recognizing that you should celebrate what you've done and appreciate all those special moments you can capture with family and friends.

One thing that I always remain aware of and would like to impart to everyone I can impact in some way, is that we are all in charge of defining our legacy. We will leave a mark on this world and it's up to us to determine what that mark will be. Great things are possible from the most unlikely sources. How do I know?

Because this boy born in an internment camp was raised to recognize that where my story begins does not have to be where it ends.

About Richard

Richard Yada was born into humble beginnings in a concentration camp for United States citizens of Japanese ancestry. After spending his first two years inside the prison camp, the camp closed and his family moved to a farming community outside Little Rock, Arkansas, (Scott, Arkansas) to work as sharecrop vegetable farmers. There his father, being a farmer in California before being incarcerated because he was Japanese, introduced farming techniques yet unused in the South. Eighteen hour days became the norm as his parents worked to save money in order to get their two sons a college education. The great people of Scott, Arkansas were extremely supportive of the seven Japanese families who settled in Scott. To this day, those who still remain or return to Scott, continue to be some of Yada's family's best friends and confidants.

To broaden Richard's horizons, he transferred to Forest Heights Junior High School in Little Rock where many new friendships were developed and a completely different way of life was observed (city life vs. farming life). Through this transition, Richard continued to realize what his parents taught him – that he would have to outwork his peers and nothing would come easy. He was enrolled in Little Rock Central High School in 1958. However, because of the segregation/integration crisis, it was closed for one year. He was fortunate to be re-assigned to North Little Rock High School, where new friendships were made and relationships continue to this day. After graduating, he attended the University of Arkansas at Fayetteville, majoring in accounting.

After graduating from the University of Arkansas, a big decision had to be made. The Vietnam War was heating up and the draft was in play. Richard decided to join the Air Force and continue the tradition of the 442nd Regiment Combat Team, a segregated all-Japanese unit. (All the men joined the unit to prove the loyalty of all Japanese Americans in the United States. Even though their parents and family were still incarcerated behind barbed wire, they became the highest-decorated unit in World War II.) He completed his tour of duty and commitment in 1970. He was a navigator in the B-52 aircraft, completing 50 combat missions. Richard received an honorable discharge with the rank of Captain.

Richard worked in corporate accounting for ten years, achieving the position of Vice-President and Chief Financial Officer. This profession was very good to him and enjoyable. At 40, he joined Merrill Lynch as a Financial Advisor and remained there for over 20 years. Richard is now affiliated with an independent Broker/Dealer and continues to spend many hours helping his clients achieve their goals, and rejoice in their financial successes as they enjoy life.

While in the Air Force, Richard married his gorgeous wife, Barbara, and they had three daughters. Richard continues to enjoy his life with many friends who have supported him throughout the years. He gives credit to his friends, his wife Barbara, their three daughters, and their five grandchildren, for any successes that he has enjoyed.

CHAPTER 4

CRACKING THE CODE TO EMAIL MARKETING

BY LINDSAY DICKS

Ever since the first email program was developed way back in 1971, email has become one of our chief communication tools. With over 205 billion emails sent and received each day, it's still an essential tool for marketers to share information with current and prospective customers.

It wasn't always easy, though. Kids today will never experience the excitement and anticipation of listening to the hiss and whine of a telephone modem connecting to the Internet. They'll never understand the joy of paying for Internet access by the minute instead of by gigabytes, or the frustration of spending your minutes downloading an inbox full of spam. Just think how bored they would be if they couldn't send pictures with their emails. Such was the Internet during those heady days of the 1990s.

EMAIL IS STILL RELEVANT

Fast forward to today and email is still with us and going strong. Some media experts believe email will be replaced as early as 2020 by some yet-to-be-named website or app. Don't believe it. Oh sure, 100 years from now, marketers may look back at email like we view the horse and buggy today – quaint, yet crude. But the numbers just can't be ignored. Email use is still on the rise, averaging an increase of 3 percent each year.

Sure, social media has changed the dynamic for how we interact electronically with consumers. Of course, using email and social media is not an either/or proposition. The best e-marketing plans include email, Twitter, Facebook, and any number of other social media sites. But keep in mind, email has been shown to convert more contacts to customers by an almost 2-to-1 margin.

Email marketers today also need to be aware of the mobile revolution. Almost half of all emails are opened on a mobile device. Just like your website needs to be responsive to multiple devices, your emails should be adaptable to tablets and smartphones. Some steps you can take to ensure readability include:

- Increasing font size so the copy is easier to read on a small screen

- Making the call-to-action buttons larger for easy tapping

- Designing the email in a single column for easy scrolling

COMPETING WITH SPAM AND SCAMS

Two of the biggest obstacles for marketers to overcome are having their emails considered spam, the electronic version of junk mail, or email scams trying to defraud recipients or infect their computers.

All email marketers must comply with the CAN-SPAM Act passed in 2003. A few of the more relevant aspects of the law for legitimate marketing purposes stipulate that the emails:

- Include an unsubscribe link

- Feature subject lines that relate directly to the content in the email

- Contain content with at least one sentence, not just a link

If you want to get fancy, the technical term for spam is Unsolicited Commercial Email, or UCE. Some studies estimate anywhere from 65-78 percent of emails sent each day are spam. How do you make sure your email stands out from all the clutter? To better understand that, we first need to understand how a spam filter works and how to avoid ending up in the dreaded spam folder.

There are numerous spam filters available today. Simple ones search the subject heading and email content for suspicious words, such as "Viagra," and check to see if they contain words in ALL CAPS, misspellings, and multiple exclamation points!!! Some look at the IP address of the originating email. If the email service has received spam from the IP address previously, other legitimate emails coming from that IP address could also be labeled as spam. Others check out complex sounding things like Reverse DNS Lookup, Domain Keys and IP Throttling to make sure the emails are legit.

There's no way to guarantee your marketing emails will never be flagged as spam, but there are steps you can follow to help your emails reach the inbox:

- **Communicate at regular intervals** – Don't wait six months between emails. Your recipients will be less likely to remember you. First, you have to decide what constitutes a regular interval for your emails. Above all, keep it relevant. It's easy for a retailer to send out emails about sales or new products, but what can an accountant do besides sending a reminder about April 15? Think about what's on your calendar that your followers might be interested in. The accountant could keep people updated on the late filing deadline, a reminder to submit flexible spending account receipts, and any changes to IRS regulations.

- **Segment your list** – Depending on your business, you may want to divide your email list into different interest groups. A pet store would want to segment the pet owners on their list by animal. A cat owner that receives offers geared toward dog owners may get fed up and unsubscribe or report your emails as spam.

- **Use a third-party provider** – Companies dedicated to processing marketing emails ethically follow all the laws governing email marketing. They also have intimate knowledge of the inner workings of spam filters to reduce the chances of your emails getting canned.

PUTTING IT ALL TOGETHER

So now that we've talked about getting your emails across the Internet, let's take a look at the elements of an effective marketing email.

I. A Campaign is Only as Good as Its List

The most important part of your email campaign starts with your email address list. Your address list is like a fish you just bought at the grocery store. If you let it go too long, it starts to stink. You want to keep your address list clean and fresh. How do you go about doing that? First, you need to manage your list from the very start.

The best method for procuring email addresses on your website is to employ a double opt-in process. This is a two-step process to collect the addresses that involves the contact filling out an online form on your website. Once the email address is collected, your website sends a follow-up email to the person asking them to click on a link in the email to confirm their contact information. There are a couple of reasons why this is the best strategy to collect emails on your website. First, it verifies the email was input by the contact without any typing errors. Second, it legitimizes an ongoing relationship with the person. It also reinforces their participation in receiving emails from you.

There are other means to procure emails depending on your business and customer base. Trade shows, community events and networking opportunities are several ways you can supplement your online leads. Keep in mind, these contacts are probably not as invested in you or your business as much as someone who takes the time to fill out your contact form on your website.

Once your list is compiled, keep it up to date. You'll want to pay close attention to several measurements after you send out an email campaign. Check to see how many people haven't opened your email after a certain amount of time, say 30 or 45 days. Take those addresses out of future emails, but keep them in case you want to invite them back at a later date. You'll also want to keep tabs on emails that bounce, that is, are undeliverable. There can be several reasons why the server was unable to deliver your email to the recipient. The person's inbox capacity may have been full, or the email address is no longer in use. Again, take these emails out of your active list.

II. Create a Scintillating Subject Line

De-spammed? Check. Clean address list? Check. So now you've got to get the recipients to open the email. You'll first need to consider how long to make the subject. Keep your subject heading short and sweet so the whole thing is visible in the inbox. I'd recommend around 50-60 characters. Good subject lines take some time and thought but can lead to a higher open rate. Some of the best subject lines can include some of the following information targeted for recipients:

- How the information benefits them

- Asking or answering questions

- Lists such as "3 Ways to Improve Open Rates"

Email marketing, like all marketing, is a work in progress. One question up for debate is how personalized you should make your emails. Should the subject line and email speak to the recipient by name or should it be more general. With traditional direct mail, studies have shown that using a person's name on the envelope and in the salutation of the letter are more effective than generic openings. So if you have a credit card through your bank, they would send you a home equity loan solicitation addressed directly to you. The e-newsletter service MailChimp suggests that personalizing marketing emails improves open rates.

However, a study done by Temple University's Fox School of Business found that 95 percent of recipients of email marketing responded negatively when addressed by name in the email.

In my experience I haven't seen personalization affect open rates one way or the other. I strongly believe personalization depends on your relationship with the people on your list. For example, if you belong to a fitness center, it would probably address you differently than your financial advisor would.

One of my best email campaigns had the subject heading of "Hey!" That was it. But that underscores the relationship I have with the people on my list. They're familiar with the conversational tone in my emails, so seeing my name and the "Hey" was enough to get them to open my email. Keep in mind, I've built that relationship over years. It's not how you would want to address your contacts in your first email to them.

But don't take my word for it. Test it yourself and see if personalization clicks with your readers. Whichever way you decide to go, email marketing is flexible enough to accommodate different preferences. It makes it easy to personalize both the subject line and content if you choose to.

III. Create Inspiring Content

OK, you've finally gotten your contact to open your email. The clock is ticking. Studies show you have 15-20 seconds to get your message across before the person moves on to the next email. Make the next step crystal clear for them. Do you want them to attend a free webinar, visit your store, or save 10 percent if they place an order today?

With that amount of time, you'll want to have shorter copy with graphics that reinforce your message. Keep in mind, though, pictures sometimes get filtered out of messages, so make sure your copy can sell the offer on its own. Put your offer at the top of the email so your contacts won't have to scroll to see what you're selling. Also, when speaking to your customers, use "you." Who will benefit from this offer? *You* will, that's who.

Try not to clutter your email with too many offers. A good rule of thumb is one offer, many links. Give the reader multiple ways to reach your intended destination using both text and graphics.

IV. When To Send It

There isn't one best or worst time to send emails, although weekdays tend to do better than weekends. There's also some data that suggests the best time of day to send emails is around 10 a.m., but it's not significantly better than other times of day.

I've found that it all depends on your business, your market, and what you're trying to accomplish. The beauty of email marketing is you have the analytics available that show you when your recipients opened your emails, so you can easily determine the day and time that's best for your contacts.

FULFILLMENT AND FOLLOW-UP

Congratulations. You've successfully launched your email campaign. You now need to follow through on your offer and review your data. It's time to send out your e-book or ship out customer orders. You also want to give some thought to how you can grow your relationship. For example, let's say you do online marketing for a seed company. You have a customer who bought several packets of tomato seeds. You've set up your system to send out an email offer for herb seeds to anyone who buys tomato seeds. After all, nobody eats a tomato by itself.

It's also time to perform your after-action review. Among other things, your email analytics will be able to tell you:

- How many people opened the email

- When they opened the email

- How many people clicked on a link

Based on these analytics and your call-to-action responses, you'll be able to calculate your ROI to measure the success of your campaign.

EMAIL – STILL GOING STRONG

Whether your email marketing campaign is geared toward sales, downloads, or just informational, you'll find that a well-designed campaign that includes an up-to-date list, an eye-catching subject, killer content, and a clear call-to-action will produce positive results for your company. No matter what the "experts" say, email marketing is still going strong and will continue to be an important tool in the marketer's utility belt.

About Lindsay

Lindsay Dicks helps her clients tell their stories in the online world. Being brought up around a family of marketers, but a product of Generation Y, Lindsay naturally gravitated to the new world of on-line marketing. Lindsay began freelance writing in 2000 and soon after launched her own PR firm that thrived by offering an in-your-face "Guaranteed PR" that was one of the first of its type in the nation.

Lindsay's new media career is centered on her philosophy that "people buy people." Her goal is to help her clients build a relationship with their prospects and customers. Once that relationship is built and they learn to trust them as the expert in their field, then they will do business with them. Lindsay also built a proprietary process that utilizes social media marketing, content marketing and search engine optimization to create online "buzz" for her clients that helps them to convey their business and personal story. Lindsay's clientele spans the entire business map and ranges from doctors and small business owners to Inc. 500 CEOs.

Lindsay is a graduate of the University of Florida. She is the CEO of CelebritySites™, an online marketing company specializing in social media and online personal branding. Lindsay is recognized as one of the top online marketing experts in the world and has co-authored more than 25 best-selling books alongside authors such as Steve Forbes, Richard Branson, Brian Tracy, Jack Canfield (creator of the *Chicken Soup for the Soul* series), Dan Kennedy, Robert Allen, Dr. Ivan Misner (founder of BNI), Jay Conrad Levinson (author of the *Guerilla Marketing* series), Leigh Steinberg and many others, including the breakthrough hit *Celebrity Branding You!*

She has also been selected as one of America's PremierExperts™ and has been quoted in *Forbes, Newsweek, The Wall Street Journal, USA Today,* and *Inc. Magazine* as well as featured on NBC, ABC, and CBS television affiliates speaking on social media, search engine optimization and making more money online. Lindsay was also recently brought on FOX 35 News as their Online Marketing Expert.

Lindsay, a national speaker, has shared the stage with some of the top speakers in the world, including Brian Tracy, Lee Milteer, Ron LeGrand, Arielle Ford, Leigh Steinberg, Dr. Nido Qubein, Dan Sullivan, David Bullock, Peter Shankman and many others. Lindsay was also a Producer on the Emmy-winning film *Jacob's Turn* and sits on the advisory board for the Global Economic Initiative.

You can connect with Lindsay at:
- Lindsay@CelebritySites.com
- www.twitter.com/LindsayMDicks
- www.facebook.com/LindsayDicks

CHAPTER 5

SUSTAINABLE SUCCESS: SUCCESS DEFINED, REFINED, AND UNCEASING

BY CATHERINE O. ENAOHWO

I watched as they drove past me in their brand new air-conditioned cars; sleek, stylish in their smart sober coloured business suits looking fulfilled.

Three branded cars drove past me as I left school that graduation day; clutching the bag that held my Bachelor's degree while I wiped the sweat that ran profusely down my forehead. "I must work with this bank and be successful," I muttered to myself. And with that determination I walked briskly towards the bus-stop on that hot afternoon in 1999.

A year later; after months of written tests, exams and several interviews; I finally received an offer. I skipped out of the bank after collecting my Employment Letter thinking to myself:

Finally! I have made it!
I have achieved my life ambition of working in a new generation bank. I shall now be chauffeured in sleek air-conditioned cars, work in tastefully finished offices and earn a salary that will satisfy all my needs...
I have become successful! ...Or so I thought!

I was wrong! That job lasted for all of seven working days.

I handed in my resignation on day eight having been completely wrong about my assumptions of self-fulfilment and job satisfaction. Now, this wasn't because the bank was 'bad,' but because my ambition to work with that bank and the success I had attributed to it didn't align with my Life Goals.

If Success is defined as the accomplishment of an aim or purpose; why, then, did I not feel accomplished after achieving my aim? Was it because 'man's needs are insatiable', according to Economics, or was the problem with my aim not being aligned with my life goals?

After many years and many jobs, searching for a role that will truly give me satisfaction and make me feel both fulfilled and accomplished, I realised one thing:

I must first determine my purpose in life to achieve 'sustainable' success. The question now becomes, "What is sustainable success?"

Seek to add value and make a difference! And not just to make money.

My boss walked in like a man on a mission. He had assembled all the top performers at the company to address the deficit we were faced with.

"Welcome to the 'war room,'" he started. "We must turn this around. We are known for the 'Can do' spirit. We can do this!" he continued. He went on to make a presentation on a transaction he wanted us to run with. It was going to bring the company 'ridiculous' earnings in fees that will not only fill out the deficit but will be sufficient to pay all participating employees very generous commission. It was tempting. I quickly made a mental calculation of the volume of business I could bring in and how much commission I would earn. The money was good and I needed it.

Like a bull, I rushed into the arena. I wanted to know more. Asking questions that I anticipated any of my clients would ask. I was determined to cover all the bases and be fully prepared to generate volumes that will surpass the commission payment I had anticipated for myself. As I continued to question my boss, it became increasingly evident that it was a *no-value* transaction.

My heart sank! I had many clients that depended on my recommendations and won't even review the documents themselves once I declared them 'a-buy'. It was tempting to go along. I hesitated for a moment then decided mentally that I won't be a party to this. I thought to myself that if I added value I would get repeat business. Repeat business brings stable earning. That in turn leads to success.

I was not going to jeopardise future transactions and relationships for a quick gain today. It was painful but I walked away from that transaction. Like a prophecy, the transaction went burst and so many quality clients' relationships went down the drain. This was confirmation that I had done the right thing. I refused to be moved by quick gains but sought to add value. And at the end; it paid off.

In all that we do, value addition is most important. Value keeps it going and will eventually lead to financial gain. Whereas if we put financial gain first, it is unsustainable because there may be no repeat business. This shall erode the client base and earnings as quickly as they came. With 'Value first', everything else will fall into place.

LIVE FOR SOMETHING, IMPACT OTHERS, LEAVE A LEGACY

To achieve sustainable success, we must also determine the value that our life's goals can bring and align our ambitions to it. We are here for a reason. To be successful is identifying that reason and working towards achieving it to the best of our ability.

I believe every life must be remembered for something. Impact on others, society, future generations... This is not just about the acquisition of wealth and being the richest in society, but the utilisation of this wealth regardless of the size of it.

I have asked numerous people what their idea of 'success' is and many times I have heard... "Success is having sufficient money to take care of my needs."

So if my 'needs' are insatiable, does that mean I will never be successful? And is the acquisition of money really success, or a means to Success?

My motto is: 'enhance thyself; enrich society'.
I believe money is not just money!

To some, it can be half a dozen luxury items and to others a gift that they share with the world. I have seen it be retirement earnings, children's school-fees or even the quality of healthcare or change to the lives of many less privileged people around the world, or the required resource for a ground-breaking disease, prevention or cure.

Many will say the value of money I have is too little to make an impact! I disagree:

Success is not dictated by how much you have, but the impact you make with what you have: whether little or much!

DETEST MEDIOCRITY
STRIVE TO BE BETTER...EVEN AT YOUR PERCEIVED BEST!

If success is impacting others and leaving a legacy through what we have; then it is pertinent that 'we have' something to give. Tangible or Intangible!

I raised my head as the clock struck 5:00pm on the dot. "Time to go home," he said, as he walked briskly pass me with a relieved smile. Daily, he came in at 8:00am, signed the attendance register as required and took his seat to commence whatever work was mandated of him. I watched him carry out this ritual for weeks.

When I couldn't take it anymore, I summoned the courage to ask him. I walked slowly to his desk, unsure of how to commence the discussion. I settled for an ice breaker.

"How is your daughter"? I asked turning my gaze to the picture on his desk. "She is so pretty, how old is she now, does she finish school at 5?" I hoped a compliment would soften the hard lines on his face as he raised his head to acknowledge my presence. He cracked half a smile that vanished almost as quickly as it came.

He stared at me for a few seconds, which seemed to last a lifetime, then as if he had an important lesson to teach me he said, "Sit down!" as he pointed towards the chair opposite him.

I wasn't sure if I was going to get a tongue lashing but I did as I was told.

He sighed as he started. For the next 13 minutes, he went on to tell me about how he had started out with so much zeal but as management did not reward hard work, he settled for the barest minimum. His opinion was, 'if he didn't do anything extra he will not be disappointed when he didn't get anything extra.'

That did not seem right to me, even at that young age. Mediocrity is defined as doing 'just enough.' *Just enough is NEVER enough to prepare us for the tasks, challenges and achievements we desire as we journey through life.* I approach every task in life like it is a training session for a future ambition or goal that I have. Always giving it my best shot is beneficial first and foremost to me even if I don't get accolades.

I can't see myself doing just enough. It is an injustice to me and a complete waste of the time I could spend earning invaluable experience. I strive to do my best at all times, not for the employer but for myself.

I believe life is a journey and the road we thread along forms the fabric of our strength, our knowledge and experience.

That's why we must give it our best effort each time, every time. We must all Strive to be Better – Even at our Perceived Best!

BE PREPARED

Adequate preparation is key! Otherwise we are just gambling. Doing our homework can never be overemphasised. In everything we do; we must anticipate the outcomes and prepare for them as best as we can.

I walked in like I owned the place. "If I was asked to attend to this client, I must have what it takes and be really good, even the best."

"I was born to do this," I said to my then twenty-two-year-old self. He was having breakfast when I arrived, so I was asked to sit in the adjourning living room adjacent to him, right in front of the television set while I waited for him.

"I will be with you shortly," he said politely, as I settled into my seat majestically.

"How is your boss?" he asked, trying to make polite conversation while he ate before the 'proper' meeting started.

"He is very well, Sir, he sends his regards." I responded.

The food smelt and looked delicious. I tried not to watch him eat, so I turned my gaze to the television set feigning interest even though my mind was on something else.

Noticing my 'interest' he asked; "Do you like golf?"

I responded quickly, "Not at all."

"Why" he asked?

I immediately went on a rant, as if possessed. "I think it is boring." . . . "And slow." . . . "Only suitable for lazy people who cannot play fast-paced simultaneous competitive sports like tennis or squash."

I went on and on. Even emphasizing my position by pointing out how most Nigerian golfers had pot-bellies and were usually old. I must have spoken for a lifetime. As I continued, I became aware of my environment, as if in slow-motion. I started to notice objects around the room: golf trophies, branded golf balls, golf clubs even the TV set had a golf tournament showing.

Just then I realized he had asked, 'Do you LOVE Golf TOO?' In my zeal to speak I did not hear the words LOVE and 'TOO'.

He even had the pot belly I had so fervently ascribed to golf players. At this point I clutched at the document that was sitting on my lap. All I was required to do was to get one signature and go back to the office. I may have just blown this important deal that my bosses had so carefully put together, I thought to myself.

I learnt a huge lesson that day. Preparation! I must understand the operating environment and key facts of every transaction before commencement. I must do my homework next time, every time, never taking plunges in the dark and just assuming that I am the 'best' therefore everything will fall into place. In everything we do: at work, play and life, we can't assume if it's meant to be; it will be. We have to take deliberate steps to achieve the success we desire.

RESILIENCE

After we have prepared, what happens if we don't get the results we have anticipated?

I was deflated! The meeting didn't go as anticipated. After months of writing proposals, initial meetings, preparations and sleepless nights, it ended up as a huge disappointment!

My expectation was that we would be ushered in to meet with the Chairman and he will be impressed by our brand new well-tailored suits and listen keenly as we spoke. We even bought a brand new sophisticated and expensive projector so we could look the part as we made the presentation to him. This transaction was going to change our lives and put our company on a new path.

I had gone over my 'chant' word for word. I was ready! Everything was in place! And the transaction will be sealed today.

I was wrong! He barely looked up to acknowledge us!

"There will be no need for a presentation," he started.

"I have read the summary of the proposals sent and we are not 'ready' to implement any of your recommendations, therefore, we can't proceed with your proposal" he continued; barely looking away from his computer. "We will get back to you."

With that, we were ushered out of his office! This meeting lasted a little over a minute even though we had waited for an hour and fifty minutes to see him.

We walked out feeling confused. We had done everything right. I could not fault our approach. Why didn't we get the result we wanted and accomplish our goal? I was ready to give up. But as we walked out of their office building; I saw signposts lined neatly in front. They all read:

KEEP MOVING! NO STOPPING! NO WAITING!

They indicated that cars should not stop or park there and no loitering or street trading.

I had seen that sign many times before, but have never read any significant meaning into it!

That day the words struck me like lightening. They spoke to me!

"RESILIENCE," they said! Just as I was about to throw my arms up in the air and give up!

With that, I picked up my stride, walked briskly to our cars and immediately started working mentally on our key next steps.

Although we prepare adequately and still did not get the results we want, it is important for us to be resilient. We shouldn't give up, stop or be discouraged. We must Keep Moving!

Many people assume that I have it better than others.

"You don't have my kind of problem," they say.

The truth is that I have had my fair share of life's challenges and still do today. I learn from my hurdles, take it in my stride and keep going. I dwell on it just long enough to earn an invaluable lesson and move on. I try not to complain about it, or make it my focus or let it define me. I prefer to be defined by the path that I have chosen for myself.

I keep moving. Never stopping! Never waiting!

And remember, you define your own success, so set a goal and seek to add value, do your best, be prepared and never give up!

About Catherine

Catherine O. Enaohwo is a fervent believer that we are all interconnected and therefore strives to enhance all around her as she achieves her life goals.

She is a founding member and Chief Executive Officer of Peregrino Oil & Gas Limited. Her background is in Economics with decades of experience in formulating financial strategies and solutions.

Catherine is an alumnus of Wits Business School (South Africa) and the New York Institute of Finance (USA). She has also attained the status of 'Fellow' in notable institutes such as the Institute of Chartered Economists of Nigeria (ICEN), the Chartered Institute of Professional Financial Managers (USA) and the Institute of Professional Financial Consultants (Nigeria). Catherine is also a council member of the Chartered Institute of Professional Financial Managers (CIPFM), West Africa.

She is the founder and current chairman of the board of Arete Copious Services Limited (a leading financial consulting firm), and has worked in notable local and international financial institutions in key roles that has afforded her in-depth knowledge of financial modelling for sustainable growth and profitability.

Catherine O. Enaohwo is an inspirational speaker and enjoys sharing her experiences with groups. She is also a philanthropist. In recognition of her selfless contributions towards the alleviation of the sufferings of the less privileged; she was recognized with the award of the title of Ambassador for Peace by the Universal Peace Federation; an international NGO in special consultative status with the UNITED NATIONS.

She also loves to play chess and travel to fascinating destinations.

CHAPTER 6

IT TAKES A LEADER, NOT A BOSS, TO CREATE AN IMPACT

BY KEN BRATZ

When a "common language" is created in the work environment, leaders emerge.

The main goal of any workplace, regardless of size, is to make enough of a profit to remain a viable business. We rely on the people we work with to make this happen, as we cannot go it alone. The larger a business gets, the more daunting this task can get. It's easy for managers to lose sight of the value that those employees under them have. It is also easy for management to become employee watchers, critiquing their work, expecting them to do what they have been told, and then delivering a favorable report to their manager after all is said and done. But is this effective? No, it isn't. Very seldom does this work, and it certainly isn't the best use of your employees—a resource that is considered highly valuable to all organizations.

How do we make a work environment where everyone is flowing together, knowing what to do (which most do), and having a culture where they are helping with solutions and profits, not simply just doing what they're told, without knowing why? We're talking about people, not trained circus performers! We do this by making an IMPACT.

CREATING IMPACT

An organization is at its best when it promotes a robust, higher level of performance.

We developed the IMPACT process with a singular goal in mind: to help organizations achieve a higher level of performance. To know we were on the right path, our benchmark was those organizations that were already working at high performance levels. What were they doing? And how could we carry over their strategies to other businesses, creating specific strategic steps that were for that business.

The common elements we found amongst all high-performing businesses included:

1. Clear communication channels
2. A clear strategy and plan of action that everyone knew about and understood
3. Value-added service mentality for customers, both internal and external
4. Continued questioning of how things were done, never doing something simply because, "that is how it has always been done."

The results of these efforts were clear: *the organizations got better!* This is what IMPACT is, and with it, each of us is challenged to learn and do things in a better manner. It doesn't happen overnight, because habits don't change overnight. But with commitment and awareness and new actions, in approximately one year, a positive shift in the workplace culture can take place. Everyone is participating and leaders emerge, not just people making sure that an employee "does what they've been told to do." The system fixes the system.

SIX TENETS OF IMPACT

Our actions directly lead to the type of environment we create in our lives, both professionally and personally.

We hear a lot of success stories from people who've gone through this process. The growth and learning in their work environment also carries over into their personal lives. One story, in particular, really affirmed that the IMPACT process was right on track. This gentleman was an active and engaged participant in the process and it helped him better connect to his work environment and help his organization gain results, but at home, he felt the benefits of this personally. His son had always struggled in school, more often on the brink of failing than succeeding, and with the use of these six tenets in his home life, he found a new approach to helping his son. It changed things around, guiding his son's grades toward the "A zone". And what a difference that made, not only for the son and his confidence to evaluate, learn, and solve problems in his own life, but also in the relationship between the two. It opened up communication channels and the expectations became clear. Dad was a leader, encouraging and helping, not a boss just chewing him out.

Tenet #1: IMPACT begins when a strategic plan is created, or a current one is revised, and all employees on all levels become engaged in that plan. It is no coincidence that this is where most organizations fail, as they look at this as something that's on a "need to know" basis. Well, everyone does need to know, because every employee is a contributor in some way.

Tenet #2: the working environment is challenged and changed to increase communication and to speed up the process of problem solving and decision-making. It doesn't happen overnight because it seems foreign—not the norm for most organizations. A good comparison is to think about what it's like driving on the freeway versus a two-lane highway. To achieve this tenet, there are events that take place once a month, usually about two hours long. These events are designed to promote team work and innovative problem solving. One of the most effective ways that we've seen to kick off IMPACT initiatives is by having a full-day kick-off event. People get the spark of excitement they need and steps are taken to keep the spark ignited. All too often, the enthusiasm leaves when an employee returns to the "same old, same old."

Tenet #3: it takes consistent efforts and strategies to create meaningful change, particularly relating to the way projects are managed, meetings are run, and problems are solved. This can be challenging for employees, especially those who have made their way to a management position, as they often embrace the "boss mentality" instead of "leadership mode." The results of these efforts speak for themselves, though, and can be compared to finally putting grease on a dry bearing. Performance is enhanced and some of the resistant bearings just need to be greased more often than others. And that's okay.

Tenet #4: coaching is a necessity for the process. Through coaching, people help each other get better in everything they do, because what we do does matter. During this tenet, we learn to listen better and accept that we can become better. We gain confidence in our voice and our ideas.

Tenet #5: learning how to communicate with customers better than the competition, doing what we tell them we will do with a smile on our face, and sincerity in our words. We become true partners, never taking our customer for granted.

Tenet #6: laying out the foundation through open dialogue and acceptance of ideas from all employees, at all levels. By doing this, organizations maintain their freshness in problem solving and innovations that lead to a culture where employees know they are valued and they are in a pro-personal and professional growth environment. When people feel this, they are less likely to leave and low turnover is something that most organizations have a goal of achieving.

THE RESULTS OF IMPACT

One of the most rewarding parts of what we do with organizations is hearing about the successes, and actually seeing how the enhanced bottom line speaks for itself.

While working with a large oil producer in Southern California, we were faced with the challenge of keeping the business profitable, as the price of oil had plunged downward. The company's back was against the wall—they had approximately one hundred and twenty union employees and the union, in itself, was very active. It created additional challenges. The hope: *to find a way to remain profitable without having to lay-off or let go any employees.*

With low morale, employees didn't believe that the unfair bosses they had would ever look out for them in tough times and their guards were up. Eventually, their Field Superintendent resigned to work for another company and the Director of Operations named another person to that role, and this person had been through IMPACT and knew its value. He also knew that he was up against some pretty strong convictions and negativity. Workers were not keen on cooperating, because there was no trust.

The first distinctive difference in this new Field Supervisor was that he actually walked around the field. This freaked employees out and they'd radio ahead to other field employees so everyone would know where he was. He found it amusing, but he didn't mind. He had a goal: *to create trust and increase communication.* He couldn't do that anywhere other than in the field with the people.

It was during this time that the strike occurred. IMPACT classes on measurement were also being held at this time. The workers were not excited about class, but they tolerated the process. During one of these classes, the Superintendent handed out the Profit and Loss Statement to the employees. He then assigned specific people to different P&L Statement items that were in areas they weren't familiar with, along with further instructions to create a graph and put it up in the break room on their assigned area—all while also looking for ways to cut costs. They were really de-motivated by this assignment, but a few took the challenge.

One man, Bob, was assigned to the electric bill. This was no normal bill, either, coming in at $1,000,000 per month! He went to the accountant for some additional information on the bill, wondering how it was figured and what steps were in place to determine if it was correct. The response: "We pay what is on the bill. Doesn't everyone?" Bob recruited an employee who was an electrical engineer next, and together, they looked over the multitude of bills they got each month and could not make any sense from them at all. Time to call the electric company and get an explanation.

What they found was really shocking—the electric company didn't provide them much help. Yes, that's correct. So, they went back and talked to several people about it, including the Superintendent and the company attorney. If the electric company did not know how their bill was figured, they might have an enviable position to negotiate. The meeting with the electric company netted them a twenty percent reduction in monthly cost, $200,000.

These results really fired Bob up more. He decided to attend the regularly safety meetings and appeal to his fellow employees about the electric bill. He asked them to look around and determine which switches they could leave off, without affecting operations. Bob was laughed into the ground. But... At the next safety meeting an employee reported that a project that was completed over two years ago was still pumping lots of water into the ground. Why? Because no one had been told to stop the project. This got everyone's attention and they were extremely quiet.

Bob's fire was contagious, because after the meeting, a fellow worker came up to him and mentioned that he thought there was another company's power line going across their property. Was one cheaper that the other? Bob ended up finding out that the demand rates were significantly different between the two companies; to take advantage of the lower rates they would have to buy a $150,000 switch, which would have to be switched twice daily, within a fifteen-minute window of time, in order to get the maximum advantage. It made sense to do and there was nothing to argue the contrary. These, as well as other solutions were worked through, and before year's end, the company cut their electric bill in half—a $6,000,000 annual savings.

This is IMPACT! When people want to help each other and when they are encouraged to communicate, unexpected things can occur. The company then sent their electrical engineer to all other field locations, never failing to cut the electric bill by at least 15% less at each location.

FIVE WAYS TO CREATE COMMON GROUND

By creating common ground among all employees, of all levels, the best workplace cultures are created.

One of my most favorite parts about the work I do with organizations involves the team activities, where they do experiential activities. I can take these activities to conference rooms to help people begin working together in order to solve a "fun" problem. From there, people learn to work with different types of behavioral styles and explore fresh, innovative ideas that solve problems. They find "common ground."

Here are five focuses of common ground:

1. Follow some basic principles that will:
   a. Preserve the integrity of others
   b. Put into practice active listening
   c. Be inclusive of all in problem solving
   d. Create accountability

2. Set the ground rules for employee engagement with each other that is for all levels of employees (yes, management included). These ground rules should be mindful of:
   a. Providing the "why" not just the "what" and "how"
   b. Being inclusive of all people at all levels
   c. Encouraging a culture that asks questions
   d. Giving everybody a role that will use their strengths
   e. A positive environment that is free of negativity and "water cooler complaining"
   f. Obtain the data and resources to give employees the "full scope" of what they need in order to begin finding solutions
   g. Listening without criticizing
   h. Recognizing the contributions of people

3. Gain understanding of the behavior style of individual employees, taking into account DISC (Dominance, Influence, Steadiness, Compliance) and where people lie in regards to this. This is assessed through observing "task versus relationships" and "level of assertiveness."

4. Follow an effective dialogue model that includes these elements:
   a. Understanding of the common purpose of the dialogue
   b. The specific ground rules needed to create a good dialogue environment
   c. The dialogue of asking versus telling, which relates to the "Ladder of Inference" and includes these seven rungs:
      i. Collect all available data
      ii. Select data
      iii. Add meaning
      iv. Make assumptions

        v. Draw conclusions
      vi. Take actions
     vii. Get results
   d. A focused initiative to have the end result become common understanding

5. Implement an effective problem-solving model, which will focus on five specific steps:
   a. Define the problem
   b. Analyze the problem
   c. Find the solution (long term vs. short term)
   d. Plan the solution
   e. Implement and evaluate the solution

With my facilitating of events that lead organizations to transitions that promote leadership cultures instead of the "boss" environment, it has become clear that we all have basic commonalities in our needs, whether as an individual or an organization. There are ways to bring about the best results for an organization by focusing on each individual and how critical they are to the overall success of the organization. Negativity is contagious, but so is positive action and implementation. In a world where we want to be acknowledged for our contributions and built up, we are better able to do that when the right mindset and structure is in place. Instead of having employees feel like they are constantly on the "firing line" – let them know that they are surrounded by leaders who are making a positive IMPACT.

About Ken

Ken Bratz is the principal of Ken Bratz Consulting. Ken started his consulting business over 46 years ago, with the intent of providing individuals and organizations resources for developing a high-performance environment. The offerings include Strategic Planning, Communication Tools, Team Experiences, and many others. Ken has worked as an executive coach as well as providing a culture change process (IMPACT) for large organizations. Through the years, many courses and intervention strategies have been developed to meet the clients' needs.

Ken is a graduate of Texas A&M University. His hobbies include piddling, reading, and amateur radio (WA5JUM). Ken is also a Business Chaplain.

Ken has been married for over 50 years to his wife, Patsy, and lives in Palestine, Texas. They have three daughters and nine grandchildren.

1-800-657-2235
www.kenbratz.com

CHAPTER 7

OUR HABITS DEFINE OUR DESTINY

BY SHERJUAN 'SHERM' BROWN

The habits we create trickle down into all parts of our lives
and impact what we can offer others.

I'll never forget the day that I first really understood what a true struggle was. I was quite young and my brother and I were already home from school in our small apartment. My mom walked through the door and I looked up. She was limping and trying to hold back her tears. "What happened?" I asked. She explained that she'd stepped on some glass and it went right through the bottom of her shoe, puncturing her foot. Some dirty old newspaper was the only thing between that wound and the soul of her shoe. The pain on her face was so intense, and it was both physical and emotional pain.

"Why don't you get a car, Mom?" I asked. She replied with a weary voice. "Son, if I could afford it, I would. Money is something we don't have, son." Her words were impactful, because my mom was a very hard-working woman. She worked three jobs and raised two sons on her own. My "father" was a non-existent presence in our lives.

At that moment, I told myself that when I was old enough, my mom would have a car and she would never want for anything. Nor would anyone else I cared for.

Then I got older…

We all go from a place of want to where we must "figure it all out."

Most people want money. Where most people struggle is that they have no idea how to get it—the right way. I knew I wanted wealth, but it took me years and many life cycles to figure it out. I had yet to learn the importance of being resilient and committed to what was worth achieving, for whatever the reason may be.

Think of how young kids respond to a new day. They're instantly excited. There are toys to play with, things to build, and lots to do—all before going to school. On the contrasting end, many adults feel just the opposite. The day starts slow, they struggle, and it's so challenging. What's the difference between the two? Mindset! Children see life as a wonderful experience filled with opportunities and adventures, and somehow adults' transition into a mode of existence, losing the motivation that keeps life an amazing opportunity to experience.

THE "MOVE LIFE FORWARD" CIRCLE…

Everything we choose to do to create positive
change in our life is beneficial.

When we are motivated by something greater, we can gain clearer vision on how to begin making changes with the inner drive and energy that are essential. This circle creates the story of our life and is held together by our motivation to not just exist, but thrive.

Accountability

Accountability is a word that many people just can't grasp. Often enough, accountability gets confused with responsibility, but there is a big difference.

I had a job at the airport after high school where I was making $4/hour and feeling pretty great about it. It was more money than I'd ever had before, totaling about $500/per month. It made me feel wealthy in a way, because growing up I didn't even have lunch money. Now I could help

Mom out a bit, pay for my pager, buy some shoes, and save some too. I still wanted more.

One day at work, I saw a newspaper ad for "young entrepreneurs." It referenced how you could be young and get into business for yourself. This was a highly appealing message to me and I checked it out. It was for selling vacuum cleaners door to door. I wanted to give it a try, even though I'd have to take a bus to get there since I didn't have a car.

When I got to work one day it was past 8 AM, the time I was supposed to be there, and my boss was waiting for me, displeased. "Why are you late?" I looked at him and started to explain. "I catch the bus at 7 AM. The bus was backed up. I had to run a half mile..." He stopped me short and said, "I need you to be here at 8 AM every day. If you're done working at 12 noon, you have from 12 noon to 8 AM to get here. Who said you had to leave at 7 AM? You can leave your house at whatever time you need to get here by 8 AM. Do that tomorrow or you won't have a job." At the time I thought, rude! Today, I think, true!

No one puts limits on our time aside from us. We are accountable for our actions. Blaming others and making lame excuses does not work for us, ultimately. Accountability is personal responsibility. You must take control of your actions, regardless of if they are good or bad. It's all perspective. See the positive over the negative so you can gain a different, more beneficial perspective.

Reject being the victim

Once you learn accountability, doors open and you disable your "victim button." Years ago, I taught an anger management class and personal accountability was a big topic within it. We discussed how we become victims through keeping violent and abusive relationships and actions in our life. We think that's just the way it is, or justify our behaviors. This is not true.

I had a friend who was addicted to being a victim and playing the blame game. It was always someone else's fault. They cheated. They didn't try. They were not committed. Finally, I asked, "When are you going to grab a hold of your life and get what you want out of it; to not allow others to define your happiness?" She was thrown off by this, but needed to hear it. I wanted to rattle the way she was thinking. From what I understand, it helped. She did move on to wonderful, uplifting things for her life.

Treating ourselves well

Our bodies, minds, and attitude are connected and help us to either remain motivated or deflate us. For me, being physically active and athletic is important. I still play in a football league, and work out every day. I'm as youthful as some of the college kids running around with me, and I can still run faster than a great many of them. Why do I do this? Because I love it and I know it makes me better. I want to treat my entire being well.

People frequently ask me to train them. I'm glad to do it if they are personally motivated. I emphasize this point! Part of gaining this motivation is tapping into childhood-like energy and also knowing why you want to do something. Furthermore, it's okay if it is a negative experience that motivates you.

I had a best friend in high school who was huge, at least 350 pounds. He ended up getting married shortly after high school. Like so many friendships, we grew apart over time but could easily catch up if we saw each other. I'd heard through the grapevine that he was having some marital problems, as his wife had left him and he was doing pretty-badly emotionally. I saw him about a year-and-a-half later and saw a different guy than what I remembered and heard about. He was down to about 180 pounds, looking great. I asked him about it and he said, "After I got divorced, I wanted to prove to her that I was every bit the man she said she was leaving me for."

Spurred by a negative event, he found positive motivation. Through regular workouts and watching what he ate, he made the changes he wanted to experience. He was motivated! In fact, he ran into his ex a few years later and she showed a great deal of interest in him again. He'd moved on, but it felt great for him to see her take note of what she'd left behind.

Goal motivation

When we want something, we can find the motivation to succeed. This is how we build goals and achieve them. I have always been motivated in life by the fact that I had no father present – it committed me to being the best father possible for my four children. I'm there in their lives, engaged and involved. And they know it—without a doubt. I wouldn't trade it for anything. This motivates me endlessly!

There are two main types of motivation we can tap into—financial motivation and emotional motivation. You can dig motivation up anywhere. Just start digging! The great Michael Jordan is an excellent example of this. When someone asked him how he got fired up for road games against teams who were not good, he shared a secret. He would dispatch scouts to the cities he'd be traveling to and have them dig up anything that suggested someone in the game was better than he was – maybe faster, maybe smarter. Then he'd go and give that team his Michael Jordan best effort.

Small things can fuel our fire, and by creating motivation we can get out of bed and start our pursuit of achieving goals. I am a firm believer that amazing things stem from a good competitive spirit and carry over into all aspects of our lives.

Make your plan

I work in the financial industry and we often talk about wishers and dreamers versus action. Remember the excited kid in the morning? They had lofty goals and embraced them. Then they got older and found out those things take work—reality kicked in. As an adult, you still need to have a childlike dream, but you must begin implementing plans in order to succeed. Don't stop seeking out that treasure or seeing the world as a playground of opportunity. Far too many adults abandon making plans and settle for the 9-5 job where they can robotically go about their day.

Within the plan exists the call-to-action. In my life, I've needed to create my own competitive edge. With work, I began looking at my industry and paying attention to the rankings. That motivated me and I not only wanted to see my name in them, but to be at the top of the list. For you, your motivation may be something involving having children, wanting a better lifestyle, relationships, etc. Goals are limitless.

Everything we do should be focused on positive benefits and abandoning negative habits. Plus, knowing that nothing says that we have to stick to a plan no matter what—it can be adjusted, but only if you know you really tried to act on it. Never abandon a plan out of fear.

Take action

I was always taught to be the smartest person in the room, not literally, but in mindset. To do this, it required taking action and continually educating myself, and growing into what I wanted to become. We should all do this. It's necessary so we don't grow complacent, which is a cozy companion to surrender and stagnancy. It doesn't matter what situation you are in or what your profession is, you can still learn something and gain experiences every day.

Winston Churchill said, "Success consists of going from failure to failure without loss of enthusiasm." The key is understanding how to use what you learned from the failure in order to succeed on the next try. There will be failure in business, in fact, there may be quite a few of them; but if you take the lesson from failure and learn and grow from it, you're going to be more successful.

Keep in mind that not everyone around you wants you to succeed. Some want you to stay behind and not get ahead of them. Remember, your actions show who you are and define you, first and foremost. To really enhance this, surround yourself with likeminded, smart people who are vested in your success or at a minimum, are not vested in bringing you down.

LEADERS COME IN MANY FORMS...

Our actions to pay it forward in this world are necessary.

Creating something that outlives my physical existence here on earth is important to me. To do this, it takes leadership from me, and leadership is an attribute which everyone has the potential to demonstrate.

There are a few types of leaders. There are Leaders, and there are those who Lead. Picture someone like Kobe Bryant. Kobe chooses to lead by his own example. He tells players what he's doing to get better and leaves it up to them to participate. "I'm going to be at the gym at 5:00am with or without you. With or without "the others", he's going to keep improving his game. The second type of leader is more like LeBron James. He's the guy who says he is going to the gym at 5:00am so he'll be at your house at 4:30am to pick you up—so be ready. Both Kobe and LeBron are leaders and two of the best players the NBA will ever see, just with different styles.

What style of leader are you? To me, it's important that what I do shows that I care. I want others to be inspired, but I'll never "make them do it." This is reflected in how I choose to give back, as well. I don't need to announce it and force others, but I want them to see what is happening through what I do.

For example, being a kid raised in the Boy's Club system taught me so much. Today, I want to pay it forward for other kids so they can have those same chances that I have had. I do this by sponsoring drives to help those who may not have the means to help themselves. And my goals don't stop there. I have goals and plans of action set in place for many other things in the future. My personal inspiration is to touch those areas of my life that were most impactful to my childhood experiences.

These messages of how to create a meaningful life experience for people and how to start living in the cycle of success are important to me, and sharing them with as many attentive ears as I can find is so inspiring. Whether it's talking to young entrepreneurs or potential clients, I want them to sense that I am truly vested in elevating their lives.

About 'Sherm'

Sherjuan 'Sherm' Brown is a mortgage and financial advisor who specializes in helping people save and invest money. He utilizes safe money strategies which help protect his clients from market risks while enjoying tax-free growth.

Sherm began his career by selling mortgage loans to veterans, many of whom couldn't afford the homes that they lived in. Recognizing that there were programs that could help these veterans to stay in their homes, Sherm began providing low cost mortgage programs to his clients (even though these programs paid a significantly lower commission to him). His mindset was to help as many people achieve their dreams as possible, which would in turn, help him reach his own.

In 2014, Sherm founded Intelli-Vest Financial, LLC. His company was created with the purpose of encouraging people to "Invest Smart". Sherm has been serving families for over 15 years with a focus on making each client a personal friend. He feels that if you treat each client as you would your own personal friend or family member, you will always have their best interest at heart.

Whether Sherm is assisting people with lowering their mortgage payments or with saving strategies for their retirement goals, he understands how these things are of the utmost importance. Most of his clients are given gifts just for meeting with him, regardless of whether they ultimately engage in a business relationship or not.

You can also find Sherm involved in motivational and self-help seminars, teaching people to reach their fullest potential. He has spoken at local grade schools and universities, as well as conducted lunch-and-learn workshops to help educate people in becoming more credit-wise and financially secure.

Sherm lives with his wife and four children in the Las Vegas area. He enjoys spending quality time with his family, traveling and sports.

 For more information on working with Sherm or to discuss speaking opportunities, you can contact him at:
- Website: www.how2invest.net
- Direct: 702-204-8400
- Email: mrdebtfree@gmail.com

CHAPTER 8

TECHNOLOGY ENTREPRENEURS
HOW TO CREATE BETTER TOMORROWS THROUGH TODAY'S VISIONS

BY JEFFREY S. PETERSON

Technology is forever evolving. However, the way
it can be brought to the world is a constant.

To understand that my life's path has largely been sculpted by technology is an easy concept to grasp for anyone who has taken note of my journey. Maybe it was because I first became hooked on technology and wide area networks when connecting to the first version of the public Internet, known back then as ARPANET, through the University of California, Santa Barbara computer center as a young boy (in 1978). For many observers, they conceptualize technology as something that was most likely "born in a basement", but before those visionaries began creating with the resources they had, the idea was invented in their mind. Someone felt the potential for a technology that would be helpful to some, perhaps even to all. Dreams are expanded and extended beyond what we may currently imagine.

Something inside of me understood this long before I could easily explain it, and certainly before I found opportunities to show that I was onto something of real value. Not everyone got it, but I was determined to develop the skills to allow me to express my vision so people would understand. Most entrepreneurs will readily admit that the most significant struggle they face lies in getting others to acknowledge and embrace their vision. Add in technology—which many people fear due to lack of understanding—and it can be even tougher. For me, breaking these boundaries and opening up peoples' minds to limitless potential has always been a priority, and continues as the driving passion behind my mission today.

This is how we can extend beyond the present.
After all, our futures are only a second away.

I can hear it now. "So, Jeffrey... I have ideas. They're really sound. How do I take them from concept to cultivation?" I've completed this journey before, although I often feel like I'm at the beginning. And I remember those days where people looked at me like I was too optimistic, but I knew what I conceptualized was more than just a hope, it was achievable! Starting out was not easy and it took resilience, along with a healthy dose of confidence that I would relay the vision I had effectively. It was seldom easy to find a captive audience. But eventually I did.

Being a technology entrepreneur does take hard work, and it's not for those who are going to be diverted easily. Call it grit, call it passion, just call it what it is—incomparable determination to go the distance with your ideas (as well as adjust what doesn't work).

Having been in that place where I was forced to figure out who I could approach with the ideas I had, I found a way. It worked well for me, but not from luck. It was due to a specific course of action. Those are the steps that I want to share with you, as they will allow you to evaluate your tech ideas and determine how ready you and your ideas are. Are they viable? And, do you have it within you to give it all that's required to go the distance? All of this doesn't happen overnight; it can take years!

I. FINDING YOUR NICHE MARKET

Entrepreneurs need to find a problem and offer a solution for it.

From the time I understood technology, I loved it. Programming computers, solving logic problems, and building products was a time-consuming passion of mine. I admit, I enjoyed it thoroughly, and certainly more than I connected with any sort of school curriculum that I was forced to take at the time. When it came time to find a career, the Internet wasn't commercially viable yet. Tech jobs that actually offered a steady income were practically non-existent, so I entered into a training program with New York-based Lehman Brothers, where I learned how to be a stock broker and to better understand corporate finance. I had the privilege to work around the business of corporate finance for years during the 1990's. It was good for me and to me, offering me a great career, but it was not ingrained in me the way technology was. Until... I was doing some research and came across something that immediately piqued my interest. When it came to the internet, the Hispanic market was basically being ignored. I sensed a tremendous opportunity to help a significant portion of the population, while creating a business opportunity at the same time.

Acting with the best of intentions, I had stumbled upon a niche market that comprised nearly 30% of the US population. This was the birth of Quepasa, a company that would serve the Hispanic-speaking population by building a social network that could give Spanish speakers a place to interact online in their native language and in a place that was culturally relevant. I got to work and did a few critical things:

- Began mapping out and creating the intensive undertaking of serving the niche I'd found.
- Sought out an investor who would understand my vision and support it. No one was more fortunate than I when Gloria Estefan gave me the "yes" to the invest in 1998.
- Grew the value and concept enough to raise over $50 million privately, eventually raising over $100 million and becoming a publicly-traded company on the Nasdaq Stock Market in 1999. We were the first technology business focused on the U.S. Hispanic market to go public.

That's when I saw firsthand how serving a group in need was good for their growth, as well as healthy for the dreams and goals that I personally had. Nearly a decade later, Quepasa was taken over by a group led by then-venture capitalist Rick Scott (later Rick would become the Governor of Florida). At its peak, while I was running the business, Quepasa reached a market value of about $500 million. Quepasa changed its corporate name in 2012 and still exists today by the name MeetMe. This was pretty big, as market analysts commented on CNBC that Quepasa with its 50 million users was first social network to go public and trade on a stock exchange in the U.S. The second—Facebook.

Niches can be highly lucrative opportunities to build and grow a technology concept that truly changes lives for the better. Once you find that area to specialize in, however, you have to have a strong grasp of how to rise up to the challenge you've created for yourself.

II. THREE ASPECTS OF TECHNOLOGY ENTREPRENEURIALISM THAT SHOULD NOT BE FORGOTTEN

You will never know it all, but you can make
certain that you know more every day.

When you are building up a technology platform you must be savvy to the user experience and the lessons that you can learn from those experiences, as well as the opportunities that exist within better understanding them. It's a huge undertaking and in order to be successful at it, you need to maintain a focused perspective on three fundamentals. When planned and played together they are game changers:

1. **Continuous Training**

   Invest in learning technology and don't fall victim to thinking you either do or should "know it all". It's ever-evolving and you'll miss out on your key opportunities to finesse your concepts if you don't focus on continuous training.

2. **A Good Base**

   The base you end up with for your business is often different than the one you started with. As you learn and grow, the foundation becomes stronger and shifts into a more permanent position. One of the best things you can do is surround yourself with a great peer group that will run the marathon with you. You should all have different strengths while sharing a united understanding of the goal.

3. **Using the 80/20 Rule in Technology**

   The 80/20 Rule is focused on how 20% of your efforts will yield 80% of the results. The rest is "busy work", necessary, but not the part of your endeavor that will lead to profitability, which is a MUST in technology businesses, just as it is in other businesses.

Two points that you must remember are:

(i). Just because tech entrepreneurs work on tech-oriented things doesn't mean that they don't need customers. With a strong focus on the product and how it is going to help a specific group you will get customers, eventually. It works itself out. The earlier you can find a way to help others and get paid for your expertise, the more sustainable your existence will be. Without the first piece being right, nothing else matters.

(ii). You want to strive for putting your energies into what will help you take your product to market the most quickly. Over time, you can increase the product's sophistication and function. It may not be perfect and you may spend years tearing it down from hard lessons learned, and that is okay. What comes first is helping people. Work with the spirit of that intention in mind and you'll find the energy and drive to take care of the rest.

The results of these efforts will be that you will be paid fairly and well for your time and expertise. Providing consistent and reliable technology helps others and as a result, it boosts your confidence in your product and how to enhance it as it builds its reputation—and you build yours!

III. THE VISIONS OF SUCCESS WITH TECHNOLOGY ENTREPRENEURS

The formula for technology success can be repeated. The greatest joy comes in helping others and giving back with the knowledge you've learned and from what you've earned.

After I sold Quepasa, an incredible world of opportunities opened up for me, both as a lifelong advocate for technology and someone who finds great satisfaction in helping transform others' lives for the better.

Today, among other things, I am focusing on international markets. Recently I have been working on increasing the visibility of the Philippines in the U.S. I learned through my experience that there is endless value and potential in international markets. By helping the right people along the way, true positive differences are being made. Is everyone meant to be a technology entrepreneur? No, they aren't, but those who are, truly are gifted in abundance and graced with the visions of the potential of their ideas. This is why I focus on helping these people become viable and productive on their journey.

One of the greatest resources that I am honored to be connected with to help bring out this technology potential that exists in so many entrepreneurs, is an investment that I have with Peter Thiel, co-founder of PayPal, and Richard Rosenblatt, former CEO of MySpace, among other high profile names. Through this venture, which is called VATOR, we helped to create a Silicon Valley think-tank for technology start-ups. Through this channel of promotion, tech entrepreneurs have an opportunity to gain an audience of tech-minded individuals who celebrate this particular brand of entrepreneurialism for the potential it holds. We have all been there and gone through the process. Helping others to do the same is a truly great reward.

Entrepreneurs who are interested in technology know that there are no limits to what they can do with the ideas they have —simplistic, or complex and sophisticated.

There is no more powerful way to connect the world than by serving niche markets that are in need of a product or service if you are a tech person. You can write your own story and there are unlimited problems to solve, which leads to you creating unlimited value. This cannot be done all alone; rather, it's a group effort that allows you to have access to the best people in all disciplines related to being a technology entrepreneur. It's simply amazing to think of how profound an impact this can have on our future.

About Jeffrey

Jeffrey Peterson is a technologist, entrepreneur, and investor. He grew up in Southern California, and developed interest in computers at an early age. He left school to work at a top tier Wall Street Investment Bank in the early 1990's.

At the dawn of the original .com technology boom, 1998, Jeff launched the first nationally-branded internet community for Spanish speaking users online. His business, QUEPASA, gained international attention when it reached the #1 position in the United States Hispanic internet market, beating competitor Yahoo En Español with over fifty million users. QUEPASA made technology history by becoming the first social network to trade on a stock exchange, reaching a peak market value in excess of $500 million on the NASDAQ Stock Market.

In 2007, QUEPASA was acquired by billionaire investor Rick Scott, who now serves as the Governor of Florida. In 2012, QUEPASA changed its corporate business name to MeetMe and continued trading on the Nasdaq Stock Market under stock symbol MEET. MeetMe today continues as a thriving public company with over two million active daily users out of a total size exceeding hundreds of millions of online users.

Today, Jeff serves on a number of corporate, advisory and public policy boards of directors, and enjoys educating entrepreneurs about technology and business.

CHAPTER 9

TEN HORRIBLE MISTAKES SUCCESSFUL WORKING MUMS AVOID

BY MOFOLUWASO ILEVBARE

Being a working mum can be a bittersweet experience. Sometimes it feels like you're living two contrasting lives. On one hand, if you put in your best to finish every work assignment, attend every business meeting, visit every client, tick off your to-do list, and submit every project proposals ahead of schedule, you'd probably never go home. On the other hand, if you put 100% of your energy into keeping your home sparkling clean yourself, cooking homemade meals with the right calorie content, attending every basketball game or ballet rehearsals, and being there 24/7 for everyone, you'd probably still not satisfy all the needs plus you'd end up pretty exhausted. Enjoying everyday life comes from feeling empowered to make the choices that best suit your season of life rather than being cajoled into something you hate.

WHY LISTEN TO ME?

My life as a career woman has been jolted twice by the birth of my two boys both currently under age 10. Whether it's the ecstatic feeling of seeing those two pink lines, the first 3D scan, experiencing that first kick or finally holding that tiny piece of God in your hands, your life as you knew it will change. As a full time working mum with two adorable boys, a part time speaking and coaching business, a blogger, best-selling author, member of the John Maxwell Team and founder of two charity organizations, I've had to make major adjustments in my life from time to time to truly be the woman I was created to be. I'm devoting this chapter to working mums in leadership and business since I live with the unique experiences every day. You can also blame it on the way I am feeling right now—taking a much-needed vacation with my family gazing at the sunrise and sunset through the tiny window at this ancient retreat apartment we rented for a few days, bouncing around a rubber ball not caring too much about how I look or what time it is. What a blessing!

CAN WORKING MUMS BUILD A SOLID CAREER AND A WELL-ROUNDED LIFE?

Absolutely! With the right ingredients in place, Yes You CAN. There is really no single formula for attaining a balanced life. It is how you choose to structure your life and then fit all other elements around it. Not the other way round. So, what are my success codes for WORKING MUMS? I've decided to illustrate this by sharing 10 common mistakes to avoid.

Mistake # 1: Not Putting Things Into Perspective
Everyone is in favor of progress, but not everyone is in favor of change. Change is inevitable. It is part of life. You cannot have progress without change. So, when change happens in your life, you've got to stop, reflect and put things into perspective which could mean rearranging your priorities to either accommodate the change or manage it effectively. Whether it is having kids, a successful career, angry with your waistline that just won't fit into those skinny jeans anymore, juggling school kids with board meetings, dealing with puberty or an angry teenager, opening new businesses, relocating to other countries and embracing new cultures, change brings with it a need to transition. Not admitting life is changing and assessing what you need to do or be can create stress for you and those around you. Being open to change and transition implies that you have the ability to move forward.

Mistake # 2: Not clarifying what matters to you most
Many times when life shifts, it is easy to assume that everyone around you should have noticed. This is not usually the case. Communicating the choices you are making is crucial. This includes to members of your family, your business teams, important partners, customers or clients.

Only then can you truly be authentic. Don't feel guilty about dropping some tasks and saying NO. For example, if family is an important aspect of your life, let it be obvious. Tell your colleagues about family vacations or taking time off to watch a soccer game or to attend a parents-teachers association meeting, or the reason why you skipped that after-work event. Making them aware of the choices you are making, the things you are going to let go of, or saying YES to, can create the right channel of support and mutual understanding that you need to balance your life.

Mistake # 3: Beating Yourself Up

Just because you are having a "bad mom day" doesn't mean you are a failure in every area of your life. Just because a client fired you doesn't mean you are a failure in life. When you experience a disappointment, there is a tendency to remain emotionally stuck in the details of what happened and find it hard to get out of the valley of guilt. One way to stop beating yourself up is by isolating the loss and the feelings in that particular area of your life to be able to address them properly. After all, we are our own best critics. Have you ever felt like you're drowning in the overwhelming guilt of what you should or could have done better? You are not alone. Learn from it and move on. Lean on your support circle (a coach, a friend, a mentor) and get back on track. Your best days are in front of you.

Mistake # 4: Faking The Super Mom

The pursuit of perfection will only leave you exhausted, frustrated and disappointed and may cheat you out of living the best life ever. Getting super busy just to keep up and look good isn't worth it. Have you ever tried to justify your busyness because you saw the lives of other working mums on social media and thought they have it all figured out? My house is messy. So what? I've got birth marks. So what? My tasks for the day never get done. So what? Now don't get me wrong. I'm not giving a license for mediocrity or bad habits. I'm simply saying that sometimes messy, tired, dirty, unfinished are all part of the equation. Stop faking it when you can truly be alive, and by that I mean not being all put together, yet happier and authentic. Give yourself the permission to slow down and truly enjoy the beauty each day brings. Even God rested so why wouldn't you! Don't neglect spending time with your tribe. Take regular breaks. Laugh. Take a walk. Watch a good comedy. Journal. Declutter your mind. Choose your battles and learn to ignore the rest. Be faithful in your sleeping (you didn't think I forgot that one). What else could you add?

Mistake #5: Not Being Organized

Going through your already busy life without a strategy or toolbox can keep you running perpetually on the hamster's wheel for life. For me, setting the tone for my day begins with studying God's word and talking to Him in prayer. That's how I get my strength for the day and wisdom to guide the tasks I have ahead of me. Then, I think through the top three things that must get done that day. All these happen before checking emails, phone calls, and waking my kids. Before I get up from bed and set my foot on the bedroom floor, I kind of feel ready for the day. Planning and Scheduling are great skills that can prevent you from being sucked into other people's agenda. You could merge private and business events in one calendar. Maximize your to-do lists and not-to-do lists. Take advantage of productivity apps. If working from home and have kids, schedule work hours, nanny time or quiet moments for the kids so you can get stuff done. Avoid wasting time. Always checking email, casual internet surfing, gossiping, and long lunches are interferences that could make you less productive and work late.

Mistake # 6: Not asking for help

It takes more than a tree to make a forest. In the same way you'd come to realise that it takes more than one person to raise a family or to build a career. How well do you take advice? How often do you ask others for help? Confident working mums understand the power of relationships and the downside of saying YES to everything. "Self-care is not Self-ish. It's called wisdom." If someone else can help you, why not? Don't get caught up in being the boss all the time. Create space where everyone can function and flourish. You may be amazed at the hidden talents your employees / kids have if only you let them spread their wings and fly.

Mistake #7: Not Having An Optimistic Outlook

Whether you run your own business or work for a company, every working mum needs to build an optimistic attitude. Why is that? Well, things may not always end up the way you've calculated it. I'm sure you've seen that life sometimes springs some detours in our way. Optimism and Faith can help you to live lighter and happier through it all. A well-rounded life includes lots of faith and less of fear. It is not about denying the absence of the rain. It is about choosing to dance in the rain remembering that after the rain comes a rainbow. "The joy of the Lord is my strength" is a favourite scripture I love so much, and I have come to realise that when I'm filled with the joy of the Lord, nothing else can take that away from me. So, find the things that bring you joy and spend time doing them. Wake up every morning counting three things you are grateful for and go to bed recounting the same.

Mistake #8: Praying And Worrying

Someone compared worrying to "chewing gum over and over again." I guess they are right. That constant badgering at the same issue over and over in your mind and losing sleep can become a habit. Through my own experiences, I've found out that worry does nothing to save a situation, rather, it exacerbates it. You earn nothing positive worrying about a situation. Intentionally choosing to pray versus worry, counting your blessings instead of your inadequacies and embracing optimism and faith, will take you far on your road to success. You can't pray and worry at the same time.

Mistake #9: De-prioritising Family

What's your son's teacher's name? What's your daughter's favourite time of the day? What's the project your spouse is working on? When was the last time you ate a meal together? You owe it to yourself to nurture your relationship with your partner/family (if you have one). Oftentimes, if you're busy with work, your partner is the first to get neglected. If going out on a monthly date is tough and expensive, have an indoor date night cooking an elegant meal together, and talking about silly things apart from work or the kids. Making time for your kids is equally crucial. They grow up so fast, don't they? So, schedule it in. Have a family breakfast or a family night with board games or movies. Create activities and fit your schedule around it. When you have family outings, avoid talking about work or checking your phone. Use Skype/WhatsApp to stay in touch. Be present in their lives now before your memories become filled with "if only" and "what ifs".

Mistake #10: Comparing Yourself To Others

Comparisons!! That irresistible urge to compare your life with that of a friend, a sister, a celebrity or your new friend on Facebook or Instagram, and kickoff a pity-party right afterwards. Always comparing yourself to others can lure you into depression, keeping you from walking in authority and being the authentic YOU. Stop wasting your time comparing yourself to somebody else's life. You never fully know what they are going through. God made you in His image and after His likeness already. What else are you looking for out there? Yes, you can exercise more, eat healthier and wear vintage clothes, but if you're hung up on comparisons you'd have all that and still be unhappy. Allow yourself the right and freedom to step into your fullness and believe in YOU. If you don't, no one else should.

I want to acknowledge you, working mum. I hope you found something worth learning in these pages and at least committed to one simple adjustment you can make in your life.

To your growth and success!
Mofoluwaso Ilevbare

About Mofoluwaso

Mofoluwaso Ilevbare is a Confidence & Peak Performance Coach dedicated to empowering corporate executives and entrepreneurs who desire to accelerate their leadership/business influence and visibility without endangering love, family, and faith. Her motto is: Dare, Dream and Deliver!

Mofoluwaso is a testament of God's faithfulness. She has been to death's doorway and back as she narrowly escaped death not once, but twice! After narrowly escaping the onslaught of death via flying bullets, she has purposed in her heart to make an indelible mark in this world. She sees everyday as an awesome opportunity to help you get rid of fear, stress, and time wasting so you can truly be authentic and enjoy great success.

Mofoluwaso has a Bachelor's in Pharmacy, a Master's in Business Administration and certifications in Social and Emotional Intelligence, Conversational Intelligence and John Maxwell Leadership Tools. With over 15 years of corporate experience, Mofoluwaso helps her clients dig through distractions and overwhelming tasks to truly focus on what really matters most and deliver them with confidence and consistency. She is the author of *The Confidence Journal For Career Women, Uplift Your Productivity*, plus several other heart-centred resources, and shares this passion as a Cherie Blair Women Mentor and founder of two charity organisations herself.

Mofoluwaso is a soulful thought-leader, wife, and mother of two boys. She loves God, family, and coaching in that particular order, and has a healthy appetite for chocolate cake.

If you are struggling to find clarity on your life's purpose or achieving your goals, if you want to uplift your productivity, confidence, and leadership influence at work, contact Mofoluwaso to learn more about how she can work together with you to achieve your goals and dreams in life.

You can connect with her at:
- https://mofoluwasoilevbare.com/
- Facebook: www.facebook.com/mofoluwasoilevbareonline
- Twitter: www.twitter.com/folusoilevbare
- Instagram: www.instagram.com/mofoluwaso_ilevbare

CHAPTER 10

FROM THE USSR TO A PENTHOUSE SUITE

3 KEY LESSONS OF SUCCESS

BY LANA BROWN

How I progressed from a hard childhood in poverty-stricken USSR, to a dangerous political career involving the KGB, to successful entrepreneurship in the UK.

Not everything in life has the same level of priority… at least not today! Today I'm sitting in a Jacuzzi in a penthouse suite overlooking a Cretan Church, admiring the azure colour of the shimmering Aegean Sea. Fishing boats are passing by, catching my eye, taking me on a journey into the past or into the future. I'm a woman of 50 chronological years. This means the planet completed 50 orbits around the Sun from the moment I came into this world, but doesn't really say much about my biological or psychological age. Stewart, my husband, is by my side. He adores me, which sounds reassuring, considering I've reached the stage of life when the female body produces more testosterone than before, forcing me to make frequent waxing appointments and lift weights in a gym to fight the pre-menopausal fat.

In the eyes of society, we are 'a successful couple.' Our multiple businesses allow us to live in a beautiful Victorian house, drive nice cars, and privately educate our children. Out of 195 countries on the planet, we have crossed at least a quarter. We keep gold caviar in an American fridge among a dozen of health supplements and strategically selected foods that are 'good for us.' We keep active in accordance with experts' recommendations, drink our water, and limit consumption of wine to the social side, just enough to accompany candlelit dinners. Life is good. But it used to be very, very different…

FROM RUSSIA WITH LOVE

I was born on a cold winter morning in the small city of Priozersk in the former USSR. My mum was only 18. According to family stories I was a noisy baby, sleeping through the daytime and crying through the night. One day, dad threatened to throw me out of the window. I don't think he ever considered that 'being noisy' is the first sign of leadership. 'Being noisy' guaranteed to be noticed, hence I survived…

Mum and dad always struggled to make ends meet, making just enough money to keep the roof above our heads and put food on the table, which my mum skilfully produced from fresh ingredients on a daily basis.

We lived in a rented wooden cottage with a tiny kitchen. The cottage was next to a small lake where dad taught me to fish. "Give a man a fish, and you feed him for a day. Teach a man to fish, and you feed him for a lifetime." This is, of course, figuratively speaking, but I will never be stuck. Skills keep your stomach full; money, however, gives you a choice to practise only the skills you enjoy. This is something I figured out later.

Mum would always save pennies for my dream birthday present or to pay for school trips to the museums, exhibitions, and theatre. Education and appreciation of things beautiful are part of my Russian DNA, I suppose. The childhood was all about education, education, education. My hunger and thirst for knowledge never died since. I crave knowledge. It's my addiction. Knowledge is my butter on the bread and the bubbles in the champagne. I like getting into the depth of simple things, turning to dictionaries, Google, and YouTube to clarify the meaning of words, or to watch presentations on totally random subjects, often unrelated to anything I do. I may get curious about the engineering of buildings in Dubai, followed by the harvesting of avocados in Mexico.

When you learn something you can't unlearn it. Knowledge penetrates every cell, offers new references, and magnifies your whole understanding of the world. Knowledge is your mobile library that can be at your fingertips wherever you go. It's your power to success.

Lesson 1: It's not about location, it's about education. Knowledge is your power to success.

FROM A CUCUMBER TO A GHERKIN

Piece by piece, experience by experience, the foundations of my life were laid by fights between mum and dad, lessons they involuntary taught me, hardships we went through, and the happy memories we managed to create from simple things.

Simple things were really simple. My dream Christmas present was getting not one, but two bags of treats from Father Christmas, filled with sweets and a couple of oranges. My dream birthday present was to have a doll in a blue dress.

And guess what? My dreams always came true and I'm going to tell you how.

My grandma lived a few miles away from our little cottage. Come rain or shine, dad or mum would drop me off at her house through the week or for a weekend. Grandma's house was full of 'things forbidden': I was not allowed to touch sweets without her permission, go to the allotment and help myself to strawberries in summer time, or run wild with my friends till dawn, as she would impose a curfew. I was allowed, however, to sleep in freshly cut hay which felt and smelled like heaven, eat melted ice cream when I had a cold, listen to the radio play productions which we both loved, and partake in numerous fairy tales she would tell me till I fell asleep.

One day, Grandma and I were having a conversation about success. I tried to clarify what 'success' meant?

"I was born into a family of five," she said, "and was educated only to the age of ten. My father was a priest and spoke four foreign languages. My siblings went to Sunday and Drama schools, sang in the church choir, and learnt to recite poetry. I, however, discovered books by myself. Well, little one, when you discover books, you get into depth, and when you get into depth, you find your calling. When you find your calling, you become successful. The word 'success' comes from the Latin 'succedere', which means 'come close to'. You are a product of five people you are closest to. Chose them wisely, as you are a little cucumber that has been pickled in brine and left to ferment for a period of time. You become a gherkin, whether you like it or not."

This made me very choosey with friends, acquaintances, and even family members. I became very selective with whom to spend time with in my life.

Lesson 2: You are a cucumber turning into a gherkin. Be selective with the top five people in your life.

FROM AN EAGLET TO AN EAGLE

My strong character traits were spotted at school, resulting in leadership training in top pioneer camps. Having completed a degree in English Language and Literature, I returned to my native town to be offered a political career. Fame, she said... At 22, I was in charge of political education of youth in schools and colleges of the region. Headmasters and headmistresses were reporting to me on their performance of bringing up the Soviet youth to the required political standards. A chauffeur-driven car, perks that nobody could dream of, TV debates and newspaper coverage became part of my daily life, with a mountain of responsibilities lying on my shoulders.

August, 18, 1991. A major event, known as the August Coup, put us all on trial. Soviet hardliners attempted to take control of power from President Gorbachov, forcefully detaining him in the summer residence in the South of Russia.

I, together with two other executives, and members of the regional Young Communists Committee were called for an emergency meeting. The agenda was simple. We had to pledge allegiance either to Gorbachov or to the hardliners. There were about fifteen of us in the boardroom, all in our twenties, making a decision on behalf of thousands and thousands of others who gave us power to vote. Tanks were deployed in the streets of Moscow. We were advised by the army that the plan was to deploy tanks in St. Petersburg the next day.

After a short brief on the developing situation in Moscow, we decided to take individual votes as opposed to the majority decision. Each name and their vote were going into the newspapers the very next day.

Intensity of James Bond movies is mild compared to real-life decision making. Playing Russian Roulette is not as thrilling when you know the possible outcome. As far as I'm concerned, if hardliners took control, it would have resulted in one of the following: I would have been banned from travelling abroad, which was not any different from cutting my oxygen, or I might have never been seen again, as happened to a colleague of mine, Elena, whose dead body was found on the lake shore. The game was getting dangerous. My phone at work clicked every time I picked it up, executives of the local KGB invited me for a 'cup of coffee', and the First Secretary of the Regional Communist Party committee called me to the 'red carpet' to voice his disapproval of my support for the evolving democratic movement.

I was scared... scared for my life, scared for the future of my son, scared to be cut away from the love of my life and husband-to-be, Stewart, who lived in Scotland.

Time to vote... My mesmerised eyes were following my colleagues. My hands were shaking and sweat broke on my forehead... Russian roulette, 50/50 split, YES or NO? **But what do scared leaders do**? Scared leaders rise above The Self, they focus on the ones they lead, the ones that trust them, they take the risk of the unknown, they plunge into the unknown irrespective of fear and pain, **they make a decision**.

The emergency meeting was over. Sergey, my chauffer, drove the car to my grandma's house. I walked in pale as a blank sheet of paper. "What's wrong, little one?" Grandma asked. I told her about my day, how scared I was, how much pain I felt in every part of my body.

"Come here and listen. Listen to what I've got to share. Today I spotted an Eagle. It's not often you can see them here. Eagles don't flock like pigeons do. They fly on their own. Their eyes are five times more superior than humans'. They can spot danger for miles. They have always admired the world as powerful, free, and transcendent. Out of all birds, an Eagle doesn't seek shelter during the storm. He knows how to rise above the storm and fly over it. In the storms of life when you have to make major decisions, soar like an Eagle. You will be fine."

Making decisions is an addiction. The root of any addiction is not a substance of addiction as such, but the emotion of pleasure the addict associates that substance with. In simple terms, human brains, like other animals' brains, crave pleasure and do everything to avoid pain.

When you speak to successful people, they have one thing in common, they are addicted to making decisions and making them fast. Why? The explanation is easy – It gives them control over the future, it brings certainty and makes them happy.

Speed of decision-making is often associated with influencing people both in business and the everyday environment. If you ask successful people why their decision-making influences other people, the response is usually the same: "I take away the pain of decision-making from somebody else, who is either less willing to make a decision, or less experienced in the field, or simply relies on my decision. This keeps me ahead of the rest."

We don't always connect decision-making with emotions. A human being is not a 'human doing' and is governed by emotions, which can't be ignored. Decision making comes with a 'feel good' factor. It backs up emotions of significance, importance, certainty, and often love, connection, and contribution.

Emotional intelligence is a major ingredient of true success. Don't be fooled by associating a successful person with 'a tough guy'. Truly successful people are emotionally intelligent. 'Tough guys' are often pretenders. You can't become successful without mastering the skill of engaging the gut instinct, gut feeling, or the heart calling. Truly successful people know the secret of tapping into the universal pool of intelligence where emotions are guides to the treasury.

Lesson 3: To be successful you must get addicted to decision making.

I'm sitting in a Jacuzzi in a penthouse suite overlooking a Cretan Church, admiring the azure colour of the shimmering Aegean Sea. Colours of the sea are like colours of life, some are darker, and some are lighter. The same applies to success, it's got dark and bright sides. It comes with lessons to learn and responsibilities to take. Success has no limits, but the more you want, the more knowledge you'll need. Knowledge must be backed up by a decision. A decision is followed by an action. Taking action requires courage. But if you want to admire the world like an Eagle, and be free, powerful, and transcendent; remember, out of all the birds an Eagle doesn't seek shelter during the storm. He knows how to rise above the storm and fly over it. In the storms of life when you have to make major decisions, soar like an Eagle. You'll be fine. I'm raising a glass to your success!

About Lana

Lana's story is a remarkable story of a girl, born and raised in the in the former USSR in the remote town of Priozersk, north of St. Petersburg. To say that her family didn't have money is an understatement. At times, even a much-needed pair of new shoes was out of the question. A hard childhood in Russia, a dangerous political career involving the KGB, working with governmental ministries in the former USSR and liaising with their counterparts internationally, was followed by her move to the UK and many years of entrepreneurship in the West. Lana has learnt some valuable lessons that got her to where she is today: an inspirational role model 21st century woman.

Lana graduated from Minsk University and started her career at the time when the words "free enterprise", "business", "free thinking" were just developing in the Russian language. At the age of 22, Lana played an active role in "perestroika" (reconstruction), working as an executive for the Young Communists committee, and at the same time joining the emerging democratic movement, spreading the word of new economic and political changes in Russia, including the first private businesses led by the young entrepreneurs.

More recently, Lana has turned to public speaking, sharing the stage with selected celebrity guests. She talks on subjects of health and energy, breaking through fear, maintaining and enhancing relationships, the role of women in society and success strategies.

Her passion is to help people reach their true potential despite the problems they may face – whether you have personal, emotional, psychological, or any other difficulties, Lana will make you a success – and that's a promise!

To contact Lana today and apply for your chance to work with her, visit:
- www.HelpMeLana.com.

CHAPTER 11

STOP THE RACE

HOW ORDINARY PEOPLE CREATE EXTRAORDINARY SUCCESS

BY KIRAN VEDANTAM

Every week we read or hear about people who have taken control of their lives and have become financially independent. We see them on television, magazine covers, billboards and on streaming social media feeds. We want to be like them - successful and accomplished people.

Why are some people outstanding while most others are not? What separates the successful from the rest? What is the extra thing that gives some people an edge? Is there a formula for success? Are some people really made extraordinary?

We need to appreciate that they too were once ordinary people with dreams of success like most, but they were able to go out and realize their dreams. These are, in fact, ordinary people who moved themselves out of their comfort zones. These people are just like us who have achieved extraordinary success. When they can, why can't we?

Let me share my journey towards becoming 'them'. Our story may be similar to the millions of immigrants who crave to become the extraordinary. We started out as ordinary people coming to the United States of America from India as college students to attend a Master's program at Arizona State University. I landed here with literally nothing in my pocket but a heart filled with dreams. I did not know anyone in this country when I arrived. My hardworking and devout parents mortgaged their lone asset to get me here. The loan was just enough to buy a one-way airfare and expenses for a few weeks. My goal then was simple and clear – to achieve complete financial independence and then grow to be of help to my family – not realizing that the goal is not complete. The baby steps were to survive to graduate, get a job, pay back and support my parents, get married, buy a house, save some money, and be able to help others.

Before long, I was well on my way to my dream life, or so I thought. I met my wife to-be, Kiran Bapatla, who was doing her Bachelor's degree in Electrical Engineering at ASU. She pursued her Master's in Electrical Engineering after completion of her Bachelor's degree. Just like our names, her approach and train of thought was in sync with mine. We got married right after graduating. Intel, our dream company hired both of us as engineers where we were around many other hard-working professionals like ourselves. The pay was great, we were provided with amazing benefits and we achieved everything we thought we wanted.

We were financially comfortable and life was cruising along nicely. We bought a house, paid off debt, traveled a bit and were able to help our families. The two of us worked hard and sometimes the hours were long but life was good.

To relax, we discovered that we enjoyed spending time in our garden, which evolved as our passion. However, as time passed, we discovered that because of the long day commitments of our engineering jobs, we never seemed to have time to enjoy our garden. There were beautiful mornings in the garden that were cut short as we had to leave for work, and it was dark by the time we got home. Our weekends were filled up with many things we could not get done during the week—grocery shopping, social obligations, work around the house and errands. We found that there was no time in our ordinary days to enjoy all that we worked so hard to achieve. My wife and I were living a "rat race." We had so much energy and passion to accomplish greater levels but discovered a need to optimize our time to fulfil our pretty passions.

What we really wanted was an ordinary life, with extraordinary achievements. We wanted to be one of those who achieve the extraordinary. But how? What did these successful people do to build their extraordinary lives? We set out to find the answers. We then revisited our life goals and started drafting a "Life Plan" with key milestones for the next 10 years, involving the key areas we wanted to focus on – Finance, Relationship, Health, and Travel. It was a simple bucket list with a due date and thinking worst case and best case.

	Goal – A (with grit)	Goal – B (mediocre)	Goal – C (worst case)
Finance			
Relationship			
Health			
Travel			

Diagram 1. Life Plan Matrix

This is the story of how we took our train of thought about the future on a journey from our ordinary lives to an extraordinary place. . . a place of successful entrepreneurship, unlimited income potential, and the time to savor all that we achieved. Once the targets were set, the journey started to become pleasurable. It led us to the life we never even imagined we could have. If we, ordinary as we were, can make this journey, why can't anyone else?

For us, the journey from ordinary to extraordinary started in 2002 when we read a book by Jim Collins, Good to Great. It talked about why some companies take leaps to succeed while others do not. It stirred us into thinking about these same principles as applied to the lives of individuals. Why did some people achieve such extraordinary success?

Our train, like every train, needed an engine to get moving. We narrowed down on excelling in "financial and temporary" independence. In other words, we needed to have enough money to sustain the humble lifestyle we enjoyed, and also have enough time to spend with each other.

To support refined goal items, we had to achieve passive income to replace the income we earned as engineers. This would give us more control over our time and let us enjoy our achievements. We did not want to be bound by the limited track of corporate life which meant working long hours for someone else. Although there was stability here, the standard procedures were made available to follow. The journey along with the destination seemed unfulfilling and limited. After looking around, we realized that what we desired was a track of self-employment and to be in control of our own destination.

This thinking and the desire to have more time we could call our own sent us on a search for opportunities. The "entrepreneur bug" bit us hard and we started researching for industries that appealed to us as potential business owners.

Even knowing the potential rewards, it was hard to start that journey. At that time, working at our jobs made our life comfortable. Leaving the security of those jobs and benefits was scary, especially now that we had a family. We sat down and made a list of the pros and cons of changing our path.

After you read our list, make a list for yourself. What will your benefits be? What areas are holding you back from starting down your own track? Doing this will help you find your driving engine so you can start your journey to an extraordinary life.

PROS OF SELF-EMPLOYMENT:

1. Supreme Authority: Obviously, when you start your own business, you alone are the boss. There is no one there who tells you what to do. You make all decisions and do it your way.
2. Awareness: No one is more aware of what is going on in your business than you are. This is your chance to focus and learn everything you can about the industry you have chosen, the clients you service and the impact you will have in the local and global marketplace.
3. Tax advantages: You have the ability to deduct expenses you incur as part of building your business. Speak to a tax consultant to understand the benefits on how to structure the business and gain maximum benefits.
4. Time flexibility: Do you need a break from your work? Are you just tired of the routine? Fine - work around the client needs and get a break. You can now work on your schedule.
5. Fulfillment: Pride in ownership and all that you have accomplished

gives a feeling of fulfillment. Entrepreneurs report feelings of fulfillment in their business achievements higher than those who are only a small cog in a big, corporate wheel.

6. Higher Income: With entrepreneurship, the sky can be the limit when it comes to your earning potential. When you work for yourself, you are not restricted by the salary limits set by someone else.

CONS OF SELF-EMPLOYMENT:

1. Financial Instability: You may miss the luxury of a stable paycheck. Your salary depends on you – and at least at first, more work equals more money. There is no easy way to do it. You run the risk of losing everything you have worked hard for.

2. Capital investment: You may have to bring in an initial capital investment. In addition, there is a possibility that the return might not come through for many years. It is possible that it may never come through at all, a risk you must be willing to take.

3. Multi-tasking: When starting out as a sole proprietor, you must take care of everything by yourself. Until you are financially ready to hire employees, you are the 'chief cook and bottle washer' too. Be prepared to get a little dirty and outside of your comfort zone.

4. Extra patience: This is a virtue and a necessity now. You must tactfully deal with your clients and have loads of patience and tolerance with all those that you do business. Flying off the handle now will earn you an unwanted reputation, so just don't do it.

5. Health and Time: Entrepreneurs put in more hours especially when they start out, which can negatively impact your health and put a strain on relationships. Preplanning in simple ways can help avoid extra stress on your health. For example, it is so easy to fall into a pattern of quick, convenient meals when you are busy. To avoid this, keep healthy snacks with you at work. In the end, this will save you time, because you don't need to go in search of fast food, and you will feel better too.

6. You cannot pass the buck: You quickly learn that your decisions will bring in profit or make you lose it. There is no one to blame anymore. You take the blame and keep moving forward.

THE BOTTOM LINE

There is no doubt that entrepreneurship has its risks. But, it also has the most incredible rewards. For many, there is nothing more rewarding, both financially and intrinsically, than building a successful business. If you are tired of being ordinary, it might be time to take that jump into the life you have always dreamed of having. Self-employment is growing in much of the world and now is a great time to make it happen for you too. What could be more fulfilling than taking a journey of success? You too can have an extraordinary life.

SMELL YOUR PASSION
(It was the garden for us)

We love to spend time in our garden. During the time when we were working at Intel, it was discouraging to have no time as we rushed off to work. By the time we were home at night, it was dark and we were too tired. If we were going to have time to smell the roses – in our case, our garden – we needed to find time to stay home, and to stay home we needed to replace the income our jobs gave us. This was our driving force, to have both the time and the money to enjoy what we achieved. Listen to your inner calling and follow your instincts.

Find your driving force or main goal. Knowing this will provide the engine to drive your journey and help keep you motivated. This is the WHY you are doing this.

BETTER LATE THAN NEVER

Do not think that it is too late for you to get started on your journey. It is better to start now than to never start at all.

Remember the quote:
> *When is the best time to plant a tree? 20 years ago.*
> *When is the second-best time to plant a tree? RIGHT NOW!*

Here are the seven things to keep in mind as you start:

1. Pause:
Find a quiet place and jot down exactly what kind of life you desire. This is the most important pause of your life. We used to go to the public library and converse in quietness and take notes on what is our "WHY". Come up with your Life Plan.

2. Skillset versus Interest:

Sometimes our personal skillset isn't exactly what we are interested in starting a business with. Take us for example – we were educated as engineers, yet our first big success as entrepreneurs was in the field of real estate. During an interview, we were asked why we chose real estate and how we managed to achieve so much success in such a short period of time. These two questions are related. We became interested in the potential of earning money in real estate after we made a significant profit on our home in just a few short years. This opened our eyes to the opportunities in real estate investment. The secret to our success was that we spent time taking a deep look and researching the industry and its potential before we jumped in. It wasn't the only industry we looked at, just the one where we saw the most potential.

3. Give your best:

With the advancement in human evolution, most paths have been travelled by someone earlier than you. Research and study hard on which field works for your style that can also make money. Then, be prepared to work hard. Be prepared to sacrifice everything for a designated time and get into the focus zone. If you work hard, your clients will see it. People love working with people who communicate well and who are sincere in that communication and effort. Always give your personal best. People will notice your efforts and respect what you do. This will help you gain and keep your confidence too.

4. Partner up:

Find people you can partner up with to learn the industry. When studying real estate as a potential industry, we quickly discovered there are many people to help you along the way. We had mortgage brokers, title companies and peers willing to guide us and share their expertise and knowledge. In your potential industry, find these people and let them help and guide you. It will save you both time and from making some costly mistakes. Make friends and resonate together.

5. Being Decisive:

Another important thing in any self-employment venture is in decision making. Any self-employed individual should be a good decision maker and can make an important decision at correct times.

We decided to choose the real estate field as a new start because the field was interesting and profitable. We saved a lot of money by just sticking to the basics and not trying too many crazy ideas. As we progressed with the business, we expanded our business at just the right time to take full advantage of my investment.

6. Genuine intent to serve:
We followed Zig Ziglar's philosophy: "You will get all you want in life if you help enough other people get what they want." We also didn't keep the knowledge to ourselves; we believed in serving and to share our knowledge with everyone.

Life is a race, so pace yourself. When it comes time, be prepared to stop the race. Stop running to achieve the extraordinary in a cluster of the ordinary; rather, make your own opportunities. Become extraordinary, do the extraordinary. Gather strength and motivate yourself. Do and think out-of-the-box to earn big and get your own share of a great reputation.

The question is: What do you want to be remembered for and are you on the path to get there?

Do you believe that ordinary people can create extraordinary success?

When you start believing that ordinary people can create extraordinary success is when the magic begins.

About Kiran

Kiran Vedantam and Kiran Bapatla are a husband and wife team. After a few years into their dream job at Intel Corporation as engineers, they set out with a simple goal of being able to spend more time together without compromising on their lifestyle. They were able to replace their income and resign from their engineering jobs. They have found that real estate investing is not only easy to transact, but also can help create cash flow and profits. They are first generation immigrants from India and met each other when they came to the United States to pursue their Master's degrees at Arizona State University.

Following their entrepreneurial passion, they got into the real estate industry with no background or experience on the ways of the land. Kiran Vedantam has been a licensed realtor since 2005 and started his own real estate company Kirans and Associates Realty in 2010. They began critically studying the real estate industry and within a short time became one of the top agencies in Arizona, ranked #113 in the USA by *Wall Street Journal/Real Trends* in 2011. Kiran was ranked 4th in Maricopa County in 2011 for most closings and is in the top 0.5% of agents overall for sales dollar volume. Kiran Vedantam was awarded the AZ Real Estate Achievement Award 2013, and was also ranked in the top 150 in the country by Real Trends in 2013.

They started community outreach events from 2006 related to homeownership and real estate investments. They invited well-respected attorneys, CPAs, mortgage professionals and fellow realtors as guest speakers so that they all could share the best-known methods. Their real estate radio shows in California (KLOK 1170) and Arizona (KQCK, KAZG 1440, KFNX 1100) have been well received and got them recognition as leaders in real estate.

Kiran and Kiran Vedantam are still actively helping families at Kirans and Associates Realty. They run a team of real estate agents and are top agents in Arizona. They passionately share their vast knowledge, experience, and expertise with their clients so they too can enjoy the benefits of buying and selling real estate. Their radio interviews and TV appearances are shown on: www.KiranandKiran.com.

They also run a family fun center in Chandler, AZ called Makutu's Island, and are involved in caring for the dying at Sacred Heart Hospice in Phoenix, AZ.

They can be reached at:
- honestagents@kiranandkiran.com
- Tel: 602 550 4842

CHAPTER 12

GO FORWARD FEARLESSLY
EMPOWERMENT CONTROL & SUCCESS

BY DR. TERI ROUSE

GOING UP? THAT'S WHAT I THOUGHT

After a failed marriage, raising a daughter as a single parent, struggling to make ends meet and cover basic needs, remarrying, helping with a step child with ADHD, working full-time in an Emotional Support Special Education class, going back to school for two additional certifications, a masters and doctoral degrees, you would think that I had, or had done it all. You would assume that I had confidence, success, empowerment, a new career…happiness...and for a brief time I did. Or at least I thought I did.

THE BEGINNING OF THE END...SORT OF

I walked up toward the old stone building, gazing at the sky bright blue, white puffy clouds and bright sunshine. My heart was thumping with anxious anticipation. I thought finally, perfection. It doesn't get better than this.

A perfect beginning to the rest of my life…a perfect day, a perfect family, a perfect career, a perfect situation! I have got it going on…nothing can stop me! Finally, I had reached what I believed to be the pinnacle of life, the top of the game! I had worked so hard to get here and I believed this is where I was going to be the rest of my teaching career. I was home, or so I thought…

Time passed and I became one of the "go to" professors for students, faculty and administration. The teaching/working expectations evolved into much more than "just" the teaching time. Work was… well… it became all-consuming. I was consistently asked to do more, to spend more time, solve more problems, have more office hours, teach more classes, and facilitate more clubs. I became the coordinator working even MORE closely with over 80 students out of the classroom as well as working with the administration solving problems and putting out administrative fires.

And I said, yes. Why? Because I didn't think I could/should say no. The job needed to get done. The institution "needed "me. My students "needed" me. My colleagues "needed" me. My family questioned the amount of time that I was spending at work. MY FAMILY NEEDED ME! I spent little to no time taking care of myself. I wasn't eating or sleeping properly and I was emotionally drained.

Did I care more for the people at work than I did for my family and for myself? I NEEDED ME!

After a few years, I began to really question if I had made the right choices. Oh, but I had worked so hard for this! This is what I was "supposed" to do! THIS WAS MY LIFE'S PURPOSE…or was it?

If this is my purpose than why do I feel so out of control? Why do I feel so much fear? Why did I feel so uncertain and unworthy? Why can't I make a decision? Is this what I really wanted to do? Was this REALLY my life purpose?

THE BOTTOM FELL OUT

I was beginning to think things couldn't get any worse, however, they did! In a B-I-G way. There was a change in leadership and then there was a change in administration. Change is always challenging and sometimes for the better. But when change turns to chaos you have to wonder. In addition to all of the "regular" teaching responsibilities, advising and preparation for promotion and tenure, I became the coordinator for our department working even more closely with administration, doing administrative things and dropping the ball on my passion, teaching.

I was advising 80+ students, the advisor for 2 student organizations, teaching 5 classes. I was on 4...yes 4 institutional committees, AND I was beginning to prepare to put together my promotion and tenure package...which is roughly the equivalent of doing a master's thesis and required multiple examples of excellence in teaching, scholarship and service.

Without consideration for what was best for students (which is why we were there), it seemed that the rules changed with the new administration. There was the threat of changing the class schedule, which put students into a panic and drove them to seek more one-on-one attention.

Administration began questioning the faculty, about their time on and off campus, making the assumption that if we were not on campus we were not working. Being at the beck and call of the administration and students further frustrated and devalued us.

However, the mid-level bureaucrats that were now running the show continued to expect faculty to produce more publications and research, while covering all the classes that needed to be taught – while continuously being short staffed by as many as five people and putting out the fires that they started.

I think the tipping point for me was when I offered to begin teaching in a small program which local teachers and principals were asking about. It had already been developed (I helped with the development), it received institutional approval AND was endorsed by the State Department of Education (NO SMALL FEAT). I was denied the opportunity, and yet we were still asked to create NEW programs, write more grants and publish—publish—publish, all of the while maintaining the teaching, advising, committee work, service and scholarship schedules.

To this day, I am still not sure why that request was denied because those courses are now being offered which now feels like a real slap in the face. Not only was it overwhelming and frustrating, it was devastating to me. I had helped to develop and propose the program!

I watched a friend and colleague become a shell of her once vibrant and exciting self. I watched friends become foes, departments divided and, demands for additional work with little appreciation and NO thanks.

Like many places, we were overworked, under-staffed and very much unappreciated. But now voices, which in the past, had been heard, if not considered, were being disregarded as non-existent. It didn't matter what needed to be done for the students or faculty. A new administration was in town and they were going way beyond flexing their muscles. The new authoritarian rule was in place.

FINDING ME IN ALL THIS MESS

As a former student and Alumnae, I was especially devastated, hurt and confused. I couldn't understand why the place that had educated ME, prepared ME and nurtured ME for the position I now filled, was no longer allowing me to do the job for which they had prepared me. I was not walking that path my mentors had prepared me to follow. I began to wonder if I was supposed to be there for the students or if there was some other agenda. If there was another agenda, then I really didn't want to be there. I felt like I had nowhere to turn for answers.

I began to question everything I had worked so hard to achieve for the preceding ten years. I needed to breathe. I needed space! I needed to get out but I didn't know how! I had never even considered applying anywhere else, but this thought kept jumping out to me. This was supposed to be home...forever. I was going to give back what I had gotten out of this institution. They had helped me to be me! And now...I didn't want to stay. I didn't want to give back! I couldn't give back any more. There was simply nothing left to give.

I wanted to get out of Dodge! It didn't matter if the issues were perceived or reality. What mattered was how I was feeling and how I responded to these issues. What was I going to do to remedy the situation? I hadn't looked for a job for over ten years! So the process of gathering my credentials began. I was searching for courage and strength. **I was terrified!**

However, I was so desperate to get out that I sent resumes to places up and down the East coast...from Maine to Florida...to Western Pennsylvania. But who would want me? There were thousands other people just like me – same education, same experience, same qualifications!

AND THEN... IT HAPPENED!

I started sending out more resume packets. I included everything and I do mean EVERYTHING I could think of that a potential employer might look for. I sent PowerPoint presentations, and letters of recommendation. I sent certificates of participation in conferences. I sent clearances. Anything I thought would make me stand out I sent! And then it happened. The emails and phone calls started to come in from up and down the East coast for little old me. Of course people were interested. Why wouldn't they be interested? They liked what they saw on paper. Emails led to phone calls, phone calls led to phone interviews and later face-to-face interviews. I interviewed with places close to home...and a few that were far, and would require me to spend part of my week away from my family. But I persisted. I am qualified! I am a team player! I will teach whatever you want me to teach...just let me teach!

Then came the waiting game. Would someone *actually* hire me? I waited. And I waited. I had a few disappointments... Ok, more than a few disappointments, BUT I never gave up. You know the saying: When it rains it pours? Well, let me just say that it didn't just pour... There was a tsunami! In a matter of 3 weeks I had 4 offers.

I couldn't believe it. Me! Four institutions of Higher Education wanted ME!!! I had a choice; I held all of the cards. I could and DID play each offer against the other. I bargained and negotiated like I had never done before...EVER. NOW I WAS IN CONTROL! I won! And now nothing, truly nothing, could stop me from moving forward.

The momentum felt amazing and I took that momentum to my new position where I have a voice, a valued opinion and choice. I now KNOW what I am capable of doing. And this is a great feeling. It has turned things around for me. I am physically and emotionally in a better place. I can sleep at night. I am cooking dinner for and with my family. I have started to enjoy doing the things I did before...and I don't feel guilty, or anxious, or sad. I am feeling confident, happy, peaceful, in control, AND I am finding the joy in doing what I love to do...teach.

THE EPIPHANY!

After all of this, after pulling my life back together only to have it fall apart again, I vowed I would not let this happen to me... or to anyone I had contact with EVER again. In the past I had always been concerned about what other people thought. I put their needs before my family and my own needs. In the past I was the lifter, the cheerleader, the mentor, the confidante for everyone... for everyone except me.

I learned the hard way that if I am not good to me...how can I be good to or for anyone else. I had to change my mind about ME. I was the only thing I had control over... ME!!!

SO...WHAT ABOUT YOU?

Have you, or do you know someone, that has had a similar experience? Chances are that if you are reading this, you too have yourself, or know someone close to you, who has been in a similar situation. You believe that they've got everything under control and then reality hits: Fear, uncertainty, indecision, lack of self-confidence, ignorance. These are not words or feelings that exude or project confidence, empowerment, or success. It's the confidence, empowerment, and success that we all want to feel. In order to do this, we have to change our minds about ourselves. So how do you do this?

I was very fortunate. Things did turn around for me, but I have seen many people whose situations just don't improve. I began to wonder why? Why don't they just do this? Why don't they just change? And then it hit me. That could have been me. Why was I able to get out and someone else was not?

I have been a teacher for a long time... 30+ years in fact. I have taught children with very specific and special needs for 10 years, have a doctorate in Education and I am an Applied Behavioral Analysis and endorsed Behavior Specialist consultant. I've taught preschool through graduate level college students. I have worked in preschools, public, private schools, urban schools, suburban schools and rural schools. I have taught at small colleges and larger universities. I have taught children two years of age all the way up through adulthood. I have served on a school board and I have been a Positive Behavior Support coach. I lived through my own personal perception of hell, and here I am today.

I needed to take a giant step back from the chaos in my life and look at what I had let happen to me. I needed to identify the things that were occurring that eventually rose to the tsunami level. I needed to analyze my own behaviors and attitudes:

- What did I do right?
- What did I do wrong?
- How did I respond?
- Who else was involved?
- What did I ultimately want to happen?
- What were the turning points that could have made a difference?
- What did I do to turn things around? Could I quantify it? Could I duplicate the results that led to the change?
- Could I help stop someone from going down that destructive road before they started and save them years of fear, pain, a feeling of worthlessness?
- Could I help someone else to go forward fearlessly?
- Could I help friends feel more empowered and get more control over their lives?

These were the questions that kept rummaging around in my head. I needed to know. I wanted to be able to tell other people, friends, family what I did and why. I wanted to break it all down in a way that was easy to explain and to understand, so that others would NOT have to endure the hell that I lived through.

I DID IT!

It took some time, research, planning, testing, analyzing and then some more testing, but I finally did it. Based on my own life experiences, years of working with students, changing behaviors both in and out of the classroom, a doctorate in Education and my training in Applied Behavioral Analysis, I developed a simple three-step framework that anyone can use to eliminate fear, indecision, feelings of unworthiness and give someone the control they want and need in their life. I called it: **Dr. Teri's GO FORWARD FEARLESSLY EMPOWERMENT CONTROL & SUCCESS SYSTEM, FECSS UP!**

My new goal in life is to go forward…FEARLESSLY, and help as many people as possible to go forward fearlessly, to be personally empowered and to achieve the control over their lives so that they can experience their personal and professional success.

Will you help me achieve my goal? Can I help you achieve yours?

About Dr. Teri

Dr. Teri Rouse began her teaching career long before she ever went off to college. She started as a swimming instructor at the local pool, working with children and adults as well as people with special needs.

She is the mother of a 20-something-year-old daughter, as well as a dog mom and wife to husband, Dr. Fred Rouse.

Not only do children have a special place in her heart, so do furry creatures. With her two rescues, Lilo and Mulan and her two labs, Mickey and Minnie, she can often be found in the yard working in the garden or down the shore with her toes in the sand.

She has authored *Julian's Gift*, a children's book inspired from her over 20 years in the classroom. She has taught grades Pre-K through 8th and spent the last 15 years working in Special Education classes as a teacher, Behavior Specialist and Early Interventionist. She is currently a professor at Widener University in Pennsylvania where she specializes in teaching Special Education to the next generation of Teachers.

Dr. Teri Rouse earned her Master's in Education from Chestnut Hill College and a Doctorate in Education from Arcadia University. She is a Certified Autism Specialist and received her Applied Behavior Analysis (ABA) endorsement from Penn State. As the Managing Director of KIDS Interventions & Direct Services, UBO she provides direct services to children, their parents as well as background and support for their classroom teachers.

Dr. Rouse, through her own life experience, noticed a need for people to break the shackles of fear and take more control of their lives. She developed *Dr. Teri's Go Forward Fearlessly, Empowerment, Control & Success System, FECSS UP!* In her signature system, she helps people go forward fearlessly for personal empowerment and more control in their daily lives as well as achieving their ultimate destiny without guilt, fear or confusion for their personal success in less than 20 minutes a day.

Dr. Teri crosses the country every year giving presentations at various organizations including the American Horticultural Therapy Association, Center for Scholastic Inquiry and Educators Rising. She works with various community groups and activities including: The Council for Exceptional Children (CEC), "Light It Up Blue" for Autism, Walk Now for Autism Speaks: Philadelphia, and Lily's Loop of The Lily's Hope Foundation. She is an advocate for people with disabilities through her association with the American Association of People with Disabilities (AAPD).

Dr. Teri Rouse has been featured on ABC, CBS, NBC, FOX News, *Miami Herald*, Bay Area, CA, Boston.com and more.

If you would like to learn more about Dr. Teri Rouse and how she could help you or your child, you can contact her through her web site:

• http://drterirouse.com

CHAPTER 13

CLIMB OUT OF YOUR EMOTIONAL DUMPSTER FIRE AND INTO SUCCESS

BY TRACY MARTINO

This is how it starts. . .

Your smartphone alarm goes off. You immediately grab it and check your messages, emails, and social media. Your heart rate creeps up from your peaceful resting rate to an erratic fast-paced one. A feeling of falling off your bed occurs as anxiety now blankets your being. You hear the voice of your therapist, coach, and friends telling you to meditate, but your "to do" list is too big. There are 200 emails to reply to, a presentation you have to complete and a conference call you have to lead in 10 minutes.

Then it happens. An "Urgent" email appears. It discusses the lack of follow through you had fulfilling a marketing request. You notice both his manager and your President are copied on the email. Anger, frustration, and rage build up as you believe you are being attacked. "As if I don't have enough on my plate!" You say to yourself. "I have sacrificed my family, my health, and my happiness for this job!" You lose it. You begin to type a response to the urgent email, typing so fast you feel your fingers are going to bleed. "I'll show him!" You continue as profanities fly out of your mouth. When you come back to consciousness, you notice the email you have written is a full-page email, packed with emotion. You stop. You have landed into an Emotional Dumpster Fire.

The Emotional Dumpster Fire is:

1. A complete emotional disaster where it is challenging to access your emotional intelligence.
2. Emotional events or triggers that sabotage your efforts.
3. Difficult emotions you avoid or don't want to deal with.

The self-created reality of the Emotional Dumpster Fire originates from fear, stress, and worry. When someone finds themselves in the fire they are completely overwhelmed, burned out, defensive, reactive, and running their life in a status quo state. It's no surprise that publications, from Harvard Business Review to Forbes, discuss how emotions affect the bottom line of success for all levels of employees, from entry-level to CEOs. There are stories of how an emotional virus can bring down a company, to working with a non-emotional narcissistic boss.

Emotions hinder problem solving, creativity, resilience, and motivation. With increased workloads, depleting resources, and a changing economy, it is no surprise that professionals are at their limits.

The scenario mentioned in the beginning of this chapter was a real circumstance one of my clients experienced. He contacted me when he received the urgent email and was in the process of writing an emotionally-infused email response. It was clear from our conversation he felt threatened and wanted revenge for the accusation and humiliation.

When someone is drunk with emotion, it is challenging to create effective communication – whether it be in person, on the phone or in text. Getting to the point takes longer, tone can be taken the wrong way, there is limited capacity for empathy, focus is lost, and problem solving skills are debilitated. The overall energy of communication is tainted.

My client started his email, "I am writing this while on vacation with my family." Understanding he was drunk with emotion, I encouraged him to change the sentence. Telling his co-worker he was taking time out of his vacation to respond to his email created a negative tone. His message could imply he didn't feel the needs of his co-workers were important enough to disrupt his vacation.

As we reviewed his email, I noticed a trend. He felt the need to prove himself. The email produced lines and lines of defensive rhetoric explaining why he didn't get back to his co-worker. He dramatically explained his increased responsibilities, pressure from his directors, and expanded travel schedule. I encouraged him to take out his proof and get to the point. In reality my clients increased work load isn't a concern for his co-worker. He has a job to do as well. In the end we scripted a communication that resulted in his President applauding his response stating, "I appreciate the well written email, you are the man for the job!"

Imagine what kind of outcome my client would have had if he sent his emotionally-charged email. His President may have questioned his leadership abilities, his thought process, or wonder if the position was a good match for him.

How do you stop sabotaging your success, get an emotional edge, maintain emotional intelligence, and get out of the Emotional Dumpster Fire?

The following techniques are three ways you can climb out of the Emotional Dumpster Fire and climb to success.

1. Master the Art of Recognizing Triggers and Patterns.

Our environment shapes our patterns and is an influential mechanism that creates our triggers. This fast-paced society has caused us to be oblivious to the power of emotional patterns and triggers. They shape our perception, our reaction, and our world.

How can we make these behaviors work for us and not against us? It starts with building awareness and willingness to change.

Triggers are any stimulus that reshapes our thinking and creates a strong emotional reaction.

The area of the brain responsible for this, the amygdala, triggers your emotional response faster than your conscious mind. Since you are being emotionally hijacked you begin to feel out of control. This is a result of living in a face-paced world of overwhelm with increased demands,

131

decreased resources, and the need to constantly prove ourselves, we become numb.

We become unaware of our triggers. Triggers reinforce emotional patterns creating a "Trigger-Pattern" Continuum. The mind, by way of the amygdala, monitors patterns. This is how it worked for my client. First, his mind sees/hears the stimulus, someone being critical of his performance. His amygdala highjacked his mind within 20 milliseconds, causing him to react aggressively. His amygdala was doing its job of protecting him. Subconsciously, he felt threatened. He did not have awareness of his reaction because he created patterns based on emotional triggers. This is why, without consciousness, he started writing the emotionally-charged email response.

It is important for you to create new awareness by exploring your triggers and patterns. In one column, write down everything that sets you off, from traffic to being late, to someone micro-managing you, to someone sending you an email in all capital letters. Next to this column, write down how you currently react and ask yourself, "What results am I experiencing from this reaction?" Keep adding to the list. Reflect on what gets in the way of your desired outcome. You will start to build awareness of how you react and why.

Through our coaching sessions, my client revealed he lived and operated out of fear. He felt it. . . "gave him a competitive edge." This pattern of fear, enhanced by his triggers, created a perception that he was being attacked. My client grew up and continues to be a highly competitive, Type-A individual who doesn't like to sit still. It was challenging when I asked him to go deeper and look at his life from that of an observer.

2.   Know Who is in Charge.

When we are in the Emotional Dumpster Fire we are so burned out we have no idea who is in charge. Is your company in charge? Is your doctor in charge? Are you in charge of you? Stepping outside yourself and observing your behavior around situations is enlightening. It allows you to separate thoughts and patterns created by your ego. Since our ego is the source of our self-esteem, self-confidence, self-importance, self-worth and self-image it has the power, if we allow it, to make or break our success. There is a component to the ego, created by the subconscious, that drives our behavior.

Welcome the Inner Commentator. Think of it like a sports commentator. It is the voice inside your head that is giving you a play-by-play commentary of your life based on subconscious patterns and beliefs. There are three ways the Inner Commentator tosses you into the Emotional Dumpster Fire.

The Inner Commentator will create lies.
Inner Commentator is sneaky, devious and loves to lie to you.
Since it is based on emotional perception it doesn't reveal reality. For example, when someone gives you a strange look your Inner Commentator may think, they don't like me. In reality that person may be having a bad day. If you feel this happening to you, ask yourself, 'Is this true?' If not, it is your Inner Commentator telling you the story.

The Inner Commentator does not want peace it loves drama.
It does this because it feeds our addictive behaviors. Our Inner Commentator, which is part of our ego, believes our identity lies in our drama. It creates a soap opera feeding off the ups and downs of the characters. It may be bored without the highs and lows. In reality your True Self wants peace. If you hear your Inner Commentator creating a soap opera out of your life ask yourself, do I want peace or drama?

The Inner Commentator loves to obsess!
Obsessing over anything is exhausting. You become a prisoner of your thoughts. The Inner Commentator doesn't want you to be free. The stories start to have a life of their own and you start to believe the lies based on perception of the Inner Commentator. To break free of the Inner Commentator's obsession, first be aware that it is your Inner Commentator speaking, not you. Then go back to steps one and two and ask yourself, 'Is this story true?' Do I want peace or drama?

My client's Inner Commentator was telling him a story that wasn't true. It told him his co-worker was out to get him. It told him he wasn't doing his job. It told him he wasn't enough. This story caused a lot of pain and frustration for my client. It prevented him from fully accessing his potential because he obsessed and reacted from the Inner Commentator's narrative. Once he was able to understand the Inner Commentator's role in his decision making he was able to move on to the next step. However, he still didn't have the tools to bounce back and deal with stress and anxiety in the moment.

3. Establish Your Edge with Emotional Harmony.

Many people, like my client, are so used to running off of stress, they feel it is the new normal. In reality it becomes a constant energy drain on the body, mind, and spirit. When someone constantly runs off stress, they become cortically inhibited and can't access their higher brain. Their perception and reality become limited. The Emotional Intelligence component of Self Awareness and Self-Management becomes obsolete. As I stated earlier, when you are in the Emotional Dumpster Fire, it is challenging to access Emotional Intelligence.

We have been discussing Emotional Intelligence, since its discovery, for the past 20 years. Most corporations have implemented some form of Emotional Intelligence into their training programs. On one hand I am thrilled there is still an emphasis on Emotional Intelligence training, on the other hand I am still baffled that I haven't seen a huge increase in the practice of Emotional Intelligence. My client had gone through many different leadership training programs that contained an Emotional Intelligence section, but had yet to implement the foundations into his life.

Achieving real changes within an individual, starts with accessing the power of "Heart Intelligence" along with Emotional Intelligence. Heart Intelligence is the flow of intuitive awareness, understanding, and inner guidance we experience when we are in harmony. The heart isn't just a beating organ that keeps us alive, it is the largest source of bioenergy. In fact, it is 40 to 60 percent stronger than the brain. Neuroscientists have discovered the heart and mind are in constant communication. When this neurological pathway of communication is mapped out they discovered individuals are able to access higher brain function and create optimal performance. Therefore, when individuals add even just five minutes of Heart Intelligence along with Emotional Intelligence they increase awareness and are able to adjust behaviors accordingly.

Adding Heart Intelligence to my client's tool box was a game changer. Through weekly coaching sessions we were able to create coherence and transform his thought process. Using HeartMath tools, my client shifted his fear-induced triggers from his mind to his heart. This became a place where he was able to observe from a place of detachment and experience a shift in his reality. My client still falls off the wagon from time to time, but the more he practices accessing his Heart Intelligence, the more resilient he becomes.

My client is a different person today than he was when I first met him. He still is a driven, type-A individual with an endless supply of energy and a never-ending 'to do' list. Because of our work together he no longer ends up in an Emotional Dumpster fire. His drive comes from purpose and passion and not from a place of proving it. He has focused on being proactive instead of being reactive. He doesn't allow his "Inner Commentator" to be in charge. My client understands it is up to him to change his perception and reality.

To make changes that are effective and sustainable it is valuable to practice the tips I have outlined for you in this chapter:

1. Master the Art of Recognizing Triggers and Patterns.

2. Know Who is in Charge.

3. Establish Your Edge with Emotional Harmony.

Emotions make us human. They can make or break success. Being in the Emotional Dumpster Fire is counterproductive, but like anything else, it is an opportunity and a learning experience. It allows us to grow and develop a side of us that is powerful. Be a master of your emotions and you will be unstoppable!

About Tracy

Performance and Executive Coach, Tracy Martino helps her clients access their most valued resource, their mind, to achieve optimal performance in their personal and professional world.

She understands how an overwhelmed, burned out and debilitated executive can hit rock bottom and undermine their own success. As an award-winning sales executive and trainer, Tracy struggled with balancing a high-pressure career and her personal life. Ignoring the signals her body was giving her, Tracy continued to push through and ended up in the ER with chest pains and palpitations. This dark night of the soul was the catalyst that allowed Tracy to re-evaluate her life choices and create a new freedom. During this time, she immersed herself with understanding the power of the mind. Tracy researched and studied epigenetics, neuroeconomics, unethical decision making, emotional intelligence and heart intelligence.

As a result, T. Martino Brands, LLC was born. Tracy's goal is to create a bridge for her clients that connects high performance to happy. She does this through her signature programs: Predicting Success with the Intelligence Matrix, Re-Ignite the Rep, Rep Intelligence, Moving from Proving it to Purpose, and Burnout Recovery 101. Tracy's clientele spans over many different industries from CEO's of small businesses to physicians.

Tracy is also partner at Linx Consulting. Linx Consulting is a global leadership and performance consultancy that helps organizations develop dynamic cultures, comprised of actively-engaged, mindfully-inspired, and functionally-equipped leaders capable of achieving critical organizational results.

Tracy provides the greatest value to organizations that:

- Have challenges with onboarding Millennials.
- Want to prevent unethical decisions and emotional viruses.
- Have leaders intent on making a fast and significant organizational behavior impact.
- Are facing significant changes driven by either external forces or internal shifts.
- Have high aspirations for leadership and/or have performance potential not being fulfilled.
- Have a cultural tolerance for status quo and/or mediocrity that is resistant to change.
- Are launching a new business unit or have critical business initiatives that simply cannot fail.

- Recognize the need to transform the culture and create commitment around a unified vision.
- Are dealing with integration issues, whether before, during or after M & A activity.

Tracy is a graduate of University of Wisconsin-LaCrosse where she studied Economics and French. She is a certified HeartMath Coach and a Health Coach with the Institute for Integrative Health. Tracy is a speaker, poet, and writer. Her articles have been featured in *Huffington Post, Positively Positive, Rock Creek Living, The Master Shift* and *Elephant Journal.*

You can connect with Tracy at:
- tracy@tracymartino.com
- www.tracymartino.com
- www.facebook.com/t.martinobrands
- www.twitter.com/tracy_martino
- www.linkedin.com/in/tracymartino

CHAPTER 14

HOW TO HAVE A SUCCESSFUL DOCTOR APPOINTMENT

BY FELECIA FROE, MD

Having a "successful" doctor appointment isn't something that most of us think about. We think about going to the doctor for a checkup or a specific problem, but I doubt many think about what would be a successful outcome to the appointment. In business, every meeting has an agenda and the leader of the meeting has an idea of what they want to accomplish, what will make the meeting successful and worth the time it took to have it. I propose that your doctor's appointment is your meeting. You scheduled it and had an agenda. It follows that you should know what would make you feel that the meeting was successful.

LET'S START AT THE BEGINNING

You have decided that you need to set up a meeting with your doctor. You call to schedule. Like in business, you must find a time that is convenient for everyone who needs to be there. AND, you need to set an expectation of the time that will be needed for the meeting. Most of us take whatever the appointment desk will give us for a time and date. Many appointment times for doctors are 15 minutes long. That may or may not be enough for you. If you do not think that it is enough, ask for more time. You do not want your doctor to feel rushed and you certainly do not want to feel rushed. Are you thinking, "But what do I do when the receptionist won't give me what I want?" It could happen.

139

The receptionist is working by a "rule book" given to her. She has a certain number of appointments a day and generally is not allowed to do something different. If you cannot get what you feel you need and this is the doctor that you want to see, ask for a manager to help. Be polite, know that the receptionist is doing her best. If you still cannot get the appointment that you want, your options are to make more than one appointment, maybe even on the same day, or keep looking for another doctor that you can work with. If you really think that this is the doctor for you, make that first appointment an interview appointment. Go with the expectation that no medical problems will be solved. You are going to get to know the doctor and the doctor will get to know you. It will be a different experience for your doctor and you may have to pay for the visit out of pocket as there will be no code for the doctor to use to bill your insurance company. You may want to ask the cost of your doctor's time before you go in to avoid sticker shock.

LET'S GET READY

You have your appointment time and date. Now it is time to prepare. You scheduled this meeting, you must set the agenda. Remember, there is a time limit so it may not be practical to review everything that is bothering you. What is most important? What is one thing you need to have answered? Then the second thing, the third, etc. Please realize the complexity of issue number one, how your doctor is thinking, and how well the two of you are communicating on the day of your appointment will determine how many of your issues you and your doctor are able to address.

Issue number one is the most important thing that you want to discuss – the one thing that if taken care of would make your life much better and perhaps would also relieve some of those secondary issues on your list. Got it? Ok, stick it in your head. Don't fluctuate. Know that this is the one thing that must be addressed. Now, let's help your doctor help you.

Here is what your doctor should want to know:

1. How long have you been having this problem?
2. Describe the problem:
    • What makes it better or worse?
    • At its worst, how bad is it?

- Is it constant or intermittent?
- Have you had this same problem in the past?

3. How is it affecting your life?
4. What are you most scared of?
5. What do you think it is? Or what do you think is causing the problem?

Let's start with number 4 and 5. These may seem like weird questions, but when I have time, I always ask my patients this. What do I mean, when I have time? I mean, if I can get the answers to 1, 2 and 3 fairly quickly, if you come in prepared with answers to these questions that actually help me to get to what I think the problem may be, we can now get to what you think it is. Believe it or not, sometimes you are right. Many times you're not; the internet is not always the best advisor. I believe that it is important to clear your mind of your greatest worry, if possible.

WHAT ARE YOU MOST SCARED OF?

Let's say that your one thing for your health is your stomach pain. You recently read about cancer of the pancreas, and you are really, really scared that this is what is going on. This may not be one of the first things that your doctor thinks of, it may not even be on the list of options of what is causing your problem. If your doctor does not know that this is what is worrying you, you walk out still worried, with no explanation of why pancreatic cancer is not what is causing your pain. You may be thinking that your doctor didn't listen to you, does not understand. But the problem is a lack of communication. It may be very easy to ease your mind about pancreatic cancer if I know that this is what you are worried about. And, guess what, once you know why pancreatic cancer is not likely the cause of your pain, your pain may become less stressful for you.

We all have stress in our lives. How we deal with that stress is usually the problem. Stress can be the cause of many of our physical symptoms. Stress causes release of hormones in our bodies. I'm not talking just about extreme stress, like a big argument or bad news, but good news can be stressful, traffic can be stressful, all causing release of stress hormones. These hormones cause increased heart rate, increased breathing, and tightening of the blood vessels. Having tight blood vessels for a long time may cause high blood pressure and possibly less blood flow to organs such as your stomach, intestines, muscles and kidneys to name a few.

Plus, stress likely causes increase in inflammatory responses in the body, which have been found to be the beginning of cancer. But, what can you do about stress? First, think about it differently. Instead of something to avoid, accept stress as help to rise to challenges.

All those things that stress hormones cause, are beneficial in short bursts. Increased heart rate and breathing helps get more oxygen to the brain to help you to think. Turns out that there is also a stress hormone that is "helpful." That hormone is oxytocin. Oxytocin is a stress hormone that may cause us to be more social, to seek support. "So what?" you say. Studies have shown that if we acknowledge our stress and accept that the physical responses ready us to meet a challenge we can deal with it differently, we can sort through the challenge, see what oxytocin is doing for us, and seek council to help us meet the challenges in our lives. We would possibly become a more social society and have better solutions to the challenges we all live with and have less disease.

WHAT DO YOU THINK IS CAUSING THE PROBLEM?

Many times, we have an idea of what is causing the symptom that we are having. Oftentimes, patients do not let the doctor in on the thought. Some do not want to do the doctor's job or don't want the doctor to think that they are stupid about medicine. The thing is, it's not uncommon that you've correctly diagnosed the problem on your own. Sometimes it is not, so stay open to what the doctor thinks and wants to look at, but at the very least you should get an explanation of why what you think is causing the problem is not causing the problem. For example, I often have patients talk about kidney pain. I ask them to point to the area of the pain. Some point to their lower back. I can assure them at that point that it is not kidney pain because that is not where their kidneys live. If they point to the area of the kidneys, I have a little more work to do. It may take further testing to evaluate the kidneys to see if they are the cause.

HOW IS THE PROBLEM AFFECTING MY LIFE OR HOW IS MY LIFE AFFECTING ME?

Interesting question. For some people, the problem is not bothering their life, they can do everything they want to do without difficulty. For some, their life's daily activities are severely affected. Really look at this, is the problem causing problems with your life or is your worry about the problem causing the changes in your life? It may be difficult to separate these two, but it is important. Getting to the bottom of this question may take looking at the end. By this I mean, looking at what it may take to cure or treat the problem. If your doctor says you need surgery, the surgery will cause you to miss work for some period of time and you will not be able to perform your normal activities. She says that the treatment will make you worse before it makes you better, if it makes you better. You have been told that you will not die from this problem. This is where you need to make the decision. This problem is affecting my life enough to risk the treatment or it is not. It is up to you, whether or not to have a treatment is always up to you.

Now let's look at what is happening in your life that may be making you feel sick. We all have very busy, usually over-scheduled, lives. Many of us sleep and eat poorly. That's not saying we are not trying to do everything right. We are sleeping and eating poorly because we are trying to do everything right. Sleeping and eating poorly are putting stress on your body. The stress hormones are released and you keep going and going and going. You find yourself with bad digestion, weird emotional changes, you feel that you are not thinking well. Guess what, if you fill out the survey for depression, you probably fit the diagnosis. You could be diagnosed with irritable bowel or any number of diseases based on the symptoms you may perceive as most bothersome. Any of these diagnoses can get you started down a path of multiple tests and possibly medications. What if the real problem is that you need a vacation, you need a good night's or week's sleep? That treatment is safer and cheaper than anything you will get at your doctor's office.

HOW LONG HAVE YOU HAD THIS PROBLEM?

Now to the facts of the matter. This is one of the crucial questions. What the doctor is looking for with this question is, for this episode, how long has it been happening? Answers like, "I have had this for the past 6 months, but it has gotten worse in the past 5 days," are great answers. It really helps to guide the diagnostic thought process for the doctor. Something going on for 6 months and worsening may be different than something starting 5 days ago. The fact that it is worsening is a clue. Like any detective, I may not know what it means right away, but it will help to get to the answer.

DESCRIBE IT

Still on the search for clues to the problem, we are now working to characterize it. Answers like, "It is always worse after I go to the gym." or, "Maybe it is worse after I get to work." even, "Nothing makes it worse, it's just always there." are helpful. The doctor also wants to know, if it is a pain problem, if it is sharp pain or dull pain. Does it feel like anything that you have had in the past?

Really think about this before you get to the appointment. Too often, I have patients say, "I can't really describe it." This is not helpful. Without this information, I am working in the dark. This is one of those times when good descriptions are very important. Many doctors will get exasperated and order tests at this point, tests that you may not need, but what else can we do? You are not helping. I hate to say this, but it becomes like being a veterinarian.

This is one of the questions asked early in the appointment. Studies have shown that your doctor will listen to you, on average, for 18 seconds before interrupting. I guarantee that if you are giving information that is helpful to me to diagnose your problem you will get longer. If you have an organized description (what, when, how bad) you will go a long way to getting a better discussion from your doctor. It will help your doctor to stay organized in his thinking about you and your symptoms, and in all likelihood, give you more than 18 seconds to tell your story.

A good description of the issue is advantageous to you in other ways. It may also give your doctor enough information to make a diagnosis without further testing. If not, testing can be more specific to helping to confirm a diagnosis. When we have no clue as to what it could be, many more tests are ordered. Tests are expensive, medications are expensive, surgery is expensive. These are the big-ticket items in medicine, not only in absolute dollars, but also in the risks that you take. I often tell patients, the more I do for you, like prescribe medicine or perform surgery, the more risk you take. In other words, when your doctor recommends cutting you or invading your body with tools or chemicals in the form of medicine, you are the one taking risks – the risks associated with surgery and the risks associated with the side effects of drugs.

A successful doctor appointment starts with preparation and ends with communication. To have a successful doctor appointment you must:

1. Schedule the right appointment to suit your needs.
2. Prepare.
3. Consider your options after listening to your advisor.
4. Make a decision on the right course of action for you and your life.

As our mother would say, use your words. Help your doctor to understand.

Remember, your health is your responsibility.

About Dr. Felecia

Dr. Felecia Froe is a teacher, entrepreneur, real estate investor and urologist. She is a mother of two, a daughter, a sister, a friend.

Felecia has been in practice as a physician for 23 years. In that time, she won the Women Who Mean Business Award in 2001 from the KC Business Journal, was the only woman practicing urologist in Kansas City, MO from 1993 to 2004, and was the first black chief resident in her medical school, University of Missouri at Columbia. In addition, she wrote the book *Overcoming Incontinence*, published by John Wiley and Sons. She is now the Chief of Urology in her current practice.

Felecia has practiced in numerous settings including large and small single specialty groups. She founded and ran a solo practice in female urology in addition to working with a military hospital for a short time. She is currently working with a large multi-specialty group.

While in solo practice she realized that the practice was unsustainable. As expenses continued to increase she needed to increase the prices of her services or see more patients in order to support herself and her employees. She could not increase the prices of services as they were set by insurance companies. She could not pass the price increase on to her patients. Her only option was to see more patients. This meant spending less time with each patient. Trying to understand the individual's urologic medical issue, how it affected their life, and how the treatment could affect their life takes time. Time that she could not afford to take and still provide for her family and the families of her employees. It was during this very stressful time that the idea for 18 Seconds for Health came about. It was not called that at the time, but the idea of helping patients help the doctor get to know them and helping the patient come to the appointment with the understanding of how doctor's think was born.

Several years later Felecia found the book *How Doctors Think* by Jerome Groopman. This is where she learned that, on average, doctor's listen to patients for 18 seconds before interrupting. Now she is working to develop a program to give patients the ability to share their important information in those first seconds of their appointment. Her desire is that all people take responsibility for their health and use their doctor as an advisor, a teacher. She wants to make sure that all people understand that doctors are human beings subject to emotions and errors. This includes liking and disliking patients and having a bad day! Negative emotions affect communication and the care you receive.

Felecia has also been an active real estate investor for the past 12 years. Her current project, a residential care facility, helps the elderly live in home-like communities and receive the help they need to thrive.

- Website: www.feleciafroemd.com
- Email: Feleciafroemd@gmail.com
- Facebook: Felecia Froe MD
- Twitter: @feleciafroemd

CHAPTER 15

REALIZING DREAMS:
CRACKING THE CODE TO STUDENT SUCCESS

BY JIM CANTONI

Advancing Human Potential in Education and Health

Know thyself. ~ Socrates

Thanks to America's collective efforts, the national graduation rate has increased to 83%. But if we're to inspire even better results, we must figure out a way to unlock the potential in students who aren't yet applying themselves.

Several challenges that we face in closing the achievement gap are equity in education, improving reading proficiency, chronic absenteeism, and reducing dropout rates. Another important ingredient is meaningful family engagement that inspires male members of the family and community to be involved in changing lives. At the same time, there is a need to raise the performance of mid-level students to higher achievement – and provide our gifted and talented students with mind-stretching, high-impact and fulfilling enrichment.

Two of "The BIG Questions" for improving student success are:

I. How do we engage students to discover their internal drive and link to learning that motivates them to want to achieve at higher levels?

II. How do we build capacity in staff and caring adults to help students overcome obstacles as they go through important changes with social and emotional learning?

The *Realizing Dreams* foundational enrichment and step-by-step roadmap promotes success for all students and includes:

1). **7 Step Framework for Student Success** - Giving Youth a Voice and Choice in their Lives.

2). *7 Steps for Empowering Youth: Self-Awareness Developing GRIT and a Growth* moves talk to action and acts like an internal GPS that helps youth create their personal game plans for a successful future.

3). **"Me and the 9 Selfs for Emotional Intelligence"** – a self-discovery framework.

4). **7 of 15+** *Einstein-Inspired and Infused Teaching Strategies and Self-Efficacy Formulas for Emotional Intelligence* to overcome obstacles and cultivate a growth mindset.

Blending the *Realizing Dreams* research-based frameworks, engagement strategies and hands-on tools help make better connections with students. The activities provide results-based outcomes and profound insight to unlock our young people's potential. You will quickly see how to personalize learning and support what intrinsically motivates students, and identify what holds them back from wanting to achieve and succeed. An example of this is the underperforming 3rd grader at Driggs Elementary School in Waterbury, CT (a large urban school district) who wrote in his action journal during the transformational engagement, "Listen to teachers. Study. [Get] Good grade[s]." More on why and how he did this later in the chapter. We all want to advance human potential in education and health. Together we can, and will, realize more dreams and crack the code to student success.

Impact and Outcomes in a recent training; a sample revealed:
- 94% of students critically thought about and planned their futures. This sample included many young adults who lacked direction in life.

- 89% improved their decision making by changing mindsets, attitudes, and behaviors in order to make better choices with social and emotional learning through the Einstein-Inspired and Infused Teaching Strategies and Self-Efficacy Formulas for Emotional Intelligence.

Let's get started on how to take Kindergarten to college students, with the help of the adults in their lives, from one step to the next.

REALIZING DREAMS
7 Step Framework for Student Success
Giving Youth a Voice and Choice in their Lives

1) Open communication: In a game-style of play, kids and adults of all ages talk, laugh, share and learn about each other's strengths, interests, hopes, passion, and dreams.
2) Build confidence, becoming self-aware and engaging for a growth mindset that inspires student imaginations to dream BIG dreams. We need to help youth discover what they want to do and a reason *why* to do it – like the 10-year-old girl wrote in her journal as shown on p.161.
3) Use natural "calls-to-action" to comfortably and quickly move talk to action.
4) Have students create personal game plans to help overcome any fears and worries and realize their dreams. They will realize their self-worth and clearly see their next steps and path to successful futures.
5) Engage, equip, and empower students with the *Einstein-Inspired and Infused Teaching Strategies and Self-Efficacy Formulas for Emotional Intelligence* to overcome obstacles.
6) Inspire our young people to make a promise to graduate from high school, prepare for college and/or career, and be the change in the world they want to see.
7) Link the intrinsic motivation insight to learning and measure results-based outcomes. *This student success framework enables systemic repetition throughout the school district and develops leaders by having students empower other students to lead, coach and then present results to adults.*

When adults learn what is inside our young people's minds, we synchronize the energy and experience of generations. The goal is to put youth and adults on the same page so they learn from the mistakes of each other and find an easier way in life. By doing this, we can transform everybody's lives.

We all stand on the shoulders of giants. Einstein stretches our minds with his observation that:

Imagination is everything. It is the preview of life's coming attractions.

As students' imaginations becomes their life's preview; as self-awareness increases, they discover passion and dream BIG dreams – giving hope and something to look forward to.

Socrates opens our eyes with his timeless advice:
Know thyself.

Self-Awareness is the key to *Cracking the Code to Student Success.* But how? We need to open communication with student-centered enrichment that gives youth voice and choice in their lives. We need to purposefully help them express thoughts and feelings about their futures and answer "The BIG Questions" in their lives. *Then, move talk to action and guide our young people to create their own plans for a successful future.*

Give Confidence … Get Confident™
Our young people thrive when they discover their answers to:
1). Who am I?
2). What do I want to do?
3). How do I create a game plan to get there?

Confidence builds, the light bulb comes on, and lives transform as we help students (and even adults) "Know Thyself". Realizing dreams leads people to "self-actualization" as noted in Abraham Maslow's Hierarchy of Needs. That's exactly what the action journal *7 Steps for Empowering Youth* does…

7 Steps for Empowering Youth: Self-Awareness
Developing Grit and a Growth Mindset

Plan your future. Transform your life.™ *7 Steps for Empowering Youth: Self-Awareness Developing Grit and a Growth Mindset* is a reflective action journal that gives youth a voice and choice in life. The discovery activities help students answer 52 of "The BIG Questions" in their life; identify their strengths; and express their thoughts and feelings verbally and in writing about a successful future.

Students will increase self-awareness, discover passion and learn what inspires them to dream BIG dreams. Natural calls-to-action move their thoughts to action, then guide them step-by-step to confidently create their personal game-plan to realize their dreams in life. *Einstein-Inspired and Infused Teaching Strategies and Self-Efficacy Formulas for Emotional Intelligence* develop Life Skill Assets™ that foster resilience and build capacity to overcome obstacles. The purpose of these assets is for exponential achievement in school, work, life, health and play. They're all about helping students grow positive mindsets, and changing attitudes and behaviors with social and emotional learning as the focus.

Students will also reflect on 104 thought-provoking and inspirational quotes from historic and world leaders. Then critically think who is their favorite, and most importantly, journal why? Visual learners thrive seeing the four sets of 13, colorfully-illustrated positive character traits. The research-based activities give results-based outcomes. Everyone learns how to identify, set, and achieve GETTING SMARTR™ goals that help them clearly see their next steps and path to a successful future.

Community Building in Small to Large Groups: Teamwork and FamilyPlay™

You can use *7 Steps for Empowering Youth* by itself, or to scaffold learning in a game style of play using Teamwork and FamilyPlay; the action journal's companion and community-building discovery game. Both the book and the game include the same activities – 52 of The BIG Questions and the 104 Inspirational Quotes. The cooperative game uses a deck of oversize cards (5"x7") that in 2011 earned The National Parenting Center Seal of Approval for "bridging the communication divide". The family engagement game makes it fun for all ages to learn more about each other as well as themselves.

To start the game, just:

1. *Invite* people to take one of the oversized cards.
2. Take turns asking and answering "The BIG Questions" written in red.
3. Exchange cards. Repeat with another person – it's fun and that easy!

Give Teamwork … Get Results™

Then, comfortably **move talk to action.** Invite students to reflect and journal what they just talked about in Teamwork and FamilyPlay [the game] and continue to climb the *7 Steps for Empowering Youth*, together.

Step 1: Complete Your Dream Tag.

In the first minute of engagement, ask students to complete a Dream Tag™. It's simply a name tag transformed to discover the student's strengths, passions – and dreams in life. This quick and powerful activity is on the inside front cover of *7 Steps for Empowering Youth*.

Step 2: Students select their favorite character trait and reflect on the two quotes.

Tell students to go to page one and give each other a high-five and jump up to the second step. If you played the cooperative oversized card game, then using the cards in a new way, students will see the same four sets of 13 quotes, but now reflect and write their favorite quote. Some quote authors, including: Einstein on a Positive Attitude; Martha Washington on Communication; Nelson Mandela on Respect; and Dr. Martin Luther King, Jr. on Appreciating Diversity – America's greatest strength. An example is:

Creativity is the power to connect the seemingly unconnected.
~ William Plomer

Step 3: Give your "MBA" – My Big Answer – to The BIG Questions in your life.

Here, students reflect on the same "BIG Questions" they just talked about in the card game, and their journaling now gives educators and parents insight how to link motivation to learning. For example:

- What would you do if you knew you could not fail?
  - (*My MBA is to give a Ted Talks, what's yours?*
  _____)

- What is something that you were told to do, and didn't do, but later wished you had?
  - (Me? I wish I applied myself more in school. You?
  _____)

Step 4: Make a Declaration to Realize Your Dreams.

Natural calls-to-action guide students to "Make a Declaration to Realize My Dreams in Life". Students learn how to identify, set and achieve GETTING SMARTR™ goals – taking S.M.A.R.T. goals to higher levels. Educators, mentors and parents gain powerful insight about individual student focus and motivation. School counselors find that it helps students to quickly and more easily conceptualize Student Success Plans and clearly see their paths to successful futures – even starting in elementary school.

Step 5: Reflect, then select your Top 5 Character Strengths.

Strength-based interventions encourage students to focus on their strengths. Step 5 does just that. For success in school and college/career readiness, this self-assessment and feedback activity has students reflecting on and selecting their Top 5 Strengths from the 13-colorful illustrations they saw in the game, but now are in their keepsake journal. Usually in less than two minutes, students excitedly circle illustrations identifying their strengths, then number their strengths 1 through 5. This builds confidence and prepares students for that BIG interview question, what are your strengths? Adults gain visual insight on how students perceive their strengths. Step 5 also helps students self-assess areas of development.

Step 6: Select and write your "My Faves" of what inspired you most.

This one-page summary provides a summary for quick insight on what resonated most with students and helps educators and parents open the conversation to personalize learning.

Step 7: Join in MISSION: USA 2020.

College and professional sports teams know the power of being part of something larger than ourselves. In Step 7, students are congratulated for completing the activities and are invited to join in MISSION: USA 2020. Students are now self-aware with a growth mindset to reach their potential.

7 Einstein-Inspired and Infused Teaching Strategies and Self-Efficacy Formulas for Emotional Intelligence

Comfort Zones – Stretching Minds. Opening Hearts

In less than one minute, all ages learn these easy-to-remember and visual formulas illustrated in *7 Steps for Empowering Youth.* Here are 7 of 15+ leadership strategies created to develop confidence, build capacity, and foster resilience to overcome obstacles for emotional intelligence and a growth mindset. After completing hundreds of Student Success Workshops, I've found that once adults see self-efficacy formulas in action, any participant having a fixed mindset quickly gets out of his or her comfort zone upon seeing a student's excitement and hearing young people read and reflect on the meaning of each self-efficacy formula.

Let's start with **"E to the Second Power"** (E^2™**)."** It's all about what this high school freshman wrote on her survey.

"I [now] know more that will help me in the future that I wish I knew before."

At one time or another, we all heard someone older than us say, "I wish I was your age and knew what I know now."

It's time that we change that.

We all know that today's youth have more energy in their youthfulness, and adults have more experience which comes with age. It is when we arrive at that special place – everyone on the same page – and synchronize the "energy and experience" of generations, that we help youth learn the "easier way" in life from the life lessons and mistakes made by adults. Together, we can and we will improve and transform everybody's lives.

"E to the Third Power"(E^3™) gives the vision and engagement-learning objectives. It helps educators, coaches, mentors and facilitators to answer three BIG questions:

1) How am I going to engage participants?
2) What new self-efficacy Life Skill Assets™ will they be equipped with at the end of the engagement?
3) How will they be empowered?

To make the learning stick, I created the framework, **The 5 Ps of a Transformational Experiential Engagement**™.

1) Positive
2) Playful
3) Purposeful
4) Productive
5) Producible by others

THE THEORY OF OUR PURPOSE IN LIFE

"It shows how to inspire others." – an educator

Inspired students are self-motivated to achieve in school and succeed in life. **"IPO to the Second Power"** is all about *inspiring potential in each other.*

"**I**nspire **P**otential in **O**urselves so that we can **I**nspire **P**otential in **O**thers. Engage, equip, and empower youth to realize their dreams, achieve greater life outcomes, and create a legacy greater than ourselves."

~ Jim Cantoni, author of *7 Steps for Empowering Youth* and Founder of *Realizing Dreams*

Educators ask me, "What did you do? I've worked with this teenager for three years. He barely says his name. You had him for 45 minutes – he now is reading – something he is not good at (yet anyway) and presenting in front of the entire group!"

Grit, Goal Setting, and a Growth Mindset
We need to engage, equip, and empower students with "G to the third power."

G^{3} ™ stands for: Grit, learning to persevere and never give up; Goal Setting to critically think about the future today for a more successful tomorrow; and Growth Mindset – believing that you can improve and be self-propelled with internal drive to do your best in life.

Overcoming Obstacles™
Gratitude goes to Brian Tracy for the **"O to the Second Power"** (O^{2} ™)

inspiration. At one of Brian's seminars in the 1990's, he said, "Whenever there is a problem, focus on the 'How' to solve it, not the 'Why' it can't be done."

In 2010, during a conference, I asked Harvard positive psychologist, Dr. Shawn Achor, if he knew why "How" works better? Fascinated with the question, he said brain science recently discovered that when we focus on the "Why" something can't be done we get emotionally hi-jacked, letting negative stressors set in. When we focus on the "How" to solve a problem, we focus on the positive, making it easier to overcome obstacles in life.

To improve communication, The Department of Labor, OSHA, asked me to create a professional development workshop to illustrate this point. In an Empower in an Hour™ hands-on leadership development activity, I had one group focus on the "why" and one on "how" to overcome obstacles in our lives. The outcome? Everybody learned that the "How's" get more done with less stress and in less time.

ABC²™ – Helps Change Mindsets, Attitudes and Behaviors to make Better Choices

Ask who will be the first to find the ABC²™ formula in 7 Steps for Empowering Youth? Then ask:

1. What does that mean to you?
2. Why is it important in life?
3. How can ABC²™ increase your success and help you realize your dreams in life?

The impact is quick, simple, and powerful. Student/Educator surveys show this is a favorite formula.

Me and the 9 Selfs – An Emotional Intelligence Framework

To develop emotional intelligence, the framework helps students learn about self-discovery, self-awareness, self-control, self-worth and self-efficacy through self-actualization. A diagram of the framework is in *7 Steps for Empowering Youth*.

For a powerful discover activity, invite students to read and share what each of the "9 Selfs" means to them. For example, ask, "What is Self-Efficacy?" To cement their learning, weave in anecdotes that engage students. For Self-Control, ask who heard the story of the four-year-old who was asked whether he wanted one cookie now or two later? Usually someone raises their hand and excitedly tells the group that having self-control increases success in life. This activity creates a teachable moment created by the students.

7 THOUGHT STARTERS HOW YOU CAN USE THESE HIGH-IMPACT STRATEGIES TO OPEN COMMUNICATION, UNLOCK POTENTIAL AND TRANSFORM EVERYONE'S LIVES.

1) *Purposefully increase self-awareness at an earlier age.*
2) Inspire Dads with meaningful family engagement in PTA/PTO events.
3) Collective impact with community engagement in education. i.e., Parks & Recreation programming, Take Our Daughters and Sons to Work Day.
4) Empower transitions and influence Student Success Plans – again, even starting in elementary school.
5) Aid in Leadership Development for Youth and Adults – including high-impact enrichment for gifted and talented students.
6) Initiate Mentor and Mentee Synchronization.
7) Provide the basis of Staff Professional Development that transfers right onto the students.

Impact and Outcomes

The rigorous and relevant student-centered enrichment and transformational tools provide simple steps to increase self-awareness and build capacity at all ages. They give educators a framework to systemically unlock potential. They help students discover their internal drive that motivates them to want to achieve at high levels. Everyone who participates makes better connections that build confidence and trusting relationships. The added benefit of social and emotional learning for health and well-being takes the experience to a higher level.

In their own handwriting, the next two pages show what students are discovering and educators are finding.

What students are discovering:

Name: Sarah AA
Age: 14 Grade 9

REALIZING *Dreams*
Engage. Equip. Empower.

What did you accomplish in this growth mindset workshop?
Self confidence, learning myself

Am I better off? ✓ Yes ___ No If yes, why? *I am better off because,* I know more that will help me in the future that I wish I knew before

13) How did this Realizing Dreams Leadership Development Workshop influence your:	None	Some	Alot	Please explain and/or provide an example:
a. Sense of self-confidence?			✓	I feel more confident
b. Having self-control?			✓	better leadership
c. Self-Awareness?			✓	
d. Setting and Achieving GETTING SMARTR™ Goals?			✓	I know my goals
e. Having a Growth Mindset to be the best you can be?			✓	I understand what I need

Name: Natnan H
Age: 15 Grade 9

I feel like I have something I want to do and a reason why to do it.

5th Grade girl

What did you accomplish in this growth mindset workshop?
It taught me more about myself and how to plan how to be more successful in life.

	It influenced me a lot	Please explain and/or provide an example:
	✓	I can help myself now
	✓	I was really intrested and in this
	✓	I know how to stick up for myself/others
	✓	It helped me keep log/track
		I am willing to learn

16) How did these self-efficacy formulas influence you, if at all? Please explain and/or provide an e
They made me understand life

What educators and parents are finding:

MY STORY – Staff/Adults

REALIZING ★ Dreams ★
Engage. Equip. Empower.™

School/Org: Driggs

Name:

Position 3rd

I will realize my dream in life of: setting up a foundation

Because of the 7 Steps for EMPOWERING YOUTH workshop by Realizing Dreams, I feel:
I can help facilitate empowering myself and the younger population

In the Realizing Dreams 7 Steps for EMPOWERING YOUTH workshop my students:

1. ✓ Identified their Top 5 Strengths for their success in school, college and career
2. ✓ Discovered and/or wrote their passion and interests in school, work and/or life
3. ✓ Are happier that they reflected on and answered some of "The Big Questions" in their life

Name: Jessica

Age: _____ Grade Teacher

What did you accomplish? I accomplished connection
Learn about the students and the different way of thinking.

Am I better off? ✓ Yes ___ No   If yes, why? I am better off because, I was able to make a better connection with my students.

The students were excited and showed motivation in establishing their

dream and the path to achieve it.

What did the students accomplish in this growth mindset workshop? Empowerment of themselves

Are the students better off? ✓ Yes ___ No   If yes, why? The students are better off because, Because now they know what they want to do and how they can reach it.

FOUNDATIONAL ENRICHMENT

Turning the Learning Light Bulb On: Now Intrinsically Motivated to Achieve and Succeed

- An underperforming student in Waterbury, CT went from a 51 to 91 in English. How? In 90 minutes, she was inspired to change her mindset, attitudes and behaviors. In *7 Steps for Empowering Youth* she created her game plan for exponential achievement less than one week later.

- The prison pipeline lost one more inner city 3rd grader. He is now taking more initiative in his learning. During "The BIG Question" ice-breaker activity in Teamwork and FamilyPlay, this 9-year-old boy told me, "I can't read big words." I moved talk to action and linked it to learning. He created his life action plan in 7 Steps for Empowering Youth. Then he excitedly led other students in the same activities – telling them to also write in their game plans, "Listen to teachers. Study. Good grade[s]." How? After completing the activities he was inspired to change his mindset in minutes. To Driggs Elementary School Principal Michael Theriault's delight, his underperforming student read five times after-school since we had met the week before. Now more confident in his future, this student *wants* to read.

- In the first few minutes of a Student Success workshop, I could see this shy, withdrawn 14-year-old girl was lacking confidence. After discovering her goals and understanding what she needed, 75 minutes later Sarah completed her game plan to realize her dreams in life. Everyone saw her in a new light. Sarah inspired counselors and adults with how she felt and what she wrote about in *7 Steps for Empowering Youth.*

Beyond Family Engagement: *Family Empowerment*

Moms and Dads are literally more engaged in education. For example, in East Hartford, CT an inner-city dad in his 40s even completed the growth mindset activities side-by-side in *7 Steps for Empowering Youth* with his 17-year-old football-playing son. Dad created his step-by-step game plan to go back to school – making his wife smile. Unable to attend that day, during the next week mom excitedly started her action journal too.

Give inspiration ... Get inspired™

You will find it fulfilling to witness self-aware kindergarten to college students create their life action and personal game plans for successful futures. Students are planning to graduate high school, go to college, get into big data, become veterinarians, engineers, teachers, police officers, paleontologists, astronauts, a Mayor, the President, and more.

You will see kids come alive as they realize their self-worth. By focusing on "Realizing Dreams" we can "Crack the Code to Student Success." Together, we can and we will transform everybody's lives by helping schools with exponential achievement, growth and student success. After all, earlier is easier and later costs are greater.

A Collective Impact Challenge

As a society, we all want to unlock and advance human potential as The Priscilla Chan and Mark Zuckerberg Initiative's thought-provoking words inspire,

The only way that we reach our full human potential is if we're able to unlock the gifts of every person around the world.

A Preview of Life's Coming Attractions

If Einstein was right, "Imagination is a preview of life's coming attractions," we must imagine what we can become if we collaborated to unlock the gifts of every person around the world...

We can increase student self-awareness and unlock their gifts. We can develop an internal drive with focus and motivation to reach their potential. Now, imagine if every student realized their dreams and self-actualized – what that would do for our society?

Starting today... let's do as Brian Gallagher, President and CEO of the United Way Worldwide inspires us to do – *collaborate for community change though our collective impact.* We can advance human potential in education and health.

It's fun for all ages to be Realizing Dreams In Teams™. After all, isn't life about inspiring potential in ourselves so that we can inspire potential in each other?

The last BIG Question: When we look in our life's rear-view mirror, can you and I say that we "Know Thyself" and answer the BIG question that Maslow may have posed?

"Did I self-actualize?"

About Jim

Jim Cantoni is a success coach who helps people discover their passion and engages, equips and empowers all ages to dream, believe and achieve. Jim inspires potential, synchronizes generations and transforms lives in education and health. Jim is founder of Realizing Dreams and author of five motivational books. In 2017, Jim Cantoni joined Brian Tracy as co-author of *Cracking The Code to Success* – Jim's chapter is *Realizing Dreams: Cracking the Code to Student Success – Advancing Human Potential in Education and Health.*

As a capacity building practitioner in his onsite and online virtual author-guided journeys, Jim Cantoni creates and applies what research has found for exponential achievement in school, work, life and play. Jim comfortably moves talk to action in a game style of play in his student success workshops, Youth Empowerment Summits (YES!) and assemblies. Jim scaffolds the learning using Teamwork and FamilyPlay, his national award-winning cooperative discovery game that he transformed into a reflective action journal called *7 Steps for Empowering Youth: Self-Awareness Developing Grit and a Growth Mindset.* Jim's keepsake action journal acts like an internal GPS guiding students with natural calls-to-action that build confidence and help them find direction in life. In his Empower in an Hour™ workshops, Jim's results-based outcomes include 94% of students creating game plans where they clearly see their path to a successful future. In his Family Engagement in Education workshops, his goal is Family Empowerment and to synchronize the energy and experience of generations by putting children and adults on the same page.

Jim Cantoni has created eight national award-winning experiential books and hands-on tools that build community and illustrate what positive psychology has found to create the positive affect. Jim has created more than 15 Einstein-inspired and infused emotional intelligence teaching strategies and growth mindset formulas that foster resilience and build capacity to overcome obstacles. Jim equips young and old with self-efficacy Life Skill Assets™ which often inspire people to change their mindsets, attitudes and behaviors in minutes, not months.

With his company, Creative Concepts & GivaGeta, Inc., www.CCPromos.com, Jim Cantoni gives back and helps inner city students realize their dreams of going to summer camp, when businesses purchase all sorts of logo'd items to recognize, remember and reward. Jim is a songwriter, patented inventor of illuminated house numbers and creator of The New Math of Health. He helps people by not adding a pill, but subtracting the cause. Using the My Body Balance T-Chart Jim created, users increase self-awareness. This has helped many people prevent and resolve many of their chronic illnesses from acne to acid indigestion, arthritis, weight gain and more.

Jim Cantoni received his MBA from Rensselaer Polytechnic Institute, and his undergraduate degree in Business from Central Connecticut State University. Jim resides in Glastonbury, CT with his wife Jackie, and their two boys. He enjoys golf, reading, playing Frisbee on the beach, taking walks and growing garlic and kale.

To learn more, contact Jim at:
- Tel: 860.657.0770
- Email: Jim.Cantoni@RealizingDreams.us
- www.RealizingDreams.us

CHAPTER 16

SUCCESS, WHAT CHOICES ARE YOU MAKING TOWARDS IT?

BY GARY L BOYD, Jr.

We wake up every day and go about our business... Eat, Work, Sleep, and then do it all over again. Is this what you are currently doing? Have you ever asked yourself, "How did I get to this place in my life?" Are you happy with where you are in life? If so, that is fantastic! Share your thoughts and ideas with family and friends! If not, then take a moment to read the rest of this chapter, and see if anything hits home and which you feel that you can use in your life today.

Do you realize that you are exactly where you are, at this moment in time, based on the decisions YOU made? Success is an accumulation of choices that you have made and are making in your life.

What do you think of when you hear the word 'consequences'? Is it negative? What if I told you that there are POSITIVE consequences for the choices you make as well? I hope it makes you take a moment and think.

Let me tell you a story, a story about two brothers that grew up in the same house, raised in the same neighborhoods, and had the same choices to make every day. They were only about a year and a half apart from each other. The oldest was a very angry child as his dad left them with their extremely abusive mom at the age of two. His anger was with everyone.

He was always fighting and getting into trouble; heck, by the time he was ten, he was on a first name basis with several police officers! His younger brother was more of a carefree individual that everyone loved and thought he was so 'cute'. Can you imagine how their lives turned out? What do you think happened to them? They took two very different paths, even though they had the same choices offered to them. Doesn't it ever make you wonder why that is?

Those two boys were getting into trouble so much so that they had to go into a boys' home called Boysville around the ages of 10 and 9 respectively, since their mother was unable to control them.

Growing up in this type of environment, you can see the challenges started to be stacked up against them. But, one thing that was in the favor of the oldest boy, was that he loved to read. There are so many great books out there that are written that give you that "AHA!" moment – like, *The Power of Your Subconscious Mind* by Joseph Murphy, *How to Win Friends and Influence People* by Dale Carnegie, and *The Keys to Success* by Napoleon Hill.

With the time to read great works on Success, and actually putting many of those principles to work, the oldest boy had grown past his anger issues and started to see success in his everyday life. Along the way, and through many great teachings, there were several things that struck home (as I know it will for many of you), and if you start implementing some of these you will start seeing positive things happening in your life. And to be honest, I am sure you will start feeling prouder of the choices you make.

1. Do what is right!

That seems like an easy choice to make, wouldn't you agree? But why is it such a hard decision to make from time to time? You see, we tend to worry about what others think of the choices we make. We don't want to offend someone or hurt their feelings. Or the right choice might be more work than we are willing to put in, and you may do nothing. In either case, or for whatever reason you have, you ARE making a choice! So make it a good one!!! And guess what... once you start down the path of making good choices, you will get into the habit of making better and better choices. You will start feeling pride in the choices you make, and you will be developing your character so that people will look towards you as an example to emulate.

2. Learn and Master the Fundamentals/Basics:

What does this mean to you? Whatever you are doing in life, be it your personal life or your professional life, get the fundamentals down. It was said that Vince Lombardi used to start every training camp with "This is a football" . . . while holding up a football. Imagine that, the coach was telling this to a team of players that have probably been playing football for 8-10 years of their lives up to that point. As with a house you need a solid foundation. And the fundamentals give you that. Vince Lombardi, John Wooden, Phil Jackson, and Gregg Popovich are all leaders/coaches that stressed the fundamentals with their players and have established dynasties throughout their careers and raised and developed legends in the game based on laying a strong foundation on the basics. So, look at just one area of your life that you want to improve, and then start reading and implementing the fundamentals and basics. If you don't know what those are, find someone that can help you along the way.

3. Strive for Excellence:

How do you feel when you accomplish something, maybe a goal, and you just winged it? It got completed, but it was haphazardly done. Did you feel great by it? Or did you feel like you just didn't do your best and know you could have done better? How do you feel when you succeed in a project or a goal and you did your absolute best? Do you feel on top of the world and are you proud of what you did? Why not strive for that feeling every time? Just try to do your best on your next task, and once completed, feel how great it feels doing something you are proud of. Take a moment to enjoy that, and then tell yourself that you will do it again on your next task.

4. C.A.N.I. (Constant and Never-ending Improvement):

This is one that I really need to thank Tony Robbins for sharing with the world. No one is expecting you to be perfect at everything. But if you live by this saying, you will develop your fundamentals into being an expert. Think about it. What are you really good at, at this moment? It could be a sport like golf, or maybe speaking to people. Maybe you are a Leader that everyone wants to follow. Did you think about that one thing you are really good at? Now that you have it, were you always great at it? I bet I can answer that without knowing you personally, and the answer would be, "No, I was not always good at that." Am I right? You see, everyone started in a place of "not knowing" but you read about it, or someone showed you and then you practiced it over and over, while you or someone provided feedback on what you were doing and how you could improve. Whether you realized it or not, you were practicing C.A.N.I. on a daily basis! Surprise! You were already doing it! Now ask yourself, how did you feel when you were making the choices you were making and improving every day? Nice feeling, wasn't it?

5. Take 100% Accountability:

As stated earlier, you are where you are, at this very moment in time, based on the choices you made every day. Good choices and bad choices. Even when you didn't make a choice, that was still a choice, was it not? Once you realize that your life is based on the choices you make, then you can take 100% ownership of those choices and start making different decisions. This is another pride moment. At this moment, tell yourself "The buck stops here! I will take control of my life; I will take control of my choices!" How do you feel? It feels good, doesn't it?

6. Avoid Negativity:

This one is a challenging one. It is easy to be negative when it seems like everything is going to hell. There doesn't seem to be a way out. Let me ask you this, when you think back on your life, has your life been 100% nothing but positive memories? If we are living in the same world, I am going to say that you are going to say 'no'. Am I right? And were some of those negative memories some of your toughest challenges? So tell me, did you get through it? And now after time has passed, did you realize that, "Those challenges were not so bad, we have been through tougher times." No matter how bad things seem to be when you are going through them, when you look back, you would realize that you got past them by focusing on something positive that came along. Family and friends can have the best intentions, but can be negative about you accomplishing something. Focus on trying to surround yourself with people that will lift you up and give you encouragement to accomplish whatever goal you want to go for.

The Brothers' Story...

What do you think happened to the two brothers? They were faced with a very challenging life and not given many opportunities. . . Well, the older brother took these ideas and values and ran with them. He joined the military, and everything he did and every position he took, was in a leadership position, and I truly believe that every success in life was based on his choices. . . both positive and negative. The younger brother went down the wrong path and faced more negative challenges than most people have. . . I am sure that he might be questioning the choices he has made, but he knows that he can still change his future and has started making good choices in his life as he is rebuilding it into the way he wants! Yes, this was me and my little brother, someone I love dearly and know that he is making better choices today.

A little side note, I have two little ones, and every morning when I am dropping them off at school I tell them, "Make good choices!" – a constant reminder that will help develop good habits. I can't wait to see the impact this decision-making will have on their lives in the future.

SUMMARY

You are where you are based on the choices you have made in your life. If you are happy with the direction it has been going, then great! I suggest that you share your thoughts and ideas with family and friends.

If not, then now know, you can still have the success and life that you want. You just need to take action and put the following ideas and suggestions into your life today!

1. **Do what is right!** – Do what is right for you, your family and your company, and things will tend to work out for the best.
2. **Learn and Master the Fundamentals/Basics** – This is your foundation that you will build on every day as you get better and better!
3. **Strive for Excellence** – Strive for Excellence in everything you do! Take pride in your actions and work.
4. **C.A.N.I.** – **C**onstant **A**nd **N**ever-ending **I**mprovement - Keep pushing yourself to be better than you were the day before. Look for your next step.

5. **Take 100% Accountability** – Take accountability for all your actions. Good or bad. Don't pass the buck. You are the reason!

6. **No Negativity** – Negativity breeds more negativity. Surround yourself with people that will support you towards your goals and dreams – people that are willing to help you stay on track towards the right choices you make.

What do you think? Do you think this is hard? Or do you think, "This is simple and something I can do!" Guess what? This is a choice that you can take right now to start having success in your life.

There is a lot of information to process. My suggestion is for you to take it in a little at a time... Start with a good choice. . .

The choice to take action!

To your Success!

About Gary

Gary L. Boyd, Jr. helps his clients focus on developing their leadership and success within themselves. Raised in a challenging environment, he knew there had to be more, there had to be a way to get to the goals and dreams he wished for himself and his family. He developed an insatiable desire to learn. One of the things he learned was that you will reach your dreams by leading and helping others reach their successes and dreams.

Gary began learning by example, in the military, and emulating that as he began to lead as well. After 13+ years working in several leadership positions at Dell, he has helped hundreds of people grow and develop to their next level.

Gary is a graduate of the John Maxwell Team, the #1 Leadership Expert in the world! He is a person that stands by his word and has developed a very strong reputation by his training, leadership abilities, and his character.

You can connect with Gary at:
- GaryBoyd@johnmaxwellgroup.com
- http://www.johnmaxwellgroup.com/GaryBoyd
- http://www.facebook.com/GaryLBoydJr
- LinkedIn: www.linkedin.com/in/GLBoydJr

CHAPTER 17

DEFEATING ALL ODDS

BY CARLA BUTCHER

As a child I had watched my father start and grow his business. I remember he had one computer with a tiny desk in my sister's room and there he created a program for pawn shops to help them with their inventory among many other things. I saw my father's business grow and I remember waking up to the doorbell because his new employees would need to come to the house to get to the garage and go to work. I was a very proud daughter watching my dad create jobs for people and create his own income without having to go get a job. As I grew older my father's company grew and he had more employees, and I became more impressed because I understood my father was an entrepreneur. He was my inspiration and I believe he instilled in me principles that he never taught me but rather showed through example. These basic principles of hard work and dedication, along with a never-give-up attitude. My father is the type of man that does not like to complain but rather just do, finish it, and then go have fun. Today I live by those principles because today I have become a successful entrepreneur.

I can remember my very first job working for Burger King, I was fourteen years old and I loved the fast-paced environment. I loved cooking with food, and since working for Burger King I had decided to start working for other restaurants and gain knowledge in the culinary field. As I was learning how to create some amazing gourmet dishes, I would notice how poorly employees were getting treated. People were getting yelled at, no breaks were given, sexual harassment incidents continued to happen to other female employees along with myself. Then one day I realized that

I wanted to start my own company, to own a business and treat people with dignity, compassion, and respect. But becoming an entrepreneur would not happen for me until many years later.

I decided to leave home at the early age of fourteen thinking my life would get better. I left my home to experience life on new terms because tension was formed between my parents and I, due to the fact that I was born gay. From the age of fourteen through twenty-four I worked in many kitchens and learned many traits, the sad part of those years was that I began experimenting with drugs and alcohol. Was I a hard worker? Yes, I was relentless, creative, talented and I never complained. I got my work done, but I could not advance in my culinary career because no matter how hard I tried to cover up my drug and alcohol addiction, people would notice. Even though my drug and alcohol addiction was never brought to my attention because it was all speculation, I knew and they knew I was not doing well emotionally and mentally. I was using drugs and alcohol to cover up my feelings from incidents that had happened to me in the past as a child. (My book St. Marley and Friar Ted goes into further detail about my childhood sexual abuse from random adults within my family and neighbors, without my parent's knowledge.)

I was twenty-four when the attacks of September 11th occurred, it inspired me to go into the service. I believed that joining the service and serving my country would change my life and give me a career that I would have been proud of. I loved boot camp, I lost over thirty pounds, I felt amazing, strong, and I knew I was doing a noble thing serving our country. Shortly after boot camp I was assigned to meet up with my first ship. I flew to Afghanistan to meet my ship and I was able to meet and greet everyone on board. I understood I was still emotional and I still had issues dealing with my childhood but I chose to suppress those feelings because I was now a part of something bigger than myself. I had a purpose and that was to serve honorably in the United States Navy and do whatever was asked of me to do.

That day I met my rapist, of whom I will never speak his name. My rapist was trying to ask me to go venture out with him when we docked our ship, but something inside me told me to hang out with other people and so I did. It was a wonderful night of good food, good friends, and good drinks. Those good drinks became too many drinks for me. My old habits of drinking heavily were instilled inside of me and that night I became overly intoxicated. I was raped that night by my rapist. The next morning, I decided to confront him, and he knew he was going to get away with it. No matter what he knew, I still stood up for myself.

My career as of that day ended, and I was hidden, swept under the rug, just like every other woman who reports her rapist. I was flown off the very next day and sent to Virginia, Norfolk where I decided to retain a Jag lawyer. While I awaited trial I started drinking one gallon of cheap whisky every two days. Yes, for the next two years I drank from the moment I woke up to the moment I passed out. My career ended as quickly as it had begun. I had no friends because no one wanted to support me or no one believed that my rapist raped me. I was utterly alone and angry.

After hearing the "not guilty" verdict I was sent to San Diego, CA, with whatever dignity I had left. I continued to try and serve my country as best I could. With the new crew and new ship, I was able to complete our seven-month deployment. I knew my time in the military was over and I was ready to leave three months before my contract was up. I was honorably discharged, but released due to a psychologist deeming me as having a personality disorder.

After the military, my mental status continued to decline and I started using drugs again. My life became so bad that the last place I ever worked for was a run-down deli. My life was crashing before my eyes and I was watching it crumble. I lost my job, walked away from the homes I purchased, I gave the bank one of my cars, and lost my wife. I finally had hit rock bottom.

I admitted myself to a thirty-day inpatient recovery program and there is where my healing began. I was sober and seeing things differently. I met these two female doctors who finally diagnosed me with Post Traumatic Stress Disorder (PTSD), these women gave me the opportunity to learn new skills. These skills are called Dialectical Behavioral Therapy (DBT) – "Skills for a life worth living". This became a game changer in my life. These skills showed me how to deal with past issues, how to communicate with everyone in every situation and how to live life on life's terms. It was a long journey to recovery, but by the grace of God, my wife, our two incredible dogs and these female psychologists I was able to recover from all the pain I had endured all of my life.

I was invited to speak at a summit called The Truth and Justice Summit for women who were raped in the military. It was there I realized my true purpose in this world. I was to not only write my book, *Saint Marley and Friar Ted*, but to also be a voice for all women who have been molested, raped or sexually abused. I was to be their voice. I am supposed to help them heal and show them there is a way to heal, and live an extraordinary life. This is why I created the Never Heal Alone Foundation. It's a not-for-profit organization. Women and men from around the nation, especially veterans, will be able to come to retreats or seminars where therapists will be there to help teach them DBT and other life-changing skills to help transform their lives and become extraordinary.

One day my wife told me she wanted us to start a business. She said, "Honey, now you're ready to start a business." "Put your culinary experience and business degree to work, and let's create healthy gourmet dog treats to help dogs who have allergies and sensitive stomach issues, let's make them soft so that dogs with no teeth or who have missing teeth can eat and enjoy them too." Our motto is "Because they're worth it." We leave no dog behind. Together we went to work in our home kitchen, and used Marley and Teddy as our taste testers. Teddy was suffering severely from allergies and Marley suffers from overgrowth of his gums, he has been losing his teeth and could only eat soft cookies and food. We created a treat that was helping our dogs with their allergies and sensitive stomach issues. Together we created Marley's Gnarly Canine Cookies, a gourmet dog treat business that believes companies should only use natural superfoods along with natural preservatives. We are proud and believe in this cause. We tell people that we are paying it forward to my PTSD service dog, Mr. Marley, who helped me heal, and now it's our turn to help all dogs feel better from the current issues they are having. We get to wake up with purpose and much gratitude because we get to wake up and do something that doesn't even feel like work. Most importantly we are having so much fun!

Cracking the code to success has been a long journey, it started by being a student of life, and being open to learning, meaning to be coachable. The skills I have learned though my mentors and coaches have created an impact on my life. First and foremost, I invest in myself by way of personal development seminars, books, workshop, and events. I have a couple of mentors and I listen and take all they have given to me. I take full responsibility for my mistakes, failures and weaknesses, while telling myself: "I am doing the best I can, and I can always do better." I create, write, and read out loud my declarations of what I want out of my life and of who I am. I will give an example: "I am powerful; I am the creator of my universe." I create and speak out loud my thoughts and feelings as long as they are positive and powerful.

I create vision boards and vision notebooks of all my goals and dreams so I can hang them on my walls in my office or keep the notebook by my bedside to envision and see my future; to have the opportunity to day dream about my future life. I write checks to myself and look at them daily while praying over my checks. I write my goals down and I cross them off once accomplished, then I create new goals. My faith is to me my strong suit, I wake up every morning to meditate, pray, and give gratitude for my life and for what I want out of my life. I live a life of service; I live to serve others for the greater glory of God. I believe success comes when you take yourself out of the equation and focus on helping others. True success comes from living a life of purpose and creating a cause to solve problems in this world.

I have disciplined myself to wake up Monday through Friday at 5:00am, Saturday and Sunday at 6:00am. I wake up ready to take on my tasks and goals; this happens because the night before I write them down so that I have a plan for the next day. I use my DBT skills to communicate with others along with managing stress. I make sure I get plenty of sleep, water, exercise, and 'me' time so that I do not feel overwhelmed with my life and my goals. I remain honest and speak the truth. Lastly, I always believe in having fun and doing things I love – taking hikes with my dogs, going to the beach with my wife and have bon fires with family and friends. I love my fine dining dinners out, my date nights with my beautiful wife. I love cuddling on the couch with my wife and dogs to enjoy a fun night watching a movie and eating pizza. I go on many dates with my wife and we spend it doing anything we desire. Or, together my wife and I choose a destination and travel the world to see everything this world has to offer. I simply live life to the fullest and I live it with grace and gratitude. I take nothing for granted.

Today I have become a mentor, life coach, public speaker and author. I speak about truth, love, and compassion. I teach skills to help people better their lives. I mentor young entrepreneurs who are looking to take their lives to the next level by offering workshops on how to become successful in business and use the power of manifestation, visualization and faith. I teach leadership to managers about how to treat employees and how to be a leader and not just a manager. I speak of God's love and how God will give you anything and everything you need to live your best life possible.

I became successful because I never gave up trying to heal myself. I succeeded in getting my life back and creating it with purpose. I am successful because I observed other business owners' mistakes when it came to treating people and how they ran their business and to not make those same mistakes. I am successful because I am a humble student of life and I always say this: "I know nothing, please teach me." I am successful in business because I created a cause for dogs. We the dog owners want healthy dog treats for our furry babies!

I use DBT (Dialectical Behavioral Therapy) to live my life and fulfill my goals. Most importantly, I am a success because I have faith, patience, and love in my heart for humanity. I wake up with the most gratitude in my heart because I get to wake up and help those who need me. Today I am grateful, happy and free. I'm a woman who lived an extraordinarily hard, sad, painful life and overcame all odds. Today I live life to the fullest, with joy and peace. I have a successful marriage to my wife who never left me and I will always continue to thank her. Today I say, "I love you!" and "May God Bless you."

About Carla

Carla Butcher's career is centered on her philosophy that:

When you treat people with respect, dignity and compassion, people will naturally flock to you, especially those who need you.

Carla's career passions are to help heal as many women and men who suffer from PTSD and depression through her Never Heal Alone Foundation. These are programs for women and men to teach them DBT skills and other skills to live a worth living, along with married couples who also suffer from PTSD.

Carla's book *Saint Marley and Friar Ted* is a book about what happened to her in the military, and what happened after the military. This book takes you on a journey through a painful childhood and young adult memories along with her conversations with God that today she still continues to have.

Carla is a public speaker who speaks on behalf of sexually-traumatized female veterans and those who suffer from PTSD.

Carla will inspire, through her motivational speeches, to supercharge and remotivate current or new CEO's, managers and employees to be their best selves and shows them how to succeed in everything they do. She is available to speak at business events, conventions, retreats, seminars, churches, and workshops. She helps create leaders in this world to make our world a better place for everyone.

Carla and her wife Stephanie Butcher help their customers (dogs) by giving them the most nutrient-dense, gluten-free and grain-free soft gourmet biscuits. These biscuits are made with all human grade food and she uses the power of superfoods to help sooth some of their allergy issues along with sensitive stomach issues. Carla and Stephanie gravitated towards this type of business because of the love of their two dogs Mr. Marley and Teddy Bear. Carla and Stephanie sell their gourmet dog treats locally all over San Diego in the Farmers Markets, in holistic dog stores and online. Marley's Gnarly Canine Cookies is an e-commerce store and they ship all over the United States. You can order their treats online!

Carla is a member of the National Association of Experts, Writers and Speakers, along with being a member of Toast Masters International and a member of the National Society of Leadership and Success. Carla is also an Infinite Possibilities Certified Trainer from the teachings of Mike Dooley. She will be graduating with honors from DeVry University of San Diego, CA in 2017 with her degree in business.

You can connect with Carla to hire her for a public speaking event or find out more about her Never Heal Alone Foundation. If you are in need of healing or know someone who does, Carla's book, *Saint Marley & Friar Ted*, will be released in April, 2017.

Contact information:
- Carlabutcher777@gmail.com
- www.facebook.com/Carlabutcher777
- www.neverhealalone.org
- marleysgnarlycookies@gmail.com
- www.marleysgnarlycaninecookies.com
- www.facebook.com/marleysgnarlycaninecookies

CHAPTER 18

THE PROCESS OF A SALE
THE THREE STEPS OF EXECUTION

BY JEREMY M. STRAUB, CRPC, CFS®

To be the best, we have to give our best.

My dad, Joseph Straub, was a salesman turned entrepreneur when he began opening car dealerships. He had that "fire in his belly" for success, as he chose to start a family at the age of twenty-three. This meant that there was no time to experiment with success; he had to figure it out quickly. Not only for him—but also for those he was financially responsible for.

Like many sons, you take away life lessons from your father, and for me it was no different. I will always remember his words: "Jeremy, my competition might have more experience than me. They may be smarter than me. I'll just outwork them." I took that to heart and the spirit of entrepreneurialism began to show in me, too. It was the diversity of my business interests that really spurred me forward, forcing me to contemplate the following question:

How can I create success in multiple arenas with one proven formula?

I'll admit; I have always prided myself on being that honor roll student growing up, soaking up anything I could to learn and definitely to become better. Anything less than the best was not an option and I felt that I had to master every aspect of the businesses I worked in so I could achieve this. A daunting task for anyone! Through some wonderful mentorship and a healthy dose of life experiences, I finally saw something of value— most peoples' formulas for success are basically the same. You can dress something up any way you want to, making it your own version, but in the end, the objective is mostly the same—to experience success according to how you define it.

OUR STATE OF MIND ABOUT EXCELLENCE

We stifle ourselves when we strive to be the best at EVERYTHING in our business. Instead, we should focus on three things at a time to master that which will help us to succeed.

Human nature brings about many wonderful things, as well as some unnecessary struggles. Thinking we need to show perfection in all areas of our business at one time is a weakness. Throughout my life, I have tried two different approaches to garnering success in my career:

1. I have been a sponge for information and knowledge, feeling this compelling urge to perfect absolutely everything that I delved into. That 4.0 GPA, or being the best on the team.
2. I have focused in on three areas in which I knew I could excel at and make a difference in my outcome, accepting that it is okay to have three A+ marks and a few Bs.

Guess what I found? It was a lot easier to be #1 by getting there through executing option #2. This was such a relief, because the amount of pressure we put on ourselves to improve every aspect of our business is one of the largest hindrances we have. This crazy self-expectation can stop success dead in its tracks.

Early on in my career, I was trying to build a client relationship model and train myself on all the products I marketed in my business. I strived to learn all aspects of my career, and the results of my efforts meant I was adequate, at best. Then I changed my approach. I worked on all those things, but created a laser focus on only three things.

By focusing attention on three primary areas, I found success.
1). I was able to get myself in front of qualified potential clients more often.

2). I was prepared to have a good first meeting and presentation.

3). I brought in the right expert staff to offer the financial advice that would lend to clients' wellbeing and my success.

Once I recognized the truth in this, I was able to take what I'd learned and create the Execution Model, which has made a significant difference in my life. Since having this, I have watched my career and other diverse businesses grow and flourish, and while I admittedly work a lot of hours every week, I could not handle it all without this model in place.

THE EXECUTION MODEL: THREE STEPS TO GENERATE SUCCESS

*A consistent repeatable system is a pathway
to consistent, repeatable results.*

In order to create a model that is repeatable for any area of business or life you need to break it down as specifically as possible. It's not about viewing a collective business—although results are reflective of this—it's about how you can identify three to five specific factors that lead to ultimate success.

The earlier example applies to my choice to offer financial advisor services and relays how I had to choose to not just be effective at prospecting and gaining an audience with potential clients through seminars. However, I still had to narrow down what my laser focus was.

With all the sales forces that I work with, particularly in my business, Coastal Wealth, I cannot afford to look at the results as just a number on a spreadsheet. It's essential to break it down to the smallest factor to hone in on—the specific strategy. This has worked, as I now have a group of 175+ financial service representatives throughout the state of Florida who achieve success through their ability to help more clients achieve their financial goals.

If you envision a funnel—large at the top and then narrowing—you can envision the three elements that make up the Execution Model:

I. **Goals and Visions are at the top.** They are your motivation and metrics to determine success in a specific area.

II. In the middle lies Systems and Processes. This is your blueprint that shows the steps and path.

III. The bottom of the funnel is Accountability and Tracking. It is here where your coaching metrics and monitoring of achieving your desired metrics takes place.

Results come from using all of the elements of the Execution Model. It's not a "pick and choose buffet," because it's a complete system that leads to the goal of achieving that consistent, repeatable system that leads to continuous success, regardless of what business arena you may be in.

I. Goals and Visions

Goals and visions are not the same thing, but they do fuel each other.

By definition, if you have a vision of something that you want it doesn't just go away once you earn or achieve it. You continue to want it be a part of your life or business. If you end up building a referral-based business, you don't want to just stop taking referrals because you've achieved success. But with goals, once we achieve a goal, it is time to move on and build up on that goal. It's a baby step that leads to the fruition of your visions and your accomplishment of bigger objectives.

For example, with referrals, if you end up reaching the goal for the number of referrals you want, it is time to hone in on that goal a bit further. Perhaps you may want to focus on better quality referrals, or even more referrals through different channels.

II. Systems and Processes

We've got to break it down in order to build it up, including down to the most minute of details.

Oftentimes with building a process, we've got to break it down in order to build it up and include the most minute of details. A good friend of mine, Jaime Frisone, told me that when building a process, you should spend the time and touch it only once so you don't have to touch it again. I've always kept that in mind as I built the Execution Model. Everything that should be focused on for success is, and with great care.

IDEAS X EXECUTION = RESULTS

If we were to rate an idea on a scale of 1 to 10 and it comes in at a 10, it will remain a worthless idea without proper execution. You cannot change this. Or on the flip side, you can have a really good idea (maybe an 8) and execute it flawlessly and achieve excellent results.

In the seminars that I've used for acquiring clients, the execution was always precise, using a methodical, well-rehearsed, and proven science.

- I knew when to send the invite out.
- Confirmation calls were scripted exactly in regards to what I would say.
- The experience that potential clients had was determined from the minute they walked through the door of the seminar.
- My presentation started at a precise time—always.
- I knew what to say in small talk with the attendees.
- The way that unwanted questions were dealt with was known and practiced.
- If there were people talking when I was speaking, I knew how to deal with that succinctly and effectively.
- My follow-up was precise and scripted.

Every little detail was planned and managed, as I knew that I had a specific vision and goal to achieve. The vision was to acquire clients that I enjoyed working with and make a meaningful difference in their lives. The goal was to acquire 40 business owners and their employees as clients. I understood the correlation between the execution of my efforts and the results that would drive.

The importance of little decisions...

When I was twenty-four, I was a First Line Manager in a sales organization. We used to run cold call sessions with the team on Saturday mornings. On one morning, I came into work, admittedly a bit tired because I'd been out late that Friday night—only getting about three hours of sleep. There I was kicking off the phone warm-up, an event where we do practice calls. It so happened that my boss's boss showed up— a legend in our industry. Eager to impress, I kept going about my process, feeling that I was doing a pretty good job. Then...he stops me in the middle of my presentation.

"Everyone, take out a piece of paper and write down what time you think Jeremy went to bed last night," Larry said. Not the most tactful approach...but this interaction was a turning point in my career.

People were kind, going for the 10:00 PM to midnight time, not the more realistic 3:00 AM time. But what Larry said next was the message I needed to hear:

> Larry went on to share that if we screw up one time it really isn't a big deal. But if we continue to screw up over time and add all the pieces together, we will definitely find that we haven't given our best efforts and it would be unrealistic to expect that we would achieve our goals and expectations, whatever they may be.

That day I was not on my "A-game". It showed more than I ever would have thought and I knew it deep inside. We all make a thousand decisions a day, some of these decisions will be the right ones and others will be the wrong ones. In those moments of choice, we decide how we will work our system and process to find our success. It's through adding up all these little decisions that we make that we will achieve our goals. After that, I grew quickly to being a consistently top-ranked person in my career.

III.   Accountability and Tracking

*You must determine what the most important gauges are in your
Execution Model so you can evaluate your success.*

By knowing key metrics, we know what to use as a measure to determine if we are tracking to achieve success, or are lagging behind. And why! Let's continue the analogy with referrals. I had an advisor who tracked not only the success of the referrals but where they came from, whether they were asked for or just given by the client. Surprisingly, what he found was that when he asked to be referred, those clients generated double the revenue for him versus the unsolicited referrals. Although this seems counterintuitive, the information is essential to know, as it helps give guidance on how to execute at an optimal level.

In regards to accountability, I learned it best from one of my mentors. We call it the "long-slow-takedown." What he would do is walk through your metrics and help you self-diagnose through a long painful questioning to determine where all the bottle necks were, and why you weren't achieving your goal. After that, he'd go into how to fix it. The process of having someone helping you be accountable to the Execution Model you put in place and taking the time to walk through the entire process is essential. This process offers an intricate look at all aspects and nuances of your Execution Model and why you might not be achieving your results, which is critical to guaranteeing your success.

PICK THREE CHALLENGE

Success is an action word, meant for the present, so delaying your thoughts about an Execution Model that can take you there is nothing more than idle wishing. You have to act!

Thinking about what your three most critical business opportunities or initiatives are may feel paralyzing, but it shouldn't be. You want to determine which three will have the biggest impact. If you struggle with that, pick the first three that come to your mind and begin by putting specific goals to them.

Next, sit down for at least an hour for each one to determine which systems and processes will help you get there, incorporating helpful and necessary steps from you really taking the time to look at your process. Determine which systems and processes should work, incorporating help when necessary and really taking a hard look at your own accountability in the process.

Then put some thought into how you can measure if you're effective in your steps and commitment. Plan on 90 days to work your plan and don't settle for less than that. You will have to make adjustments, which is why you track—so you can adjust your systems. You will succeed when you are giving your focused best efforts. Remember, success leaves clues, and the clue I am leaving you is that consistent repeatable systems will lead to consistent repeatable results.

About Jeremy

As a committed and successful Founder and CEO of Coastal Wealth, Jeremy M. Straub has shown what a commitment to the art of excellence can mean for the outcomes of any effort he's involved in. As an entrepreneur who has vast interests, he brings about a unique perspective on how one can achieve success in their professional lives, and is grateful to experience firsthand how this can carry over into one's personal life, as well. Past work experience for Jeremy includes time as a wealth manager and an executive at Ameriprise Financial. He is also a serial entrepreneur, owning businesses in multiple industries.

Jeremy says, "The way we structure our day and take accountability for our actions has a direct impact on our success." Through his work of training individuals in different businesses, he has come up with the Execution Model, a three-part formula that is geared on individual skills and efforts, guiding them to the real answers and metrics that they need in order to achieve success that is sustainable and can be repeated.

With a diverse wealth of knowledge, Jeremy has always been an advocate of learning. He has earned his BA in Business Management from Moravian College; he earned designations as both a Chartered Retirement Planning Counselor (CRPC) and Certified Funds Specialist®, and is licensed in Life, Accident, and Health insurances. He is certified in the FINRA Series 7, 9, 10, 24, 51, and 66. Awards and accolades from Ameriprise Financial include: Outstanding Leader Award in 2014, 2011, and 2009; Presidential Recognition Award for Financial Advice from 2001 through 2005, and he became a Diamond Ring Recipient in July 2014. Jeremy is also a co-author with renowned best-selling author and sales expert Brian Tracy, in the book, *Cracking the Code to Success.*

Making his home in Fort Lauderdale, Florida, Jeremy is originally from Bethlehem, Pennsylvania, and has lived on the west coast, as well. He acknowledges how fortunate he is to have his wife Maureen, who he admits, "has to put up with a lot with his crazy work schedule and lack of vacations." But when they do get to have fun, they know how to go all out, enjoying the oceans they live near via their hobbies of scuba diving, paddle-boarding, boating, and snorkeling. Jeremy also enjoys a great workout of Krav Maga, an Israeli martial art that offers an intense and vigorous experience that is wonderful for staying fit and managing stress. The causes that the Straub family is most passionate about are those involving helping underprivileged children and families.

CHAPTER 19

LESSONS FOR BETTER BUSINESS
WHAT WOMEN CAN LEARN IN BUSINESS FROM "A MAN'S WORLD"

BY CLAUDIA ZANES

Success involves maximizing relationships and alliances to form mutually-beneficial relationships.

When you evaluate the deals men put together with a neutral eye, you'll usually notice that their partnerships consist of a split of some sort. It's usually equal and very seldom is it a split that's hung up on money. They don't worry about fair, they were worry about results, knowing that the rest will play itself out in time. These men are more eager to work together with less criteria and stipulations than what women will generally have. It's more like, "You give me this and I'll give you that." They don't feel they need to be strong at everything. They believe that their collaborative efforts can eradicate the areas they are less strong in, and vice versa.

Women tend to handle it differently. We're often in protection mode, which seldom serves our purposes well. Then we get closed out of good opportunities, and wonder why. We do have something big to offer and it's of value in the business world. Women excel at doing many important things at one time—multi-tasking gurus—and it's one of the most fantastic things about us, actually. Doing many things at one time often goes hand-in-hand with holding on to too many things at one time. This is where the problem comes in, as it creates distractions that stop us from achieving the levels of success we are quite capable of reaching. Plus, it strains our happiness outside of work, because when we physically leave work, we don't mentally leave it.

I've been there, living in an emotionally-consumed state of mind. Then I'd look over at my husband and see him simply conducting business and creating partnerships—without the emotional attachment. I was curious, and I wanted to learn from it. I didn't love emotional complications, but I had definitely been existing with them. And—yes—that was very hard to admit. It's not easy to have a "coming to reality moment", but I did and learned four wonderful lessons that women can benefit from. It's not about becoming a man, it's about becoming the most amazing business woman you can be for your own sanity and prosperity.

Lesson #1: Don't Take Things Personal

Men don't take anything personal, and what a
wonderful gift that is to their wellbeing.

It's true, and enviable, that men don't take things personal. Someone can call them some colorful name or expletive and it bounces right off them. For us? We are offended or immediately retaliate. It becomes personal, instead of just blowing it off and moving on. It impacts the way a woman does business.

Men look at business as a transaction only; you move money from one place to another with no emotional attachment.

Not every business deal works out, for whatever reason. Business can fall apart despite our best efforts and intelligence. What do you do when the deal goes down the drain? That's the big question. Mostly, men will shrug it off and move on. What's done is done. Women, on the other hand, begin a brutal analysis. What went wrong? What could have been done differently? They feel personally and professionally slighted. Then they find their take-away from it, which usually involves never touching that fire again. The problem is that so much time was wasted evaluating what went wrong that you miss out on the next chance to "seal the deal."

Women get attached to business and those emotions have a price, and it's usually a loss of opportunity.

Some years back I was pursuing the purchase of a small family-owned business—thirty-six years strong. The owners wanted to retire, which meant they had to sell. The mother was very emotionally attached to the business, as it had been a huge part of her life. I was compassionate but her attachment stopped the negotiation dead in its tracks. She couldn't let go and the deal fell through. A year later I was approached to see if I was still interested. The price had been significantly reduced because they hadn't sold it. I thought, these people could have been enjoying a year of retirement already, what a wasted gift.

The moral of the story: *Missed opportunities are often the result of making business personal.*

We can have different outcomes, as demonstrated by Toni Ko, founder of NYX Cosmetics. Her mindset about business allowed her to grow a company from the ground up into an impressive $120MM in a single year. The opportunity to sell to L'Oreal surfaced and they offered her a $500MM deal for the business—a tremendous opportunity! Did she love her business and have a lot vested in it? Of course. The difference was she was able to detach her personal emotions from her business savvy, and it certainly paid off. She decided not to stay on after the sale, stating some impressive words of truth and wisdom: "I didn't know a single entrepreneur who stayed on and was happy. I got paid and said farewell to my baby."

Lesson #2: Lock-in and Stay Persistent

Men have an incredible ability to "lock-in" and go for the kill, once they've spotted what they want.

When your sights are set on something, the determination to succeed sets in. It's an incredible trait to have. Being able to fearlessly pursue something without over-evaluation is a time saver that allows you to begin the race before many others are even out of the gate. As much as there is talk about and focus on "following your intuition," women tend to shy away from this magnificent gift. They over-evaluate and express self-doubt, resisting taking immediate action. All for what? Just to see if it is indeed a good opportunity? Just to "see" if you want to proceed? By the time a decision is made, the opportunity is often gone.

I conducted an amateur survey of different couples I knew. I wondered who pursued who. In every case, the man pursued the woman. Never the other way around.

What does this tell us? It's simple, yet poignant—men see what they want and go for it. Women tend to weigh it out too much or just wait for it to come to them. They want it, but they wait…and wait. Thankfully, it's a life cycle and mindset that can be shifted.

Just like in life, business also goes through life cycles. In its infancy, a business needs every minute of your time. This is where the attachment often starts for women. Men work hard and give their best efforts, but again, it's "just business," not their "identity." Then the business becomes a toddler, if all goes well. It's up and running, able to do some things on its own, but still requires your constant attention and time—you are quite literally together 24/7, either physically or mentally. But finally, you are able to see how all of your work has paid off. Your business is now a young adult and it's wise and smart, making you so proud. It turns into a machine that has programming and systems in place that allows it to thrive without your constant attention. But you are hesitant to let go… just in case.

When businesses mature, what do men do? They high-five each other and are thankful that it worked out and then they move on. How about women? Due to that compassion and care we devoted, we suddenly experience "empty nest syndrome" and we cling to what we feel is missing, instead of looking forward for what comes next. We want to feel needed, because it is such a part of who we are.

Looking back, I can remember every single stage of life in the law practice. More often than not, I went to bed exhausted and frustrated about one thing or another. Then I'd wake up in the middle of the night with a thought, which would snowball into me getting up and starting to research. I do admit, however, I found some of our best solutions that way. By the time the sun came up, I already had a few hours of work done and was living in anticipation of the responses to those emails and middle-of-the-night requests. The problem, everyone else was just getting started. I drove myself crazy. But not as crazy I was driven by my husband getting up and just going to do what he did best—practice law. The moral in the lesson: persistence and locking-in on what you want does not mean that you have to make yourself so personally attached to it.

When we know what we want and what we stand for and expect, we've succeeded. Solved obstacles and won victories help women grow more attached to the business that they give their all to, while men really "expect" that it will work out if they do the right thing. A great example of this comes from the story of Jin Sook, founder of the huge teen fashion store Forever 21. Today, her and her husband are worth $1.9 billion. That is a lot of clothes! One thing about this story of success that really stands out to me and drives this point home is something I learned in *Forbes Magazine*, which states: "The fashion clothing chain has been sued more than 50 times for copyright infringement, has $4.4 billion in sales, flat from a year ago. It has closed some stores and was late to pay some vendors. But the company denies any financial difficulties, saying its business is solid and noting the planned opening of 67 more stores this year." They move forward and don't stifle themselves with "what-ifs".

Lesson #3: Be Flexible and Adaptable

Planning is smart, but don't get too attached to your plan.

A well thought out plan is a thing of beauty. It shows that you put thoughtful analysis, detail, and commitment into creating what you believe is a successful plan. The risk to the perfect plan is growing so attached to it that you either force things to fit into it or reject other ideas that would be beneficial. You have to have flexibility or you are going to run into problems that can cripple your hopes and expectations.

The amount of decisions that occur on a daily basis when you are building a multi-million dollar business is astonishing.

Planning helps business owners make decisions more quickly; however, you cannot be exceptional without considering exceptions to the plan. It just won't happen.

The moral in the lesson: when we embrace flexibility and adaptability, we keep the blinders off that lead to us losing out on opportunities that come our way—often unexpectedly.

Do you have what it takes to be flexible? About five years into the law practice, I began shifting from the do-it-all-myself mentality, and began using an advertising agency for our marketing. We had been, and still do, run television commercials to gain new clients. Producing these commercials involved travel to other states, creating scripts, production costs, etc. It is a big time and money investment. Just as we were preparing for our yearly production, an opportunity fell into our laps to buy a vanity telephone number in our market. The now famous 777-7777 number was available for purchase—for thousands of dollars! I thought, a phone number. Are you kidding me? We had a free number from the telephone company! Some time ago, someone had purchased that number much the way people purchase a .com today to resell it to the highest bidder. After the shock of it, I began to process and better understand the value of having something unique to brand. We postponed the commercials and purchased the number. Today, we are known as the "777 law firm" in our market. Even if someone has never needed our services, they know of the firm. Without being flexible, this opportunity would have passed us by and we wouldn't have that "edge" today.

Lesson #4: Be Confident

We gain a lot from becoming more confident and having the courage to say what needs to be said, make decisions that need to be made, and putting ourselves out there to be seen.

Confidence brings out a unique energy that you can sense from a great distance away. Really, you cannot help but be drawn to it. Women sometimes spend too much time worrying about the consequences of putting ourselves out there, choosing to play it safe instead. Fewer risks often do mean less reward. Men are more fearless this way, which shows in the number of men who are mega-successful in business compared to women.

Back in 2010, I committed to taking my husband's law firm to a higher level. It was going to require me being bold and putting myself out there, as I was going to focus all my time on growing the business, not working in the business. I would take on the CEO role, leaving my husband, the owner and main attorney, to be responsible for working closely on case resolutions, guiding the junior attorneys, and handling clients. We eagerly made the announcement and even sent out a press release about it. The intentions were good; the response was shocking and controversial, and definitely harsh.

The judgment and ridicule I received was hurtful, more than I could have ever imagined. Others words were tough to take, but no one was tougher on me than myself. I had to get over it and gain confidence quickly—there was no turning back!

I joined a CEO peer group, which happened to be all males, and found coaches to help me in my new position. I gained more confidence in my actions and removed personal offense from my equation.

During this time, my greatest lessons were mistakes and the more I learned from them, the more confident I became. The results proved to be worth the experience, as I began to win many business awards. But more importantly, I was able to create a thriving, profitable law practice, which allowed for the opportunity to give back to my community. To this day, we provide school supplies for 450 teachers every year, as well as support many community programs.

The moral of this lesson: through confidence all things become possible.

PARTNERSHIPS AND ALLIANCES CREATE OPPORTUNITIES

Look for qualities that help you do better business, not qualities that you refuse to do business with. Perspective is everything.

We live in exciting times. Women are more business savvy than ever. We're able to use our best qualities to create success—qualities that men don't encompass. Likewise, we are able to learn many things from men that allow us to conduct business better and remain alert to the opportunities that create successful business partners and alliances.

The time has come for you to look around. See the inspiration. Be liberal in your extractions from that "man's world of business" and make your mark!

About Claudia

Claudia Zanes is a lifelong serial entrepreneur who passionately champions for others in business, in her community and in her life. She was the Chief Executive Officer and business strategist behind one of Arizona's largest and fastest-growing personal injury law firms: Zanes Law based in the greater Phoenix and Tucson areas.

This Latina non-attorney is known for her business know-how, a laser focus on marketing, finance strategy and execution, and a deep love for community outreach. When going into a business, her motto as the Fixer is: "Be prepared to feed the baby, and by that I mean your business. When things are going wrong and the pocketbook is empty, it's your passion for what you're building that will motivate you to keep going."

Known internationally, her story of success has been published in *Cosmopolitan Latina* and *El Imparcial*, the newspaper in Sonora, Mexico. She has also spoken at Harvard University on the topic, "How to Build a Brand That is Not Only Recognized, But Loved." She has received many awards for her business and personal service to community. Some of these include 2014 RADICAL Entrepreneur, Doreen Rainey; 2014 Hispanic Business Woman of the Year, Tucson Hispanic Chamber of Commerce; 2013 Woman of Influence, Inside Tucson Business.

Claudia has set her sights on helping other entrepreneurs worldwide achieve massive success financially and culturally in their businesses including turnarounds, while still advising the law firm. Her time at the law firm allowed the opportunity to execute on many of the business strategies she learned over time from some of the best business people in the world – like Tony Robbins, Keith J. Cunningham and Jay Abraham. She focuses on bringing the most current marketing and financial strategies to companies so they reduce mistakes and increase success for themselves and their employees.

Regardless of industry, it's about applying the right techniques and getting the desired results. This means understanding the skeleton that 'fits all' when it comes to marketing and economic growth. It's to change the mindset of the business owner and help formulate the most effective strategy to move forward.

I am passionate about helping you do what I have done for my family business and my clients. I am doing what I was born to do!

You can connect with Claudia Zanes at:
- www.ClaudiaZanes.com
- Claudia@claudiazanes.com

- www.facebook.com/claudiazanes
- Twitter: @CzanesZanes
- www.linkedin.com/claudiazanes

CHAPTER 20

HOW THE GREATS CRACKED THE SUCCESS CODE
THE BIRTH OF THE MEDIAMASTER

BY JW DICKS & NICK NANTON

A thought leader is someone who creates something
before people realize that they need it.
~ Guy Kawasaki

❖ *Think and Grow Rich*
❖ *How to Win Friends and Influence People*
❖ *Awaken the Giant Within*

These book titles, which are no doubt familiar to many of you, helped create the careers of their legendary authors – Napoleon Hill, Dale Carnegie and Tony Robbins. Even though these three gentlemen were virtually unknown at the time, these books still made a massive impact.

Why?

Well, take a second look at these titles. What do they have in common?

The answer is pretty simple. They're all calls to action to improve your life in a significant way. To increase your prosperity. Raise your personal profile. Become a more powerful person. At their root, these are basic, almost primal, urges that most of us carry around with us on a daily basis.

And that is why those titles resonate with us.

It's not a stretch to say we're all trying to gain an edge in both our personal and professional lives, to become more than we are, to become richer than we are, to gain a higher measure of respect, recognition and, yes, admiration in our circles. It's just human nature. Which is why works like these exert such a pull on our population.

And yet, until the last fifty years or so, this kind of – yes, we'll say it – self-help content was routinely rejected by the powers-that-be.

The first book in this genre, actually named *Self-Help*, was initially turned down by most publishers in England when author Samuel Smiles submitted his manuscript. When he finally resorted to self-publishing the book in 1859, it was an instant bestseller and turned Smiles into an instant celebrity and sought-out guru. And he got his revenge when, about twenty years later, he was seated next to one of the publishers who had turned him down. The publisher asked, "And when, Dr. Smiles, are we to have the honour of publishing one of your books?" Smiles told him he already had the honor of rejecting *Self-Help*.

Napoleon Hill's struggles in getting his landmark book, *Think and Grow Rich*, into print have also been well-documented; at one point his publisher demanded he change its title to *Use Your Noodle to Win More Boodle*. But once again, when the book finally was released, it was a sensation – as of 2011, the last accurate count we could find, 70 million copies had been sold. And once again, its author became a huge celebrity – and, in our estimation, the first real MediaMaster.

A MediaMaster is a term we use to describe someone who has not only expertly packaged themselves to gain the biggest following, but also knows how best to juggle today's multiple media channels to their advantage. Hill was the first of these in our estimation, because he didn't stop at writing books; he also started successful magazines, taught at schools, did national lecture tours, and produced a host of other books, courses, and radio and television programs – all based on his theories of prosperity.

THE MAKING OF THREE MEDIAMASTERS

So far, we've mentioned three people who we consider to be true MediaMasters – Napoleon Hill, Dale Carnegie and Tony Robbins. As a matter of fact, we consider them to be the 20th Century's primary exemplars of MediaMastery because they maximized the use of the media they had at the time to generate maximum success for their business. (Who's our 21st Century contender? You'll find out shortly.) Each of them in their own way were pioneers in this field and ended up defining the concept in their own individual ways, with Hill leading the way at the turn of the century and Robbins adapting it to a new and much more sophisticated era late in the late 1900s (and well into the 2000s, as he is perhaps more successful today than ever).

So how did these three men, men who came out of virtually nowhere, with little education and no credentials, make their impacts? How did they come to occupy such influential positions?

We've researched their individual stories and were struck by the huge similarities they shared in their narratives, similarities we believe created the perfect foundation for their ongoing impact. Here are the most important of them, most of which still apply to today's MediaMasters.

1) They understood their audiences.
Napoleon Hill was raised in a two-room log cabin. Dale Carnegie was the son of a struggling farming family. Even Tony Robbins grew up in a turbulent and impoverished household, abandoned by his ne'er-do-well father, leaving him and his siblings at the mercy of their non-functioning alcoholic mother. Robbins, being the oldest, was forced to serve as the primary caregiver to his siblings.

These difficult childhoods not only motivated these early MediaMasters to achieve at an early age, but it also gave them an innate understanding of others who also struggled and had ambitions to make more of themselves. This enabled them, on an unconscious level, to appeal to their audiences' similar psychologies; they knew instinctively how to speak their audiences' language and tap into their deepest desires, creating a powerful and lasting bond.

2) They learned how to sell at an early age.

Tony Robbins began his career promoting the seminars of Jim Rohn, another MediaMaster of the time, who relied on his rags-to-riches story to connect to his audience. Napoleon Hill taught a correspondence course on salesmanship and worked in advertising (even though he saw himself primarily as a writer). Dale Carnegie sold bacon, soap and lard for Armour & Company, and he was so good at it, his sales territory ended up being the firm's most lucrative in the nation.

3) They were incredibly driven to share their message, not just to keep the secrets they had learned to themselves.

Carnegie left a very successful sales career to pursue a career in public speaking, offering to speak at the neighborhood YMCA for no fee and a cut of the gate. His interactions with audiences led him to discover that the average American wanted more than anything else to develop self-confidence. From there, he developed the Dale Carnegie Course to address that issue and stuck to it for his entire life.

Hill, despite many business reversals, always picked himself up, dusted himself off and returned to his theme of how everyday people could attract wealth into their lives. He never really strayed from that theme and continued to lecture and write about success principles until the end of his life, always leveraging the knowledge into a platform for sharing what he knew.

As for Robbins, he emerged from his training with Jim Rohn hungry to learn every aspect of self-improvement – and then he took the field to a very new level of mainstream distribution. This culminated in the physical demonstrations that really made an impact, as he used board-breaking, skydiving, and fire-walking to help his students learn to push through their fears. As he knew it would, this approach gave him incredibly compelling visual demonstrations to put into his marketing to give him the biggest platform possible at the time—TV infomercials.

4) They associated themselves with people of influence.

Hill, of course, is famous for accepting the offer of American steel magnate and philanthropist Andrew Carnegie to study the habits and backgrounds of Carnegie's rich and powerful friends, in order to discover common principles of success everyone could profit from. This, in turn, gave him incredible credibility with his work and made *Think and Grow Rich* the huge perennial bestseller it came to be.

Interestingly enough, Andrew Carnegie, in a way, plays an important part in Dale Carnegie's career as well. Even though the two weren't related in any way, Dale was anxious to give the impression they were – so he changed the spelling of his last name from "Carnagey" to "Carnegie" to make it appear he had some relation to the internationally-known industrialist. It was enough to raise his profile until his massive success brought him into contact with more well-known circles.

As for Robbins, in addition to being mentored by a MediaMaster (Rohn), he was savvy enough to draw attention by producing infomercials that utilized such public personalities as NFL Hall of Famer Fran Tarkenton and actor Martin Sheen, something that hadn't been done previously at this level. These commercials ended up being seen by an estimated 100 million people.

5) They specifically addressed Pain Points.

A Pain Point, is, of course, a problem, either physical or emotional, that nags at a group of people. What Hill, Carnegie and Robbins all did was sharpen their message to directly address a Pain Point shared by a substantial portion of the marketplace – and present compelling solutions.

Carnegie stumbled on the Pain Point that would become his focus one day during one of his early lectures. He had run out of material and decided to fill the time by asking the audience what they were angry about. Through that process, he discovered that most people really wanted more self-confidence, so he put together a series of techniques that would help them feel more comfortable dealing with other people. This led to his blockbuster book, *How to Win Friends and Influence People.*

Hill's focus, as we've already indicated, was all about building wealth. As lack of money is always a Pain Point with most, he was bound to attract followers with this approach, especially since Andrew Carnegie's circle of very rich acquaintances (one of the first official Mastermind groups) gave him insights not available to the average person anywhere else.

Robbins put his emphasis on increasing one's personal power. In his words, "How many of you have ever seen someone who seemed to be less talented than you but seemed to be more successful in business, in relationships or even in growing up? And you thought to yourself, 'How come they're so successful, and I'm not?' Well, you might want to remember this: Intelligence is nothing. Action is everything." In other words, when it came to success, it didn't matter how smart you were, it mattered what you did – a message that could resonate with millions (and still does today).

6) **They authored books that provided actionable advice.**
Finally, what cemented these men's reputations with their audiences were the books they authored that gave their readers concrete ways to get what they want out of life. In short, they offered easy-to-understand solutions, solutions that any person could carry out, that could generate positive transformation in people's lives. It's no coincidence that all those books became huge sensations that sold millions of copies over years and years – and continue to be read even now.

TODAY'S MEDIAMASTERS

All of the common characteristics of the early MediaMasters that we just listed contributed mightily to their success – and they still are important to the success of the MediaMasters of today. So, if yesterday's and today's MediaMasters have so much in common, what sets them apart? In other words, what's different about the MediaMasters of the 21st Century?

Short answer? There's so many of them!

In the last few decades, there's been a huge explosion of coaches and gurus of all sorts, hundreds of thousands of fledgling MediaMasters anxious to catch the public's eye and become the leading authorities for fixing whatever life or career problems they've decided to specialize in. And this huge explosion in self-help personalities is actually the result of an equally huge explosion in media.

While many of you reading this grew up with only a few radio stations and TV channels to choose from, today there are literally millions of media outlets out there, if you factor in all the online venues available to people on a daily basis. Most of the large expenses involved in publishing have also disappeared, thanks to online tools and social media outlets such as those offered by Twitter, YouTube, Google, Amazon, WordPress and many others.

In short, it's never been easier in the history of humanity to make your message available for the whole world to see – and to make your impact on your audience.

The vast number of media options made available by today's technology means you can achieve a similar scale of economic success as some of our media superstars, but be known by fewer people. For example, there are millions of dollars being made by YouTube superstars in their twenties (and even their teens!) who most of us would be hard-pressed to recognize them if we passed them on the street. And yet, they're making more per year than most TV series regulars!

But if you really want to identify the biggest MediaMaster success of the 21st Century (told you we'd get there), there's only one name to consider: Trump.

Trump began his march to political success the same way as Hill, Carnegie and Robbins did -- with a bestseller. In 1987, Trump released his first and biggest book, *The Art of the Deal*. It established him as a national figure and business expert, and his brash way of presenting himself on camera when promoting it showed him to be a personality to be reckoned with. He demonstrated he had the stuff to become a MediaMaster, even though there were undoubtedly plenty of other New York City real estate developers who had the same skillset. What they didn't have was the drive to make a public impact.

Trump did.

Over the years, he wrote 17 more books (including one on golf!) and, of course, was the star of the hit reality show, *The Apprentice*, for 14 seasons. He has done cameos in many other movies and TV shows and has found countless other ways to garner press attention over the years. Very few people have utilized media more powerfully than Donald Trump.

Again, as we've noted, Trump is in many ways no different than others of his ilk. There are a lot of businesspeople out there who are just as successful and just as skilled at deal-making. But what separates him from the pack is that he focused on presenting a compelling image and using memorable messaging to make himself a "yyyyuge" public figure. Just how yyyyuge? Well, in 2016, of course, he became the Republican nominee for President of the United States, one of the primary contenders for the highest office in the land, if not the world – without ever holding any other elected position in his life!

And he did it all by being a MediaMaster.

While competing candidates were blowing through millions of dollars in buying expensive TV ad campaigns, Trump managed to get over two billion dollars in free air time on all the major networks and cable channels by constantly appearing on all their news shows. And not even in person. Many of these shows would allow him to simply call in, so he could hit several morning shows in a single hour. Other candidates weren't allowed to do that on a regular basis. Plus, because he made a point of being so controversial, news networks also began covering all his speeches and campaign events in their entirety – simply to make sure they caught it if he said something particularly outrageous.

Like a true MediaMaster, Trump didn't use traditional media in a traditional way. Instead, he continually uncovered media opportunities that would cost anyone else a fortune – without paying a dime for them. And he crossed media channels relentlessly – focusing, for example, on Twitter as his main social media vehicle for issuing campaign updates, savage attacks on opponents, and attention-getting policy statements.

In the end, his MediaMaster tactics enabled him to make history. He upended one of America's two major political parties, despite the leadership's repeated efforts to stop his candidacy. But, as we've noted, that kind of entrenched opposition doesn't really matter to true MediaMasters; the people propel them to their positions of power in spite of establishment rejection. As a matter of fact, that rejection makes MediaMasters more appealing to their followers – just as it did for Trump.

Trump's impact proves beyond a shadow of a doubt that the traditional MediaMaster template works better than ever in today's multimedia climate. In our forthcoming book, *Impact!*, we'll explain more fully how to take advantage of that climate for anyone who's ready to grab all the available opportunities.

For now, we'll leave you with this anecdote. In 2015, ABC News asked Tony Robbins what his biggest fear had been when he first started out in 1986. His answer came quickly: "Not having the level of impact that I wanted to have." He knew that it didn't matter how good he was at what he did if he couldn't reach his audience in an effective and powerful way. He knew it was all about impact.

And so does every other successful MediaMaster.

About JW

JW Dicks, Esq., is a Wall Street Journal Best-Selling Author®, Emmy Award-Winning Producer, publisher, board member, and co-founder to organizations such as The National Academy of Best-Selling Authors®, and The National Association of Experts, Writers and Speakers®.

JW is the CEO of DNAgency and is a strategic business development consultant to both domestic and international clients. He has been quoted on business and financial topics in national media such as *USA Today*, *The Wall Street Journal*, *Newsweek*, *Forbes*, CNBC.com, and *Fortune Magazine Small Business*.

Considered a thought leader and curator of information, JW has more than forty-three published business and legal books to his credit and has co-authored with legends like Brian Tracy, Jack Canfield, Tom Hopkins, Dr. Nido Qubein, Dr. Ivan Misner, Dan Kennedy, and Mari Smith. He is the Editor and Publisher of *ThoughtLeader® Magazine*.

JW is called the "Expert to the Experts" and has appeared on business television shows airing on ABC, NBC, CBS, and FOX affiliates around the country and co-produces and syndicates a line of franchised business television show such as, *Success Today*, *Wall Street Today*, *Hollywood Live*, and *Profiles of Success*. He has received an Emmy® Award as Executive Producer of the film, *Mi Casa Hogar.*

JW and his wife of forty-three years, Linda, have two daughters, three granddaughters, and two Yorkies. He is a sixth-generation Floridian and splits his time between his home in Orlando and his beach house on Florida's west coast.

About Nick

An Emmy Award-Winning Director and Producer, Nick Nanton, Esq., produces media and branded content for top thought leaders and media personalities around the world. Recognized as a leading expert on branding and storytelling, Nick has authored more than two dozen Best-Selling books (including the Wall Street Journal Best-Seller *StorySelling*™) and produced and directed more than 40 documentaries, earning 5 Emmy Awards and 14 nominations. Nick speaks to audiences internationally on the topics of branding, entertainment, media, business and storytelling at major universities and events.

As the CEO of DNA Media, Nick oversees a portfolio of companies including: The Dicks + Nanton Agency (an international agency with more than 3000 clients in 36 countries), Dicks + Nanton Productions, Ambitious.com, CelebrityPress, DNA Films®, DNA Pulse, and DNA Capital Ventures. Nick is an award-winning director, producer and songwriter who has worked on everything from large scale events to television shows with the likes of Steve Forbes, Ivanka Trump, Sir Richard Branson, Rudy Ruettiger (inspiration for the Hollywood blockbuster "Rudy"), Brian Tracy, Jack Canfield (*The Secret*, creator of the *Chicken Soup for the Soul* Series), Michael E. Gerber, Tom Hopkins, Dan Kennedy and many more.

Nick has been seen in *USA Today, The Wall Street Journal, Newsweek, BusinessWeek, Inc. Magazine, The New York Times, Entrepreneur® Magazine, Forbes,* and *FastCompany.* He has appeared on ABC, NBC, CBS, and FOX television affiliates across the country as well as on CNN, FOX News, CNBC, and MSNBC from coast to coast.

Nick is a member of the Florida Bar, a voting member of The National Academy of Recording Arts & Sciences (Home to The GRAMMYs), a member of The National Academy of Television Arts & Sciences (Home to the EMMYs), Co-founder of The National Academy of Best-Selling Authors®, and serves on the Innovation Board of the XPRIZE Foundation, a non-profit organization dedicated to bringing about "radical breakthroughs for the benefit of humanity" through incentivized competition – best known for it's Ansari XPRIZE which incentivized the first private space flight and was the catalyst for Richard Branson's Virgin Galactic.

Nick also enjoys serving as an Elder at Orangewood Church, working with Young Life, Downtown Credo Orlando, Entrepreneurs International and rooting for the Florida Gators with his wife Kristina and their three children, Brock, Bowen and Addison.

Learn more at:
- www.NickNanton.com
- www.CelebrityBrandingAgency.com

CHAPTER 21

THIS ISN'T YOUR PARENTS RETIREMENT
PLANNING IS ESSENTIAL

BY JAMES HAMILTON, CEO
- Forecast Financial Group

A nice pension and Social Security are no longer enough to make sure your retirement years are wonderful years.

Serving in military combat and peacekeeping zones heightens your awareness of details and appreciation for strategic planning. Although I was unaware of it at the time, gaining those experiences was a catalyst for my journey into the financial services industry. There are few areas, outside of retirement, where lack of planning can be as devastating. The concept of working hard, saving, and investing wisely so you can relax and enjoy retirement is more complex than it was when most of our parents were in their pre-retirement years.

The Gulf War and Operation Desert Storm were set into motion around the time of my basic training, quickly altering the landscape of my military career. Enlisting as a way to escape the ghetto was quickly replaced with the goal of staying alive—every day. Through the intensity of our missions, the skills to plan and implement strategies for specific outcomes were essential.

After eight years of service, it was time for me to leave the military. I didn't know every detail of what my return to civilian life would include, but I did know that whatever career I chose would include providing a service that really made a difference for people. The most direct and rewarding path would be an entrepreneurial route. Just like I had a concept for success in my military career, I also had one for success in business. Through observing other entrepreneurs, it appeared to be a simple, three part plan:

1. You have an idea and start a business.
2. You work hard, take appropriate risks, and grow that business.
3. You sell the business so you can retire and live out your years comfortably.

I had no reason to anticipate anything other than success. I didn't shy away from the hard work that is always a part of achieving it. Together with my wife, we found a passion in the mental health industry, serving a clientele that we believed needed access to resources. We grew our thriving company to over 400 hundred employees. At our disposal was a financial team to help us—and our employees—with our assets for growth and retirement. Great visions were on the horizon, and the new century was showing an extraordinary amount of promise. Until…

Mid-2000 changed everything, practically in an instant. Not just for our business, but for almost everyone in business that had followed that same pattern of growth. Our reality quickly revealed improper planning.

This experience taught me what happens when you put all your eggs in one basket as a business owner.

It was surprising to see what happened with our investments and business from the stock market shake-up of 2000. It shifted everything, because during events like this two things are sure to happen:

- The market decreases rapidly and rebuilds slowly
- Banks stop lending

Thankfully, with some hard work we found ourselves rebounding from this; approaching our business a bit smarter and more aware. Welcome 2008—a year that made 2000 appear pretty mellow. Again, we adjusted strategies and saw significant growth. Eventually, we were able to sell that business with profits that exceeded our expectations.

After the business sold there was available time for me to reflect on lessons learned and how to use that knowledge to help others. I thought about how I'd relied on a single strategy to guide all the decisions of the business's financial investments. I wanted to participate in the decision making process for the investments we would make with the profits from the sale of our business. I became a student of finance; learning, growing, and seeing the industry from the inside. I quickly realized why most people don't enjoy the retirement they imagine for themselves. That was it. I was hooked and the entrepreneurial spirit kicked back in and a new company was born.

I received the pertinent licenses and training for investing and immersed myself in the industry. What I found both excited me and amazed me.

There was this entire area of finance that evolved around tax-free retirement that was not fully tapped into, at least not by anybody that I'd ever known. That spark inside of me to be of service to others was reignited in a powerful way, and I knew exactly what I was meant to focus on: offering tax-free retirement products to business owners. It was a better way—a way to grow money without loss. Today, my family's life has changed significantly in how we are protected from market shake-ups that are beyond our control, and also the lives of many hard working Americans that I work with, too.

THE BASIS OF SAFER RETIREMENT PLANNING

It would be a great disservice for anyone to think that having a 401(k) and pension plan means they "have retirement covered."

Because of what I'd gone through with my own business, I found I had this connectivity to other business owners, a very underserved market, particularly in the African-American community—where there are incredible entrepreneurs doing great things. By helping these business owners, I am also helping their employees and the families they serve. Everyone benefits, or at least has access to knowledge about the pertinent information that may give them a chance to be less impacted by those unanticipated market shifts that have become commonplace in the US markets.

And as it turns out, those significant market events aren't quite as unpredictable as what most of were lead to believe over the years.

Most people align a 401(k) with their retirement picture and it can work, but it is monies invested in the market. The condition of many peoples' 401(k)s is likely to be more favorable if their advisors were proactive in taking on the challenges that come with the market. The market is great for long-term growth. However, the market and a 401(k) should not be a singular strategy for retirement. Here's why:

401(k)s have a big challenge on the fee side, more so than the growth side. The fees will eat you alive and you may not even realize it until it's too late. Say you have a fee of 2% on the account. Not a big deal when you first start, but what about after you accumulate money in it? After taxes, fees, and all the other expenses that come with your 401(k)—since it is tax deferred dollars—your $400,000 account could very well end up netting around $200,000 when all is said and done. That's a lot of money for most of us, and what's most startling is that many don't recognize this until they are in the process of planning retirement withdrawals. This is why it's one of the most major themes of the seminars I give about this topic. I call it the "Tax Bomb Shell" and if you don't detonate it on your own, it's going to blow up in your face at some point.

The 401(k) information makes sense and certainly presents a compelling argument. Most people's next thought is regarding Social Security Income. Well, I have that so I'll be okay. It'll all work out. Sadly, despite contributing to it, Social Security is highly unlikely to do for us what it did for our parents. Will it go away? No, but it certainly isn't going to go toward your cost of living like you might have imagined. Currently, it's projected that within the next ten years, 100% of peoples' hard-earned Social Security Income checks are going to go toward one expense—their healthcare. And unless our healthcare system gets fixed quickly (fairly unlikely) this expense is our reality. About the best thing you can do is plan and hope you can start drawing on your Social Security at the cut-off age of 71 ½ so you can receive as high of a percentage as what is available and hope it lasts as long as you do.

Do you feel like this is maddening yet? Well, that's why I am here for you. Teaching people how to navigate the information and their options is what I do. It's called a tactile approach, and it is a sounder approach.

Where there is 401(k) and Social Security Income uncertainty, there is something more stable that is beneficial—tax-free retirement planning. This strategy goes against what most of us have been taught for so long and is part of an exciting approach called tactical investing. Your parents likely never did this, but you want to consider it.

Are you thinking, "Tax-free"? It doesn't sound possible.

Most of us have been taught that there is no way around taxes. They are an inevitable part of investing and retiring.

Taxes are mostly scary because there are no guarantees that they will even remain at the same rate as what you prepare for. Tax rates from when you're 20 are sure to be different than when you are 65. So, it's logical to see why tax-free growth is an appealing objective. Tax-free growth takes place through: allowing your money to grow with the market, while it isn't actually in the market.

The method that allows people to benefit from tax-free growth lies in something that has existed for extended periods of time—approaching finances like insurance companies approach their investments. With this approach you are taking after-tax dollars and allowing them to grow tax-free income in an efficient manner. And you make withdrawals tax free!

UNDERSTANDING THE ROLE OF A TACTICAL STRATEGY WITH INSURANCE INVESTING

Insurance companies invest money on index strategies, and consumers can do the same.

Most people don't question if they should have insurance because they see how it protects them. They purchase it for their car, their health, their home, their life, and many other things. However, they hardly ever think of insurance in regards to their largest asset—their retirement. Tactical investing creates the insurance component to this valuable asset.

The way this works is that when you invest monies on index strategies the money is not "in the market"; it's "against the market". This means that a cap is set for the maximum and minimum index. You only anticipate the cap, through the use of software. Maybe it's 12% high and 0% low, which means that if the market goes negative you're capped at no growth. You never lose money. **Zero's your hero!** I'm not talking "all-in" with this strategy, but smartly allocating a portion of your retirement to it.

By considering a portion of your investable monies for insurance investing and other types of alternative markets, you eliminate a major decision that comes from everyone who invests in the standard markets: when do you buy, sell, or stay put?

It's easy to feel that pit in your stomach swell when you see the market going up and down and you know that it's linked to what your future looks like. You can end up driving yourself crazy and as a result, you may make rash decisions in the moment that are not good for the long term. With insurance investing, you can at least know that you won't lose anything with that money, thereby protecting your retirement wellbeing. The tactical strategy is what will lessen the risk of loss.

A tactical strategy involves you giving the money manager the ability to make predictions that give them insight to know when to get out—often months before. . . a market crashes.

This is done through software and the money manager's sole job is to evaluate what is happening within your parameters and make any required adjustments. As the client, you also have access to this information so you can see what is happening all of the time. Through this approach the aspirations that people have with their money can play out better, including important things that many people used to take for granted, such as:

- Paying for their child's college. Parents used to consider it an honor and a joy to help pay for their children's college. It was the essence of the American dream. Today, college tuition increased 30+% in just 5 years and continues to rise an average of 6% per year. For most parents to help with college today they are required to withdrawn from their retirement plans—a scary proposition for most, if it is even feasible.

- Retire with the same type of lifestyle they currently have. Far too often retirement means downgrading homes, plans for fun, and even the healthcare decisions that a person makes. Through better strategies based on today's world, this can be better circumvented. It all starts with a plan and a partnership with a money manager.

Today, we do live in a different America and a new set of challenges exist for Baby Boomers, as well as Generations X and Y, and eventually the Millenials, too. We all get older, the key is to get wiser along the way.

WINNING AT RETIREMENT

Through understanding alternative ways to invest we are dividing our eggs into several baskets. If one basket breaks, we no longer have to be left with nothing.

With a better understanding of alternative investment instruments and how they work we can gain a better understanding of the market, allowing it to work for us. Most people don't understand that strategies such as this are often the main difference of how the wealthiest people in America really invest their money. They don't put it all in danger, because they want to keep it—just like the rest of us!

There's a demand for this information and this is where I help people meet that need. My mission is simple, because I have everyone's successful retirement as the catalyst for what I do every day. When I meet with people I want a real conversation, but also a productive conversation. They have to learn something so they can grow. Through looking at investments differently, we have our best chance to do better than our forefathers and parents did—something that seems unlikely to a great many people today. This is a different America we live in. Whether we think it's good or bad is not relevant when it comes to creating a favorable retirement scenario. So, you may not be ready to "change", but you should at least be ready to look at the big picture from all the angles, right?

About James

After serving nearly a decade in the United States Army, James Hamilton has achieved success in the business world as an entrepreneur, creating and leading several corporations. In less than eight years, James grew a corporation from inception to $20 million in annual revenue. He is now focused on creating strategies that help individuals plan and achieve financially-stable futures for themselves and their families.

As CEO of Forecast Financial Group, James leads a team that is committed to providing clients with financial education and resources to help identify their retirement goals and forge a path to create and preserve predictable income in retirement years. The foundational premise of his business model is building strong, professional relationships with his clients.

Under his leadership, Forecast Financial Group has implemented the philosophy that every client deserves to be empowered through financial education. Clients are empowered to create a safer financial future, based on their current assets and future goals, by positioning their portfolio for growth with little to no risk of loss. He also spends much of his time traveling the country and training other retirement and asset strategists to do the same for their clients. In addition to his educational seminars and financial services business, James is a motivational speaker and business consultant.

James and his wife Matisha have one daughter, and reside in the Raleigh, NC area. They are very active in their community as leaders and philanthropists.

He can be reached at:
- Tel: 800-678-2045,
- Email: james@forecastfinancialgroup.com.

CHAPTER 22

OUTRAGEOUS ENTREPRENEURIAL COURAGE
NO LIMITS TO SUCCESS

BY ANTHONY CALIENDO

Do you have any idea of what entrepreneurial success is all about? Is it simply starting your own company? NO!

Is it about starting your own company and realizing a return on your investment? MAYBE?

The startup world is an attractive, shiny and optimistic place to be. Creative, entrepreneurial minds are constantly trying to invent something extraordinary and buzzworthy enough to change the marketplace and the world. Building a brand plus achieving financial independence and security are key reasons to take that leap of faith to business ownership. Risky? YES! High, calculated risk can mean high reward. That's what makes venturing into entrepreneurship worth the sacrifice. That's how the most successful entrepreneurs remain determined and driven at all costs. But it's also about realizing your potential to dream and exceed beyond your own expectations, taking the chance and going beyond what the average person feels are limits to success. Sure, it all starts with an idea. What's more, entrepreneurship starts with driven and focused individuals that decide they have a story to tell and want to reap the rewards from sharing it with others.

But the true code for success is your own perseverance and tenacity that fuel our desire to drive through barriers. More importantly, entrepreneurial greatness only comes from your willingness to be bold and take bold action toward achieving your business vision. Bottom line, it has everything to do with an outrageous entrepreneurial mindset; how committed you are to changing the world.

Let's be clear, in my estimation there are no limits to my capability, desire for success and bold challenges that I will take on. I will admit failure is always an option, but it will not come from my self-imposed limits. It will not come from my fear of defeat. Placing limits on ourselves is a natural aspect of life. All entrepreneurs need to become Sales Assassins: they are people who are incessantly driven, have outrageous focus, discipline and commitment to sales success, and have razor-sharp instincts to navigate through cycles and trends. Yes, personal doubt and fear are major factors that are natural to human beings. These factors cannot simply be managed, they only disappear with a fierce tenacity to win, succeed and get back up when you are knocked on your ass. There are no limits except your own mind. It's called possessing Outrageous Entrepreneurial Courage. This is the key to cracking the code to success.

I admit that I have been knocked down, but I get back up the next day because I have no limit. I have no limit and I have no fear of defeat. I'm known as the Sales Assassin – an "entrepreneurial marketing machine" and this is my mindset of S.A.M (Sales Assassin Mastery)!" There is no stopping my commitment to achieving my passion, my commitment to achieving success and supporting my family! I might be down today, but I am always up tomorrow. It's not easy! How I have achieved success is not complex. But it is about my willingness to overcome adversity and never relinquish myself to defeat and the tough days of entrepreneurial life; Outrageous Entrepreneurial Courage!

Great entrepreneurs must be great leaders that organize, manage and assume risks with the willingness to absorb defeat, but rebound immediately from the challenge and continue the drive to success. They believe there is no excuse for defeat and we overcome all the odds! There are no limits to what we can endure and no limit to what we achieve!

EIGHT OUTRAGEOUS WAYS SALES ASSASSINS LEVERAGE OUTRAGEOUS ENTREPRENEURIAL COURAGE

1. **Become the World's Leading Expert.** Be the best and the one with more knowledge than anyone else. Everyone loves being with, working with and buying from the best.

2. **Be Remembered or Be Forgotten.** Differentiating you and your business is reinventing what you offer in relationship to the competition. No matter what that is, you have to make an impression. Be unique. Be distinctive.

3. **Anticipate Set-backs.** You will face constant obstacles that could be deadly to success. It's how you handle the obstacles that set you apart from the rest. A Sales Assassin always focuses on what he or she can control. Obstacles are mere pit stops on the way to the next score.

4. **Never Ruin Your Personal Brand.** Never compromise yourself for a quick buck or win lest you become perceived as the industry scumbag; rebounding from it is nearly impossible. Always strive to develop and maintain Leadership Integrity.

5. **Own Up.** Life's lessons are powerful and rapidly become the foundation of your success. Recognize them, if you fail, be accountable for the role you played, and learn from it.

6. **Use Your Instincts.** Learn when to cut your losses and move on to bigger things, other ideas or strategies when necessary.

7. **Change your Mindset / Change your Lifestyle.** Consistently make conscious choices and changes needed to drive, achieve and sustain desired results.

8. **Load, Lock and Aim:** Continually achieving higher status and upward mobility means setting goals and outlining strategic plans for consistent achievement. Trying to build success without measurable, attainable goals is like running a race without a finish line.

EMBRACE THE POWER OF ENTREPRENEURIAL CONSUMPTION

Who are the entrepreneurs? They are not simply people who continuously come up with new ideas, start a new business, fail, and then start another business. An entrepreneur is a person who thrives on the challenge of innovation, and is willing to plan, struggle and commit to what can be the all-consuming drive for success. My code for success starts with an entrepreneur's willingness to consume and strategically utilize knowledge, success and failure as precious resources, using at every moment the lessons of experience as a core foundation.

Entrepreneurial Consumption is the building of your energy to pursue the odds of success and failure, the drive to find solutions and discover the path to success.

The challenge of Entrepreneurial Consumption is to understand that the impact is not only your business initiative, but will most likely engage and challenge your personal and family life. The vision of that rainbow of entrepreneurial success can be a powerful magnet that will draw you and consume every moment of life. Your challenge is to give your all, but find the place to ensure how you will engage and balance life.

I will not try to give you a formula, because each of our circumstances are different. Nevertheless, **Entrepreneurial Consumption** is a massive commitment of life. Family must be an integral commitment to your achievement. Entrepreneurial Consumption can destroy families, but when managed properly, it can become the fuel and power of the family. YOU MUST BE CONSUMED in your commitment, and your family must also be consumed in the commitment.

There are three key points of Entrepreneurial Consumption:

1. Family must be integral to your commitment and entrepreneurial commitment.
2. The Lessons of Experience must be used to inform, mold and shape decisions.
3. Entrepreneurial Consumption must fuel your commitment to pursue the odds between success and failure.

Embrace the Authentic You… You Can't Fake It!

You cannot fake being an entrepreneur and you cannot fake success. I have a colleague whose son, now 39 years old, shocked his parents after they paid for five years of college, and after 6 months of work at Career Builders, he announced that, "I want to be an entrepreneur. I have so many ideas and I want to work for me." Ten years later this young man has developed and sold two companies and is now developing his third. Regardless of his parent's reservations, he embraced his dreams and found success by committing to his authentic-self.

You Can NOT Fake IT!

Being the "authentic you" is an individual commitment, demonstrating your personal drive and your personal values and mission in life. More importantly, the 'entrepreneurial you' provides your own frame of reference to your own political, social and cultural frame of reference. The key point in finding the 'authentic you' is not duplicating others, but instead finding your own Distinctive Nature to Achieve, your "S.A.M. DNA" of what you want to do. This is not a moment in life, but rather how you will lead your entrepreneurial existence through the best and worst of times, adhering to your process and business strategy. Don't fake it! It's your process…Your authentic you…Your instincts are informed as a result by all the great inputs of others in your life, but the bottom-line is you and your decisions, and the business commitments you are willing to make.

BE A HEAT-SEEKING MISSILE LOOKING FOR B.S. AND SUCCESS

You have to be a *"heat-seeking missile looking for the bullshit of business"* that separates you from the average person. A heat-seeking missile in real life is fired from an aircraft for the purpose of destroying the enemy aircraft. The analogy is simple. The most successful entrepreneurs are heat-seeking missiles overcoming the normal business challenges that you are going to face, and more importantly, they sort out the verbal garbage and B.S. of others who talk about success more than ever achieving entrepreneurial greatness.

Your "Entrepreneurial Missile" must be able to change direction at a moment's notice, adjusting to the market place demands when the facts, circumstances and your gut tell you to move now…move quick and never relinquish the competitive edge.

The B.S. of entrepreneurs is amazing. I have a theory. The more people talk, brag and tell you about their success or tell you how much money they're making, there is a strong likelihood it's all B.S. There is no need to challenge or debate them. You have no time to acquiesce to the nonsense of life.

OUTRAGEOUS PIONEERS OF CHANGE

Let's get real. We have all tried the scheme to camouflage that we got fired or severed from a job by announcing I decided to start my own business. Creating your own business is NOT a substitute for your severance from a company. Ok, this is life and you need to recover. But don't assume that creating a company and doing some fancy social-media marketing will convert your best skills to a successful entrepreneurial enterprise. Its not that simple.

The best entrepreneurs are **Outrageous Pioneers of Change**. They are masters of creating paradigm shifts that affect themselves and affect others. But we must understand that change and achieving our best are the results of capacity to push through what may seem like natural limits. We are surrounded by people who accomplish greatness by pushing through seemingly insurmountable challenges and amounts of physical and mental pain to reach the greatest pinnacles and incredible goals.

Being an entrepreneur and owning your own business is not a job. It's a way of life. Achieving and maintaining ultimate entrepreneurial success is a lifestyle and never deviates from idea to idea. The failure is not understanding that you must have real business expertise, a product or service that solves a real need and/or solves a problem. It has a risk of success and failure and is NOT a "stop-gap option" for a severance deal. Remember that the true code for success is your own perseverance that fuels your desire to drive through the big barriers, shielding success. It's about being the authentic you. It is the authentic you that becomes the heat-seeking missile that 'separates the bullshit from reality.'

There's a reason why I'm known as the Ultimate Sales Assassin. I am the entrepreneur of my life and my business. I have self-control and I make no accuses. I am responsible for my own success and my own failure. This is the authentic-me and I am a heat-seeking missile looking for bullshit. I am successful because I am outrageous and I have no limits to my ability to achieve success.

Outrageous Entrepreneurial Courage is not complex, but certainly is not easy. This is the key to cracking the code to success! You cannot compromise and must realize there is no limit to what we can endure and no limit to what we can achieve! More importantly, entrepreneurial greatness only comes from your willingness to be bold and take bold action toward achieving your business vision. "Dream Big" and achieve your dreams!

About Anthony

The business world changes around us with relentless speed and intensity. It takes great vision to not only see these changes, but to also anticipate and react with the tenacity to sustain success. Few business leaders possess the innate skills to maneuver the modern-day challenges of today's business. Anthony Caliendo is one of these self-made men, an entrepreneur and corporate visionary. To thrive in business and beyond, Anthony learned to look ahead and understand the trends and dynamic forces that shape his business to move swiftly and prepare for what's to come.

Anthony is a professional salesman, marketing machine, and sales leadership coach with supersensory sales skills, proven success in sales strategy and corporate leadership, and has generated hundreds of millions in sales revenues; he trained thousands of sales pros in various industries over 25 years to define him as the Ultimate Sales Assassin Master! Today he is a motivational sales speaker and author of the international best-selling, USA Book News Best Book and Indie Book award winning book: *The Sales Assassin: Master Your Black Belt in Sales.*

Anthony discovered his entrepreneurial instincts early in life, which piqued his desire for success and fortune. At 18, he became the youngest manager at that time to oversee Chicago Health Clubs and with his mentor, Al Philips, built the World Gyms with Arnold Schwarzenegger. Afterwards, Caliendo went on Wall Street as a stock broker where his instincts and thirst for sales domination accelerated. With financial success on Wall Street plus a number of notable business ventures, Anthony mastered the art of personal branding when he became known as "The Main Man" in the mortgage business, architect of one of South Florida's most successful mortgage and real estate companies and a local celebrity regularly featured on TV and Sports radio.

In 2008, during one of the U.S.A.'s worst economic downturns, Anthony reinvented himself and became the #1 Italian Cheese Salesman in the USA, known as the "The Big Cheese." He directed his manufacturing plant's national and global expansion initiatives and doubled the company's revenues inside of five years.

Anthony defines himself as an "outrageous and relentless sales professional." With his outrageous and relentless mentality, he constructed a fail-proof sales model encompassing specific skillsets and concepts that became the foundation of sales training for his brokers, salespeople and the sales staffs of his clients. The concepts and motivational themes of his sales experience inspired him to write The Sales Assassin and become a sales motivational speaker and sales coach to salespeople in all industries.

Anthony has discussed his sales strategies on radio and TV on CBS, NBC, ABC and FOX. He has been quoted in industry mags including *Salesforce, Small Biz Daily, The Canadian Business Journal, Focus Magazine, TK Business Magazine, AMA Playbook, In Business Magazine,* with a spellbinding book review in *Digital Journal.*

Anthony lives and works in South Florida with his wife, Lynette and their eight children.

To connect with Anthony or for more information on motivational speaking, coaching services or media opportunities please visit:
- www.thesalesassassin.com
- Tel.: + 1-561-265-1405
- Email: info@thesalesassassin.com
- Facebook.com/TheSalesAssassin
- Twitter.com/1SalesAssassin
- LinkedIn: https://www.linkedin.com/in/anthonycaliendo1

CHAPTER 23

MANAGING PERSONAL HOUSING CRISES
FINDING HOME SOLUTIONS THAT HELP PEOPLE

BY WILLIAM ROLL

*In a world where more people experience trouble with their housing,
I work with them to solve their problems, one family at a time.*

We are living in times where our dreams and dignity don't always align with the economics of our lives, or the world around us. It's tough to face the financial challenges that significantly alter your life, and nothing is more pressing than the issue of where you live—the place you call "home."

Without a home, we are lost, and throughout my life, I've become the person who has taken an active interest in helping people in crisis manage transitions that must take place in their housing. Whether someone has recognized that they are 'in over their head' and struggling to avoid bankruptcy, trying to rebuild from a bankruptcy event, or being forced to realign their obligations due to job loss or lesser income, I want to be the one who helps them. When doing this, I am vested in protecting their interests and wellbeing, while also addressing what is necessary from my end to remain in the business of helping others.

THE TRANSITION OF REAL ESTATE FOR THOSE IN CRISIS

Through the years, the struggles to assist those who are in dire straits with their properties has grown more complicated. However, the angst that these troubles can cause a family seem to be consistent with all generations.

It was quite by chance that I came into the business of helping people who were struggling with the properties they owned. I was a General Contractor for many years, doing remodels and other projects that would be typical of a guy in my field. I had a cousin who was in real estate and a common hindrance he faced when trying to help people sell properties that they were either at risk of losing or in upside down on (negative equity), was a lack of options. There was little he could do that that point... And that's where I came in.

The process was pretty simple at first. In fact, it was 1, 2, 3.

1. I would assume their mortgage (take over payments).
2. I would fix up the property to make it more marketable.
3. I would sell the property.

The people would move on and start anew. This was well before "flipping homes" and going into real estate investing became so trendy. It was a good business, but equally so, it was a good service to offer people.

That was then. This is now.

Today, because of the number of "players" in the field and the financial housing bubble repercussions, in conjunction with an economy that hasn't been favorable to the American worker, I am still offering the same skills and expertise that I have for decades. However, the rules are different, and the options are more complicated than they were once upon a time.

The biggest adjustments that have lead to significantly different approaches to helping people in crisis with their properties include shifts in:

- The weight placed on credit history. Credit scores were a "non-factor" until 1989 with the introduction of the FICO score by the company FICO (Fair, Isaac, & Company).

- Tight restrictions placed on banks due to negligent practices, more aggressive loan programs, and fewer programs with assumable mortgages than what once existed.

These changes have been tough for many banks who, by the way, are often the challenge in these situations, for a variety of reasons. Don't get me wrong, we need them, but it is inevitable that their challenges become the consumers' challenges, as well.

What does it all mean to someone like me? I am determined to help as many people as I can, because I know how to do it and am not afraid to do the honest due diligence to help people in an authentic, lawful manner. Ideally, I could still do it the way I did in the 70s…but thankfully, I am not resistant to change—that much.

It's important to keep the goal in mind—address living needs and help people start rebuilding with their new circumstances. Lessen the "dire" and determine the "direction".

Aside from assuming a loan, the other options that most consumers have today from dedicated professionals in the housing solutions business are:

1. Lease Option (possible purchase down the road)
2. Contract for Deed (known as a Land Contract in some states)
3. Rent to Own (a portion of rent and/or sweat equity goes toward downpayment)

The best method depends on what the client's circumstances are. This would include:

- What their objective is
- What their history is
- What their ability to pay is

I've taken steps to show people that I am more than someone who wants to flip their house and turn a profit. I am invested in their wellbeing, because without them being good, I can't feel good about what I do. A big step toward demonstrating this, as compared to just "talking the talk" came when I became a Certified Affordable House provider. This is a nationwide accreditation, dedicated to letting consumers who have real estate needs know they are working with someone who does things the right way.

WHAT HOME OWNERS IN CRISIS MUST KNOW

Today's financial issues do not have to stop tomorrow's goal of responsible home ownership.

Every housing transaction, regardless of the circumstances, is an individual thing. There is no "one-size-fits-all". However, there are some common areas that all homeowners should know if they are struggling and looking for housing solutions. The last thing you need during a highly stressful, down-on-your-fortune time is to make things worse by making one of the most critical decisions of your life solely based on emotion.

STRIVE FOR A WIN/WIN SITUATION. THEY DO EXIST!

My personal objectives are to not get rich quickly, which is the appeal of this business to far too many individuals. Rather, it is to just supplement my income while helping others in need. This is what drives and inspires me, as well as what compels me to give you forthright information that helps you—the consumer. There's a slew of "big wigs" looking out for everyone else.

1. **Do not settle for working with anyone who will not have a "real" conversation.**
   The first step usually involves a phone conversation where the goal is to determine what someone's exact situation is. From that point on, the path of action is determined.
2. **If you don't talk face-to-face, you cannot create a favorable scenario.**
   Solid information and numbers cannot be exchanged without having a look at the actual property. Don't be fooled into thinking otherwise! It's kind of like that ice cream shop with thirty flavors. You go in and are not sure what you are going to get until you evaluate all your options. Everything must be reviewed and you cannot know your options without crunching the actual numbers.
3. **Research the property and get absolutes with the numbers.**
   Researching the property's history of activity is mandatory and

skipping this step is neither protective to the consumer nor potential investor. There's no way around it and you learn a lot—and often reveal a lot. The two ways to find out what "baggage", a/k/a liens, mortgages, judgments, violations, etc. on a property are through:

a. Running a title report: this is done through a title company, also known as an escrow company in some states.

b. Personally researching the public record of the property and individuals attached to it: by doing this, I can find out exactly what is showing on public record (often before going to the property to meet with the current owners). It is a time saver and lends to a more productive conversation. Plus, you'd be surprised at how many people are not aware of what all is attached to their property. And on occasion, they have even been making payments on paid off notes due to them being sold to various servicers. Hard to imagine, but true.

After all of this, if a logical and mutually beneficial agreement can be arranged, the first and best choice is to always assume the mortgage. To assume it, the criteria that generally must be in place are:

- To not be excessively behind on mortgage payments
- To have a mortgage that is assumable (it's in the recorded mortgage wording)

In this "best case scenario", the consumer can walk away from their property and begin a fresh start with their life.

FROM MY PERSPECTIVE: WAYS TO ENSURE BETTER OUTCOMES

The more parties that need to be involved in helping people sever their ties with a property, generally, the more complicated the process becomes.

It's not a matter of hiding information from people, it's a matter of solving problems without involving more entities than what are necessary to reach a fair and just resolution. This is real life playing out in an emotionally-charged environment. There's stress, and streamlining can alleviate much of the tension, and for someone like me, it allows me to help in a transaction and end it with a favorable impression and an outcome we are all grateful for.

People are busy dealing with their lives. They are trying to work and make ends meet, and raise a family. As a result, things they should know get put to the side—like educating themselves on handling all finances. High school and even many colleges don't teach this, either, which does not help. The fact is that we can believe we're doing our due diligence and the right thing, and when we find out we didn't, it's often too late to correct our course of action before we're in a challenging position. On the other hand, isn't that the very reason we hire professionals in these areas to look out for our best interests? To be our source of knowledge? Someone we can trust...

I'm dedicated to teaching people how it all works and working to have them as informed as possible. They won't get a do-over, but they have the opportunity to get a do-it-right.

Aside from true affordability, the biggest thing that I help customers with is guiding them toward the best resources to help repair their credit.

There are some fantastic organizations out there—many non-profit—that help consumers clean up and improve their credit so they can gain a more favorable position for future mortgage financing. But more than that— they help them to learn all the nuances that are important in managing one's own credit and ensuring that it can lead to more favorable options and opportunities for their lives' needs that require financing.

With an improving credit history, I have the ability to help people take that next step to home ownership again. That sense of permanency means everything in regards to the way that many hard-working, good people perceive their own lives, and the quality of it. Oftentimes, living in a property that is going through foreclosure or a rental property leaves people feeling distressed about their situations. It's hard to focus and it's scary. Strategies to improve credit open up the opportunities for me to connect people with properties on terms that will work for them, whether it is a Lease Option, Contract for Deed, or Rent to Own. And equally important, we can find ways to structure these things so that a boat-load of cash is not required (remember the sweat equity). Everyone wins, but most importantly—dignity is rebuilt and can be maintained.

AS LONG AS PEOPLE ARE IN NEED, I'LL BE IN DEMAND

My goal is to fit the right people with the right homes.

We've all heard the stories about how many "everyday Americans" are in financial trouble, particularly with their housing. The need for helping people get into affordable housing also extends far beyond that.

As part of my way of giving back and continuing to educate people, I am now seeking ways to connect challenged adults (due to disabilities or limited mental capacity) in group homes where they can gain a sense of independence in a more secure environment. The same concept is also being evaluated for some of America's greatest heroes—our veterans. When people need a guiding hand and a trusted source to help them in this world, I hope to be their guy in the Portland area.

To do this, it will require gaining more inventory to connect people with homes that meet their criteria and budget, in places they want to live. Dignity is essential, and I'd settle for nothing less. What do I mean by that? Just because you had a tough time with your credit history or a home in the past doesn't mean that you should have to live wherever the available home is that will accept that situation. We can make it work everywhere, giving people a home that they can be proud of in a neighborhood that they enjoy.

As each day starts and I begin the work that I do, I am always mindful of this message, as it's a driving force in my life, as well as personal philosophy:

When you have a good feeling about yourself you are going to be willing to go out and do something more—and give more, too.

I wish that wonderful feeling of accomplishment for everyone!

About William

William Roll, who is referred to by friends and family as "Uncle Bill," learned at an early age what work was. At the time, it did not seem like work.

Since he was raised on a farm, his summers were spent working with the family. He learned how to make do with materials at hand, as it was 20 miles to town to buy materials.

After graduating from high school he went to work for the local utility company up until the Vietnam War, then he joined the Air Force. Upon returning, he then went into the construction industry which led to him owning a residential remodeling business.

It was during this process that he was introduced to the works of Zig Ziglar, Brian Tracy, Steven Covey, Dale Carnegie, Tony Robbins, Bob Proctor, Jack Canfield and many more. It was these individuals that helped Uncle Bill to develop a more positive attitude.

It was during the 80's when a wave of bankruptcies occurred, that Uncle Bill learned how to help people who had property and were about to lose it, that he developed a win/win philosophy.

Uncle Bill has been in the Real Estate industry and has seen many developments over the years, but this latest with the subprime lending and the effects that it has had on people has created an even greater desire to help people with their housing needs.

He feels blessed that he was able to be included in this book with his friend and mentor.

CHAPTER 24

KEEP DIGGING TILL YOU FIND GOLD

BY DR. GEORGE AYEE

INTRODUCTION:

My quest for gold – have a great life, fulfil my potential, and achieve my dreams, started years ago when I left my country of birth in Africa for a better life. My parents ingrained in me at the time that knowledge through education was the best way to achieve my goals and be successful. I enrolled in a university outside my country. There was a catch though. My parents did not have the money to support my education, so that meant looking for work to pay my way through school. The University was gracious to put me on a Work-Study program to help pay part of the fees.

I visited different organizations to ask for financial support with no success. On one occasion, I visited an organization and was advised by the leader of the organization to just go back home and find something else to do. I talked to my parents about my challenges in getting financial support and the struggles I was going through. As you can expect from any loving parent, my dad suggested I return home to work for a printing and publishing business he was thinking about setting up. This business never got off the ground. I told my dad I was not returning home till I achieved my purpose for leaving home. I took whatever job was available at the university through work-study and completed my bachelor's degree.

After completing my bachelor's degree, I looked for a job but could not find any. The excuse from the potential employers at the time was that I did not have any work experience. In my naivety, I asked one of the employers, "If you don't give me a job, how you expect me to get the work experience?" to which he said, "We are not a charitable organization; I don't care what you think; we have no job for you." I volunteered to work for a charitable organization and got my first work experience to put on my resume. I did more volunteering for other organizations and got more experience.

Still, with no job in sight, I applied for a Master of Business Administration degree in England. I was accepted and commenced the MBA program. I found a benevolent catholic priest who promised to pay part of my fees, and in return I would go to work with him in Africa. Once again, I requested for work-study at the university to pay a portion of the fees and got office cleaning jobs to keep me afloat for a while. Whatever money I was making was inadequate to fully pay the rest of the fees and so I was in arrears. The university administration gave me an ultimatum to pay up or they would let me go. I remember doing all that I knew to do, taking on more work, going to class half asleep because I worked all night. I went to the MBA director's personal assistant with the suggestion to quit because the challenges were too much for me. Her words to me were so clear; "George, do not quit now. If you do, you will regret it for the rest of your life. You have come this far and I know you will finish. Don't give up on yourself now." I took her advice and continued with the courses, worked various jobs and completed the master's program.

On graduation day, I was awarded the MBA director's Award of Distinction with the following accompanying words from the professor, "George, use this degree and award to change and influence your part of the world." These words resonated with me and are now part of my personal vision statement, which says: "I release champions and inspire each one to greatness." I have since obtained a doctorate degree in business administration, worked with international management consulting firms, started two private universities, worked with multinational corporations, set up a consulting practice providing training and consulting services to for-profit and non-profit organizations, set up a health and wellness business and now providing professional speaking and coaching services to clients in various countries. That's why I insist, "Keep digging till you find gold!"

My purpose for writing this chapter is to provide you with six strategies from my experience to use in digging till you find your gold. My story is not to impress you, but rather to impress upon you that you can achieve your potential, dream and success in whatever you want to accomplish in life. I also want to remind you that success and achievement is not for a chosen few, but for all those willing to pay the price for success and advancement. In speaking to thousands and conducting seminars around the world, I came to one conclusion: we give up too soon. Success and achievement are not for a select few, but for all those willing to keep digging till they find gold. Your gold is waiting for you, so go find it!

I. DEALING WITH DISCOURAGEMENT

Discouragement is not the absence of adequacy,
but the absence of courage.
~ Neal A. Maxwell

There was never a person in the world that did not experience a stint of discouragement along the path of success. History is dotted with stories of successful people who went through discouragement several times before achieving their goal. Discouragement is part and parcel of success and therefore part of the story to success and achievement. On your path to your gold, you will encounter discouragement. You will have discouraging thoughts especially during periods when things don't go well, when you miss the target, when the sales fall through, when you don't make the grade, when the business proposal is rejected, when you don't get the promotion and when things fall apart. Learn to travel light.

The key to dealing with discouragement is to be committed to your goal of finding gold, recollect past victories, successes, and how far you have come. The fact that you are still alive, pursuing your dreams, is a testament of your tenacity, and courage, weathering the storms of life. Dealing with discouragement is to commit yourself to staying focused on your goal no matter the challenges and setbacks. Commitment is about starving negative thoughts and focusing 100% on what you want. Make commitment and courage your greatest ally. When discouragement takes a hold of you, shake it off and focus on your gold. Don't let the failures of yesterday deter your vision. Adversity is the food of champions.

II. DELAYS ARE NOT DENIALS

Time ripens all things.

You know what you want; you have clearly identified your gold and set specific goals and milestones for achieving your goal. For unexpected reasons, you have missed a few deadlines, milestones, and now finding your gold is elusive. You start thinking, Am I in the right place, do I have what it takes, am I delusional in in what I want to achieve? Perhaps pursuing and digging for gold is not for me. I should just move on to something else. Be warned! Finding gold and achieving your goals take time. Someone once told me that time ripens all things.

The delays on your path to success and achievement are not denials. Delays test your commitment, courage, quality of your ambition, character, and patience. Delays also refine your personality, provide growth and development to be able to handle the stresses that come with having your gold. Delays are a gift from God to position you well for your gold. Any time you encounter delays on your path to success, remember delays are not denials. Various life episodes may cause delays on your journey to success; however, never lose sight of your gold. A great way to deal with delays is to visualize the prize at the end of your digging. Imagine living the life you have always imagined, living in the home of your dreams, running that successful business with significant growth. The gold that lies ahead of you is unlimited. Nobody can take it away from you but you!

I have experienced various delays along my path to success, and I can tell you without any reservation whatsoever, that those delays have made me stronger, wiser, and capable of handling whatever life throws at me. Use delays to your advantage by reframing their meaning and for honing down your skills.

III. THE GIFT OF 'NEXT'

To find your gold, you must learn to appreciate and accept the gift of 'NEXT.'

I have come to appreciate the word NEXT. During my days of looking for scholarship and financial support for school, any time I was turned down by a potential donor, I told myself NEXT. When I was selling insurance, and was rejected by a prospect, I said NEXT. When my proposal for a consulting or training work lost the bid, I said NEXT, when a particular business I invested in lost a lot of money, instead of whining and complaining I said, NEXT. I love the gift of NEXT because it's a reflection of hope, faith, courage, tenacity and the belief that all things are working together for my good and that there is a major conspiracy in the universe to bring good to me. We live in a world of opulence and there are so many opportunities available to help you find your gold.

The gift of NEXT says that there is someone out there ready to help you find your gold. When you develop the mindset of NEXT; develop an unshakable belief that there is more than enough to go around and that what you require is to operate from a creative plane in digging your gold. We make the mistake of operating from a competitive plane which says that there is too little to go around and resources are scarce. This mindset breeds discouragement, despondency and despair. The gift of NEXT is on your side and the people you need to find your gold are waiting for you. Print the word NEXT and place it in conspicuous place where you can see it as a reminder. Explore the word NEXT and begin to move in the direction of your gold.

IV. DON'T WASTE YOUR PAIN

Pain is just temporary, if you give up it becomes eternal.
~ Dexter Lim

While pursuing my master's degree and struggling to make ends meet, I remember on one occasion I had to go to school and take an exam. All I had on me was a one-way train ticket to go and write the exam. I finished the exam and boarded the train to return home but this time without a ticket. Somewhere in the middle of the journey, an officer approached me and requested to see my ticket to which I responded I don't have one and pleaded for mercy. I believe the officer was in a very bad mood that day or perhaps he was just doing his duty. When the train arrived at the next station, the officer threw me out. I was embarrassed with the whole ordeal, shed a few tears, and was scared, in the middle of nowhere wondering how I was going to get home.

These were the days when there were no cell phones to call and ask for help. I waited several hours and got back on the next available train, but this time on the lookout for any person resembling an officer. I finally got home and promised myself never to allow this experience to be repeated in my life. Out of this pain and experience I resolved to pursue my goals with gusto, never give up on my dreams, to keep digging till I find my gold.

What is your pain? What are you going through on your path to success? What are the discouraging episodes in your life? Turn your pain on its head and let it motivate, inspire, and propel you in finding your gold. There are those who crash under the weight of pain let this not be you. Don't waste your pain.

V. CELEBRATE MILESTONES ALONG THE WAY

Celebrating says you are grateful for your achievements and successes.

Don't wait for everything to be in place before you celebrate your achievement and successes. When we were kids, we were always fascinated when it rained. My favorite part was when it rained after school, over the weekend or during the school holidays. We developed a tradition as kids of playing in the rain or dancing in the rain. We never waited for the rain to stop because we liked playing in the rain. There was something about dancing in the rain that was fascinating to us as kids.

May I suggest to you that it's time to be a kid again? Learn to celebrate the small and big successes on your path to finding gold. You don't have to wait for the rain to stop. You don't have to strike gold big time before you start celebrating key milestone. The journey of finding your gold takes time and so it's important that you celebrate the small gains along the way. These celebrations provide encouragement, motivation and inspiration to keep digging. Take a break to encourage yourself along the way. Whatever success you achieve, irrespective of how small it may appear, celebrate it. No accomplishment is too small to ignore. Any time you achieve a milestone, reward and spoil yourself and your family.

VI. FOCUS ON YOUR GOAL 1 MILLION PERCENT

Whatever you dwell upon grows.

The word focus means emphasis, attention, concentration or single-mindedness. Oprah Winfrey said, "What you focus on expands, and when you focus on the goodness in your life, you create more of it. Opportunities, relationships, even money flowed my way when I learned to be grateful no matter what happened in my life." That means we get more of what we focus on. When you are digging for your gold and you begin to think about how hard it is, verbalizing the difficulties and dwelling upon these challenges, you will certainly get more of what you are focusing on. There is a law regarding focus. This law states that whatever we dwell upon grows. Discipline yourself and focus single-mindedly on digging your gold. You will be amazed at what happens.

When you focus 1 million percent on the things you want to accomplish, these thoughts will come to saturate everything you say and do. The more you focus on what you want, the more determined you will become to achieve it. When you focus on thinking about the things you fear, worry and are anxious about, overly concerned about what tomorrow will bring, these fears will soon grow bigger and dominate your thinking and behavior.

Focus continually on the person you want to be. Do everything in your power to be the very best person you can possibly become. Resolve to keep your mind, your conversation and your activities away from anything that is inconsistent with what you want in life.

Dig until you find your gold!

About Dr. George

Dr. George Ayee is a consultant, professional speaker, coach and trainer. He helps his clients to unleash the full power of the organization and employees for maximum results. George works with organizations and people to unlock the power of change and transformation for optimal results.

George's philosophy is that successful change and transformation is a precondition for optimal organizational results. Organizations and people who learn to anticipate, embrace, engage, exploit, navigate change and transformation successfully are the leaders of their respective industries and careers. In alignment with his philosophy, George spends his time facilitating change and transformation programs, coaching leaders, and people to work through change and transformation faster and successfully.

George's passionate, inspirational, and high energy call for action liberates and engages his audience for action, change and transformation. His electrifying seminars on leading change— personal change, as well as resilience in change, organizational transformation, and personal achievement, motivates his clients and audience to immediately take required actions to achieve their vision, strategic objectives, and goals.

Dr. George Ayee will help you go through change and the transformation process faster and successfully.

With a doctorate in business administration, an MBA in International Business Administration and his BSc in Finance/Accounting and decades of experience, George works with world-class companies, oil and gas, banks, insurance, non-profit organizations, government institutions and people who want to succeed, follow their passion, exploit their potential, make more money and achieve organizational objectives.

You can contact George at:
- www.georgeayee.com
- info@georgeayee.com

CHAPTER 25

HOW TO SUCCEED WHEN OTHERS SAY YOU CAN'T!

BY ANGELA BRITTAIN, M.Ed.

How do you accomplish your goals when everyone around you is telling you it can't be done?

How do you make a better life for yourself and your infant son when you are only 18 and have no education and no role models? These were questions I had to ask myself.

At an all too early age I found myself in a situation with divorced parents and little supervision, so I turned to my boyfriend for the love I was seeking. I found love and then found myself pregnant while still in high school which in the 70s was highly unacceptable. I was asked to leave school.

Fortunately, I was blessed to have a built in stubborn curiosity from childhood which translated into a love of learning as I entered school. This love of learning has never waned throughout my years. Something in me at that time told me that education was my way out of the poverty I was facing. I read everything I could get my hands onto and listened to motivational speakers on the radio. I couldn't afford a television.

Going to bed hungry in order to ensure there would be food for my son was wearing me down along with the two minimum wage jobs I was holding. One of the jobs was at a fast food chicken restaurant on the evening shift because they allowed you to take home the food that was left at the end of the evening. We ate a lot of chicken in those days. I dreamed of steak dinners while seeing myself walking across a stage and being handed a college degree. How that would happen didn't matter to me as I held onto that dream. It became my vision. I had plenty of people around me telling me all the reasons I could not accomplish my dream, none of them offered support or help.

Nowadays, I think most people have heard of Visualization and how it works, but in the '70s I had never heard of such a thing. I only knew I had to make a better life for my son, and so obtaining my college education became my vision of how it could be done. I began with baby steps. It started by going to a local community college to see about taking a class or two. They informed me that since I had not finished high school, I would have to take a test and get a G.E.D. before I could enroll. I studied up, took the test and obtained the G.E.D. Next I was told I should take a placement exam of which the results surprised both me and the counselors by my scoring at the sophomore college level. My vision was becoming a reality little by little, but working two jobs, going to classes and raising a son continued to take a toll. My son went from daycare to night care and my lunch breaks and dinner breaks were spent devouring books rather than food. There isn't much nourishment in a bag of chips and a caffeine-laden cola. When I found myself unable to walk up a flight of steps, I was diagnosed with malnutrition and forced to quit school. In spite of the odds against me I didn't give up on my dream for I knew with certainty it would happen, but it had to be postponed. At that time, I had not heard of Brian Tracy, but as he says:

Whatever we expect with confidence becomes
our own self-fulfilling prophecy

Whether out of self-preservation or an innate wisdom that staying with the low-paying jobs would never get me to the point of the security I was seeking, I job-hopped, and frequently. And with each new job paying a little more and requiring new skills I slowly but surely learned more and became more experienced. I became more valuable to employers and my self-confidence grew as I also learned to tune out the negative comments from my "friends". It seemed to me at the time that a secretary's job was the goal to achieve. To be honest, without any role models and a lack of experience in the workplace, I didn't know of any other goals to shoot for.

Oh sure, there were the traditional girl roles to choose from – ballerina, nurse, veterinarian, and teacher, but one by one they were ruled out.

Ballerina seemed unlikely for a girl who was frequently told she had two left feet and was nick-named "Grace". Nurse was certainly not an option for someone so squeamish to minor cuts and blood. Veterinarian ruled out for the same reasons as nurse. Only 'teacher' had possibilities as I had been a helper in grade school to kids in a lower grade to work one-on-one with those who struggled to read. Helping others was a joy and made me feel needed. And I loved learning.

Even though I couldn't attend college right away, I read books and listened to self-help tapes from the library to expand my mind. I read *The Wall Street Journal* at the library and numerous other business magazines. My friends called me weird and made fun of me. But they weren't struggling and didn't understand how I struggled and dreamed of a better life. Most didn't have kids to support and if they did, they had husbands and family to help.

After getting my nutrition and food intake leveled out and myself healthy, I continued with small steps towards my goal. Instead of taking three classes a semester, I took only one. And I'm forever grateful to the forward-thinking administrators at the local community college who allowed me to miss the one class each month when my work schedule conflicted with the class schedule. I would then make up the work on my own.

I got discouraged more than a time or two, but when I considered the alternative to not achieving my goals, my motivation increased. I remember thinking at the rate I was able to take classes it might take me six or seven years to obtain my degree, but then I would stop and think if I didn't work towards the degree, where would I be in six or seven years; obviously older and without a degree. I didn't like that option so I studied to learn all I could and to prove to myself and those around me it could be done.

Not only did I obtain my Bachelor's degree in Communications but I graduated Summa Cum Laude. I was inducted into the prestigious honor society of Phi Kappa Phi. I had achieved my goal and it felt fantastic. But then I chose to push myself a little further and went on to get a

Master's Degree, an M.Ed., in Instructional Design. My love of learning and teaching was then able to be shared.

So just how do you accomplish your goals when everyone around you is telling you it can't be done?

You must have a determined focus on your end results. Have a clear vision of where you will end up. Don't focus on how you will get to the end results, or how much hard work it might take, as that can overwhelm and discourage you. Instead imagine your life as it will be after you have accomplished your goals. Imagine having a steak dinner and living in a luxurious home. Imagine the joy and self-respect you will feel for accomplishing your goals. See yourself on vacation in an exclusive resort, laying poolside or on the beach. Believe in yourself and believe your dreams can come true!

It's important to also note that while you are focusing on your end goal, don't lose touch with the present moment you are living in. Enjoy where you are now, find joy and have gratitude for the little things. Try not to make statements like, "I'll be happy when I get my degree. I'll be happy when I get the promotion at work. I'll be happy when I get married." Don't forget to look around at your life now and find things to be happy about. The choice of happiness is yours. When you find yourself saying things like, "She makes me so mad", realize you are giving your power to someone else. Know that you always have a choice in the ways you react to the situations where you find yourself. You are in control of your life. You have the power to change your life and your situation. Don't give control of your life and emotions to someone else. *And along the way, don't be afraid to fail a few times on your journey.*

Albert Einstein did not speak until he was four years old and did not read until he was seven. His parents thought he was "sub-normal," and one of his teachers described him as "mentally slow, unsociable, and adrift forever in foolish dreams." He was expelled from school and was refused admittance to the Zurich Polytechnic School. He went on to win the Nobel Prize in Physics.

Walt Disney was fired by a newspaper editor because "he lacked imagination and had no good ideas." He went bankrupt several times before he built Disneyland. In fact, the proposed park was rejected by the city of Anaheim on the grounds that it would only attract riffraff.

Thomas Edison's teachers said he was "too stupid to learn anything." He was fired from his first two jobs for being "non-productive." As an inventor, Edison made 1,000 unsuccessful attempts at inventing the light bulb. When a reporter asked, "How did it feel to fail 1,000 times?" Edison replied, "I didn't fail 1,000 times. The light bulb was an invention with 1,000 steps."

Probably the greatest example of persistence is **Abraham Lincoln**. If you want to learn about somebody who didn't quit, look no further. Born into poverty, Lincoln was faced with defeat throughout his life. He lost eight elections, twice failed in business and suffered a nervous breakdown. He could have quit many times - but he didn't and because he didn't quit, he became the 16th president of the United States and one of the greatest presidents in the history of our country. Lincoln was a champion and he never gave up.

Read the stories of these great men and others who failed numerous times before they reached their goal. You only fail when you stop getting up and continuing the journey towards your goal. Never quit. You must stay focused on the end-results. See yourself celebrating your accomplishments. Focus. The focus will enable you to tune out the naysayers and in some cases you may even find you have to leave some of your current friendships behind, and that's ok. Those will be replaced by better and truer friendships with people you admire and who believe in you and encourage you on your journey. Find people you admire and emulate them.

Dress for success. With today's casual attire in nearly every workplace you can still dress to impress. Make sure your clothing is freshly pressed and is styled in a classic manner. How do the successful people you admire dress? Follow their fashion lead. Even if you are in a department where everyone is prone to wearing blue jeans, by not wearing blue jeans you will stand out and impress. My belief is you should always dress for the job you want, not the job you have.

Perform each job you are in with all of your attention and talent, even if you know this is not your dream job. Act with confidence, not cocky, but with friendly confidence. Learn everything you can about the job you are doing. Always do your very best work. It's good training for when you are in your dream job. And besides, wouldn't you want and expect your own employees to do the same? Make excellence a habit. It will serve you well when you go into business for yourself.

Believe in yourself, your beliefs shape your thoughts and shape your expectations. If you find yourself thinking limiting thoughts, flip the channel and change your thoughts to something more positive. Take time out each day to find a quiet place and take a few deep breaths, close your eyes and let the feeling of happiness and peace surround you. This may not feel easy at first, but with practice it becomes easier. This will help to focus your mind. Find little things to be grateful for. I'm grateful I don't have to go to bed hungry. I'm grateful for the ability to see and hear and smell the world around me. There are so many small things and big things I do not take for granted. Make your own list. It seems the more we appreciate the moments in our lives, the more moments we are given to appreciate.

Be kind to others and yourself. Our self-talk can sometimes be critical and demoralizing. Things we say to ourselves, we would never dream of saying to someone else. What would your best friend say to you in the situation? What would you say to your best friend if they were in a similar situation? Then be your own best friend and speak kindly and with encouragement to yourself. Forgive yourself for past mistakes. Be a good friend to yourself.

Don't wait for the "perfect" moment to start your journey. Don't wait for everything to be just right and line up perfectly to begin. That "perfect" moment doesn't exist, it will never come. Begin your journey now, because NOW is the time. And if something causes you to hit the pause button, that's ok. Pause, and then begin again. You have to start in order to get there. If you map out a road trip to your dream destination, but never get in the car and start the trip, it's guaranteed you won't arrive at your destination. You may have a flat tire along the way or run out of gas, or encounter a detour or two, but those are just part of the journey and only deserve a small amount of your focus. They don't cause you to change your destination. You stay focused on the destination and you keep going until you arrive. Life is a journey full of choices. Choose to succeed at your life. Enjoy the ride.

What we expect to happen usually does.

Expect the best!

> *Only those who dare to fail greatly can achieve greatly.*
> ~ Robert F. Kennedy

About Angela

Angela Brittain helps her clients move into their power to create the life they love. She uses techniques and resources gained as a Certified IP Trainer by Mike Dooley. Using the principals outlined in Mike Dooley's Infinite Possibilities program she coaches her clients to understand just how powerful we each are in reaching our dreams. Angela also incorporates her training in Healing Touch and Pure Bio-energy to further assist her clients to find a harmonious balance in their lives while achieving their goals.

Angela is a graduate of McNeese State University in Louisiana where she graduated in the top 10 of her class. She earned her Bachelor's degree in Communication and her M.Ed. in the design of training programs. Angela was included in Who's Who in American Universities and was inducted into the prestigious honor society of Phi Kappa Phi. She is a business woman whose first business plan she created in order to successfully obtain a bank loan and open a gourmet candy/gift store, was used by the Business Department at MSU. She was also the Editor of the University's yearbook for two years while being active in several community groups such as the City Christmas Lighting Event and involved with the Mayor's Committee, among others.

Angela's past experiences include Director of Marketing for the Lake Charles Convention and Visitors Bureau where she travelled to various cities throughout the USA speaking and bidding to bring conventions and business to Lake Charles. She was the manager of Human Resources for a major USA retail chain where her intuitive nature served her well in hiring, training, counseling and sometimes the termination of employees. She has years of experience in the meeting planning industry including working with BMW North America on the launch of one of their cars in 2014. Angela handled local publicity and public relations for Kenneth Feld productions which included the *Disney On Ice* shows and *Ringling Bros. and Barnum & Bailey Circus* productions.

Angela's love of people and her drive to expand her view of the world and live life to the fullest, has led her to become a Visionary member at Project Positive Change. She has travelled to several countries including South Africa, Italy, France, Honduras, Guatemala, Mexico, Netherlands, Columbia, and Principality of Monaco and most recently to Belgium.

Her joie de vivre is genuine.

You can connect with Angela at:
- www.facebook.com/angela.brittain.77
- www.ippinspire.com

CHAPTER 26

BE THE MANAGER PEOPLE WON'T LEAVE

BY JAN MAKELA

People tend to be promoted to management for three reasons: a specific skillset they possess, a technical ability, or seniority in the organization. The assumption is that when an employee has been successful in their current position, it would be logical that they will be successful managing others. Obviously this is not very solid logic. To complicate matters, the new manager is already viewed as successful, so little consideration is given to offer any extensive management training to better prepare them to manage their new team. You can probably predict the outcome.

Managing people requires unique skillsets that may or may not correlate with the talents that have made the new manager successful in their previous position. The soft skills managing people is hard work. In fact, poor managers are consistently one of the top five reasons people leave organizations (even above money). Front line managers can be compared to either the accelerator or the brakes in a car – they are the drive behind the motivation, effectiveness and ultimately, the success of an organization.

It is no secret that employee turnover is costly. It is estimated that when an employee leaves, it costs the company 150% of the employee's salary to fill the gap, recruit, hire and train a replacement. Managers who can't keep and grow their employees actually cost the company money because some of the best talent doesn't stay and as discussed above the cost to replace them is high.

When speaking to CEOs and company Presidents, I often hear, "our managers are just fine and doing a great job!" However, when I follow with, "How do you know?" They have no evidence to back up their claims. Just because everyone appears happy and there haven't been any negative reports to HR doesn't automatically mean all is well in the organization. To ensure that a management team is truly performing and enhancing the value of the company, there needs to be a tool to measure it by.

My career as a manager started as a company commander in the U.S. Army. As a commander, if I said, "Jump!" my troops would respond, "How high, sir?" At that time and in that organization with such a strict culture, having the title of boss was all that was needed. When I left the military I was asked on several occasions to be promoted to manager. I didn't take the offers. I liked what I was doing and I didn't want the hassle of supervising others and/or being responsible for any performance other than my own. My managers kept pushing. They were confident that my success in the military would translate to the private sector and I would be able to turn around the underperforming unit.

As you have probably surmised at this point, although I was working 70 hours a week and giving it my all, nothing was improving. In fact, seven of the twelve people in the unit left. Luckily for me, I was finally matched with a mentor who helped me go from a manager that people left to one that people requested to work with. My turnover rate went from 58% to zero. I was rated in the top 10% of all managers in the industry and I was interviewed for the popular book by Gallup, First Break All the Rules. Suddenly my group was outperforming the others and we were having fun doing it.

So what is the secret? How do you or your leaders not only keep but enhance the dynamics on a team and help them to be even more successful?

Here are key pillars to success as a manager:

- Make decisions based on productivity
- Motivate every single one of your team members to take action

- Engage your team with a compelling vision and mission
- Have the assertiveness to drive outcomes while also building trust with open and full transparency
- Create a culture of accountability and cooperation

How do you accomplish these pillars?

1. Vision and Mission Statement:

What is that you want? I ask this of managers all the time and I get blank stares in return. Of course we all want to increase profit margins and be successful but what does that really mean? How are you going to get there? People say things like "I will work hard" but statements like these are too vague. Sit down and picture the future when all is going well, what will it look like and what specific steps will get you there? One of my vision statements was "I want my team to know how to accomplish goals and tasks without my direction. I want them to be a self- sufficient, cooperative team when I am not there."

Another great question to ask yourself is, "Six months after I leave my current position, how do I want to be remembered? Or will you be the manager nobody wants to be in a lifeboat with?" Use these thought provoking questions to guide your vision and mission statements.

Every team and organization has a culture. If you don't like the dynamics you see in your group, you as the manager are the only one who can change it. That culture, whether good or bad, exists because you have allowed it to be so. As the leader, you have to give thought to how your team will function and will or will not be accepted. Just like you envision the future to create your mission/ vision statements you must also develop an idea of the ideal culture for your team to maximize its potential and create a road map to make it happen. Remember – if you don't know where you are going any road will take you there. As Stephen Covey said, "Start with the end in mind." What is it you want?

2. Set Goals:

We all know that setting goals is important. The problem is that you write them down at the beginning of a new year, a new process, a new position in a workshop and you plan to commit to them. The paper goes in a file somewhere and eventually they are no longer driving your daily tasks and decisions. Not only do your goals, as well as those for your organization and team need to be posted and revisited frequently, but they also need to be measurable. As Peter Drucker, the father of modern management said, "What gets measured, gets done."

When setting goals think of the acronym, SMART. Goals need to be Specific, Measurable, Attainable, Relevant and they need to have a Time frame. It is also important to have your employees assist in the goal setting. Sit down with them individually – not only to get their opinions of just the goals but also the roadmap they will use to achieve those goals. Not only will employees feel more valued but they will also have more personal commitment into the program you are trying to establish.

A large manufacturing plant was set to be closed if it did not quickly improve its performance and safety record. This particular plant was the lowest performing plant in the company and the board could not see investing millions of dollars into a failing facility. As a last effort, the leadership team of the poorly performing plant came together and identified 22 processes that they needed to improve or change. They posted these items on the cafeteria walls and charted the progress each department was making towards it goals. As a result, the employees knew exactly what was expected and they could easily see how close (or far) they were from the goal they needed to accomplish. It sounds simple and obvious, but again this part of goal setting is often overlooked. Two years later, the plant was awarded not only the Occupational Safety Award for having no accidents, but they were one of the top performers nationally.

3. Expectations:

People will live up or down to the perception of your expectations of them. If they think you believe in their abilities and expect them to do well, they will. One of the best ways to establish and communicate clear expectations is to "level the playing field." I use this technique with every new hire and group that I have been asked to lead. I start by asking the group or individual what they expect of me? Don't be surprised if you get blank stares. With encouragement you will get some honest feedback as to what people expect of a boss. After I agree to do the things they requested, I ask them, "What should I expect of you?" Again silence but prompt them as necessary and you should hear pleasing responses. Now you have a contract that you developed together that outlines what is expected and has started to develop the culture that you desire for group behavior. Do this with each department or team that you work with. By establishing your group expectations early on, you set the bar for how the team works together and performs.

4. Feedback and Recognition:

Feedback is craved by high performers; do it a lot. In fact, in looking at the millennial generation, surveys show not only is feedback one of the top five desires for these employees, but also, this "I want it now" generation wants the feedback as soon as possible. The more feedback you can provide, both positive and constructive, the better.

Another important aspect of motivating your team is to "catch them doing it right!" If I say to you, "Great job at the meeting this morning, but the spreadsheet is screwed up." What would you remember? Most of us would remember what area we screwed up and forget what the positive we did well. We, as humans, are wired to more readily accept negative feedback. A lesson to take from this biology is when giving feedback, separate the two events in time so the positive event can be remembered. Catch and comment on your people doing right, and they will do more of the right things.

Also let your employees know, often, that you value them and the job that they do. Help them to see that positive results for the group or the company have a direct correlation to their efforts. Try saying, "I value you and the job that you do every day. In fact, without you doing what you do and being part of this team, we would not have the positive results that we do." And watch their facial expressions change.

5. Treat everybody fairly but not equally:

The people you work with are all unique individuals, and although you need to treat each one fairly, that does not necessarily mean equally. They have different values, wants, backgrounds, skillsets, experience and most likely are at different stages of their careers.

One size fits nobody.

Great managers play chess; average managers play checkers. In checkers all of the pieces move in the same direction. In chess, all of the pieces move differently and the key to success is knowing the differences between the pieces, how each piece moves and how to create a strategy that maximizes the moves for all of the pieces.

Another key piece of the puzzle is showing your team that you genuinely care about them. They need to know you have their interest at heart, people want to know that someone at work cares about them as a person.

The demonstration that you care gets to the heart of good management; if your people believe that you truly care about them, to a person they will walk through fire for you. On the other hand, if your people see you as treating them as a stepping stone to get what you want or just as a part of the process to drive profit, they will not be engaged or willing go above and beyond for you or the organization.

People who know you are compassionate and care are significantly more likely to stay with an organization. Bottom line is they can trust you. One of the hardest things to get back when it is lost is the trust of the people you work with. When I speak to groups or teams in organizations and I talk about trust, everyone shakes their head to the affirmative. Everybody agrees it is important, but can be hard to establish, especially if you are trying to be trusted quickly. Most likely your team members have previously been in organizations where trust did not exist. You can see it and you can feel it. Don't lose the trust of your people; about the worst thing that can happen to a manager is to lose the trust of his or her people. This is your bond – the glue that holds your organization or people together. Trust might be the do or die foundation of leading.

6. Provide tools and resources to do quality work:
Most people don't wake up in the morning and say to themselves, I think I will go to work today and do a bad job. Most people want to do quality work. Part of that is having the tools and resources to do a quality job. Ask your people what can you do to make your job

easier? (Reaffirming your commitment and caring to them.) If they say I need a new widget maker, well get them a new widget maker. If they say they don't need anything, your response is – "I guess I can expect quality work." You want to take away any and all reasons people can conjure up for failure. You only leave a path to success.

7. Celebrate successes:

What do organizations do when they accomplish a big thing? Well, they move on to the next "big" thing. It is important to stop and celebrate with your teams. Allow people to share the memory of what has been accomplished. Simple things like handwritten notes are important too. Write notes to your people, yes the old fashioned hand-written notes, saying thank for what they did and how their contribution lead to the overall achievement of the group. They might even post them on the wall of their work space, on their desk or possibly even on the family refrigerator! Elaborate parties are nice, but simply stopping the day or work process to say thank you with a pat on the shoulder will do miracles as well. The simple gestures are less expensive and require much less time so they can be given more frequently. These small, quick forms of recognition not only help you to keep your team motivated, but they also give the message that they are valued and appreciated.

I asked the question earlier in this chapter, how are you going to be remembered? You are going to be remembered one way or other. When you follow the steps outlined in this chapter you very well may be remembered as The Manager People Don't Want to Leave.

About Jan

Jan Makela has a long and successful history of making a difference wherever he has been. He has held a number of senior level positions in the military and private sector organizations. His background includes a solid track record of having profitably managed and grown business units, including two de novo regional offices, as well as having successfully led the turnaround of a troubled business unit. He has worked with companies of all sizes, including start-ups, and is occasionally sought out for strategic advice by senior executives and business owners. Jan is a Gallup-Certified Strengths & Workforce Solution Consultant as well as a nationally certified trainer in behavioral-based interviewing to ensure quality hires, and a trained manager in how to get and keep quality people.

He has additional experience in building sales teams, restructuring and sales force design and has managed the operations of sales forces of greater than 600 people. Jan's additional experience includes sales cycle management, sales forecasting, incentive compensation planning, as well as sales management training for both new and experienced managers.

In addition, Jan works with clients and discovering their strengths, he travels the country conducting seminars on a variety of topics including Human Resource Law, Employee Accountability, and Being the Manager People Won't Leave.

Jan is a volunteer for the SCORE organization under the Small Business Administration where he mentors 'for profit' and non-profit small business startups or struggling organizations to flourish in their endeavors.

Utilizing his strengths and extensive business experience, Jan provides valuable guidance and insight to his clients, working purposefully to assist his clients to maximize their potential and achieve their goals in order to enjoy success and fulfillment both in their professional careers and personal lives. His specialty is strength-based leadership development with a particular focus on working with senior (CEO, COO, and CFO) and mid-level executives, business owners, and professionals. He will work with companies of any size with no specific industry focus.

His promise to his clients is:

Everyone has the ability to be great at something. The trick is finding that something. I promise I will help you find your something. Engaged employees are more productive and want to contribute to the organization's success, which in turn leads to increased job performance and personal satisfaction.

Jan can be reached at:
- jlmakela@gmail.com
- strengthbasedleadership.net
- Linkedin@jlmakela
- twitter@JLMakela

CHAPTER 27

SUCCEED ON PURPOSE

BY JESSICA KUNWAR

Whatever the mind can conceive and believe, the mind can achieve.
~ Napoleon Hill

Your thoughts have measurable frequencies.

What makes this statement significant, and how can the comprehension of this simple concept help you create your ideal life?

The answer to this question will appear on these pages, but first, let us together embark on a short, but deliberate, journey; to attain the most from this expedition, be sure your mind is focused and you are engaged fully. Take a moment after each sentence to ensure that we are still walking in unison and that our steps are properly synchronized.

Let's begin.

Imagine you live a life of passion and productivity. Imagine your every aspiration seamlessly manifests itself into your reality as if by pure magic. Now imagine that all of your dreams have transcribed themselves as memories in the book that is your life—no longer are these desires things to be attained in your future; rather, you have already lived them in your past and are currently harvesting them in your present. Each and every moment of your life is dedicated to the fulfillment of the cravings of your own heart. Imagine you are the very epitome of a successful human being—you enjoy liberties and luxuries that would make fairytales jealous, and your achievements have become things of legend. What does this life of yours look like? How does it feel? What amazing feats have you accomplished? Who are you?

Now, what if I told you that by simply imagining this life, you have already sanctioned its construction? You have just taken the first step, and with it, your thousand-mile journey has already begun.

A MAP TO AID YOUR JOURNEY

As is the case of exploring any new territory, it is always helpful to have access to a map to aid your journey. But as is true of any such map, it is only useful insofar as you are able to understand its contents. For this, all proficient maps include both a legend to assist you in deciphering what might otherwise be deemed as incomprehensible and a scale by which you can then accurately judge the real territory.

Scale

Let us begin then by defining the scale by which this map is represented. By revisiting the opening statement of this chapter, you will find that the scale we are utilizing would be considered by many to be too small to be effective for such an ambitious map. After all, how can we use thoughts, things we cannot even see, as appropriate measures for the journey of a lifetime?

In addition to the aforementioned elements, there is one more vital component that is the single determining factor establishing whether or not you will even attempt to follow the map in your possession. Your willingness to employ any given map will always be contingent upon the degree of faith you hold in the mapmaker and your confidence in his/her stated prescriptions.

Let us commit then, for the purposes of this conversation, to accept as fact the assumptions given herein. If any of the concepts described within these pages feel to you as if they are expanding your horizons, that is exactly what they are designed to do. After all, what good is a journey that fails to help you grow?

Now that we have established that thoughts have a measurable frequency (something that is easily verifiable by contemporary scientific research), let us delve a little bit deeper. Everything we know of our universe is comprised of a single element—energy. Thoughts, by extension, are merely energy in one of its countless forms. The complex relationship between energy and frequency is made far simpler when we realize that the greater the energy, the higher the frequency (and therefore the smaller the wavelength). When we apply this understanding to thoughts, we can see that the stronger the thoughts (and the more intently that we are thinking them), the higher the frequency of those thoughts and the smaller their wavelength. To put this simply, when you think a thought—namely an affirmative thought—with a high intensity (something you can easily gauge by the intensity of your emotions while thinking said thought), that same thought shows up in your mind more often (with higher frequency) and reappears at shorter intervals (with a smaller wavelength). When we couple this with Einstein's equation for special relativity ($E=mc^2$, where E equals Kinetic Energy, or the energy of a moving object; m equals mass; and c equals the speed of light), we can finally make sense of the renowned proclamation that "thoughts are things!" Although a complete explanation of this concept is beyond the scope of our current discussion, it is nevertheless worth holding in your mind as our present journey continues.

Legend

Given the unorthodox nature of our map (considering that it points the way to a successful life of your own making as opposed to a literal treasure chest), we will create our legend to be congruent with the map it has the burden of defining. Although the following are relayed without any hierarchical order, each of the following should be bestowed with equal importance, as they are all pieces of the same puzzle.

DEFINE SUCCESS

Success might mean something different to different people. Although we are all human beings, there is something unique in every single one of us. Think back to our exercise at the very beginning of this chapter (when you inadvertently created the "map" of your ideal life) and remember to hold the experiences you created in your mind as you continue down this path. Should you feel the need to revisit the exercise for greater impact, now would be the perfect time to do so.

INTENTION

It should be anything but surprising that intention is an integral ingredient for success. Without the intention to accomplish any given goal, your ability to meet your objective with any kind of efficiency is greatly diminished. To aid in this process, before commencing any excursion, decide what you would like to gain from your endeavors. What is your intention for your journey?

ACTION

Intention without action is like a cookbook—it can make your mouth water, but it can never fulfill your appetite. You can be handed the most intelligible roadmap known to the capabilities of mankind, and you may well admire the craftsmanship of its maker, but if you choose to let it lay around collecting dust, you will have rendered it utterly useless.

COMMITMENT

Nothing noteworthy can ever be accomplished without commitment—nothing magnificent can ever be stopped with it. If you are 99% sure about something, you will always have that 1% nagging at you, making you second-guess your decisions, bombarding you with "what ifs," and controlling your life by keeping you looped in insecurities and uncertainties. If you find it hard to believe that 1% can really make any considerable difference, consider the wealth distribution of the world as it currently stands: 1% of the world's population currently controls over half of its wealth. The moment, however, that you are 100% committed to doing something, it becomes the simplest feat in the world.

CONVICTION

Always remember, a single person with conviction is a majority. Never allow the limitations that others have imposed upon themselves to determine what you are willing or able to do. Once you lead the way, others will follow.

FORGIVE RELENTLESSLY

One of the top two things keeping people from attaining their true potentials is all of the extra baggage they carry with themselves on a daily basis. Whether you are carrying a grudge against someone else or are engaging in negative self-talk for a mistake you feel you have made or even experiencing elevated anxiety stemming from your own lack of action, it is time to forgive everything and everyone—including yourself. The moment you truly do this, you will experience a sense of liberation unlike anything you have ever felt before—and it truly will give you wings.

YOU ARE ENOUGH

The other of the two things that keeps people from being successful is the belief that they are lacking in some way. If you have an ambition, never believe the voices saying you are not smart enough, fast enough, pretty enough, competent enough, outgoing enough, charismatic enough, healthy enough, accomplished enough—even, and especially, if those voices are your own. You absolutely are enough. You are enough to be, have, and do anything and everything you put your mind to. Know this, and then trust yourself—this is your life and you already know how to make it exactly what you want it to be.

BE VALUABLE

Far too many people focus primarily upon hoarding monetary wealth. While money is an incredible tool with which one can build almost anything else to which (s)he puts her/his mind, it should never become one's absolute goal. The amount of wealth one controls should be directly proportionate to the amount of value he/she contributes to the world. If you focus on getting more money, not only will you likely miss out on other priceless riches life has to offer, but you also will never quite have enough. If you focus instead upon adding value to the world, you will gain wealth in all areas of your life and will command greater abundance than you ever thought possible.

GIVE CREDIT

Give credit not only where it is due, but also whenever it is possible. Recognize the interdependence of our world; as Carl Sagan aptly put it, "if you wish to make an apple pie from scratch, you must first create the universe." Be grateful for and appreciative of absolutely everything. And never let your own arrogance hinder your success. You will find that the more you acknowledge the efforts of others, the more your own excellence will also be commended.

STOP HIDING

You owe it to both yourself and the world to be the absolute best version of yourself that you can possibly be. There is absolutely nobody else in the world with your exact capabilities and therefore no one can add the value that you can add to the planet. Every single person in existence is a resource—including you; and by keeping yourself shielded from the world, you are depriving the rest of humankind of everything you have to offer. It is true that alone, each of us can maybe elevate the lives of tens, or hundreds, or thousands of individuals...but there are billions of people in the world and the only way we can impact the lives of the global community of billions is by playing out each of our respective roles. Never allow yourself to believe you are too small to make a difference. You are necessary.

WHAT'S NEXT?

Throughout our lives we are faced with countless choices; because every decision opens up avenues to a unique set of opportunities, each choice becomes life altering.

As humans, we too often let our fears, insecurities, and the reservations of others keep us from taking the path that is calling out to us. We choose to stay in familiar places thinking, "at least there is stability here;" but ask yourself this: is this truly what you want your life to be? Are you merely a mirror to the limitations of your environment? Or are you ready to let your life become a reflection of the You that you have kept tucked away for so long?

> Pen your own ambitions;
> Follow your own dreams;
> Release your reservations;
> And define what your life means.

You already know that all the magic begins where your comfort zone ends. So tell me…are you ready for some *magic?*

LET THE JOURNEY CONTINUE...

If you walk away today with only one lesson engrained in your mind, let it be this: **You. Are. Enough.**

> *Watch your thoughts; they become words.*
> *Watch your words; they become actions.*
> *Watch your actions; they become habits.*
> *Watch your habits; they become character.*
> *Watch your character; it becomes your destiny.*
> ~ Frank Outlaw

About Jessica

Jessica Kunwar was born to a family of entrepreneurs and has been involved in business since the ripe age of four. Her experience spans various industries and she has more experience than many twice or even three times her age. Jessica's knowledge base transcends generations and cultures alike. For all of this, she credits her parents.

Jessica studied Communications, Sociology with a legal emphasis, and Global Studies at the University of California, Davis and has since gone on to start a number of her own businesses in various parts of the country (also spanning multiple industries) and manage many others.

Jessica believes that individuals and businesses alike should embody three primary principles; according to Jessica, they should be 1) humble in thought; 2) noble in action; and 3) limitless in achievement. In fact, one of Jessica's business enterprises is called HNL, Inc., the full form of which is Humble. Noble. Limitless.

Jessica Kunwar is what can only be described as a, or rather, the mystic entrepreneur— she is somehow not only capable, but also enigmatically skilled, at taking the most abstract of philosophical concepts and masterfully translating them into real-world applications for her students and clients alike. She uses her perfect command of these two seemingly paradoxical forces to first understand the depth and breadth of one's problems and limiting beliefs and then ingeniously design a "success playbook" which she creates specifically for that individual. If you've ever wished your life came with a manual, now it can.

You can connect with Jessica at:
- www.JessicaKunwar.com
- www.FaceBook.com/jessicakunwar3
- www.limitless0527.tumblr.com
- www.instagram.com/limitless0527
- SnapChat ID: limitless0589

CHAPTER 28

WELCOME TO THE ELITE
THE AUTHENTICALLY "YOU" BRAND

BY KARINA OCHIS

Life is beautiful when you know how to live well; you must first understand it and then relentlessly live it.
~ A philosophy of Karina Ochis

The term "branding" is prevalent in today's world, but is seldom implemented in an authentic manner. Branding must be focused, meaningful, while presenting a precise set of events. In my life, I have refined and finessed the art of branding, helping individuals create an elite brand for themselves – one that is true to them, larger than life, and results driven.

Elite branding differs from other types of branding, much like an Olympian is different from a novice athlete. Being elite requires many things – each one representing an important sequence of the whole and final picture. When achieved, it results in effortless simplicity that reveals a person's fullest potential.

This chapter offers an overview of the initial phases of branding yourself at an elite level, whether you incorporate the help of a Brand Master or not. It is an introduction to the whole process. The process, in itself, is a lifelong one requiring an intricate growth strategy that is built on a stable base. Challenging adjustments may also be necessary, such as editing your entourage, your habits, and your overall manner of conducting your daily affairs, business, and life.

Proper branding gives direction and insight. As a Brand Master, together with my team, we help individuals with the process. My results-oriented process is called KO by Karina Ochis. Be mindful that elite branding is an action verb, a mindset where passivity is unwelcomed. It only stops growing when you are unwilling to continue vesting into growing it. Our inner self must be reflected in our outward brand.

ANALYZING YOUR ELITE BRAND OBJECTIVE

Fine living implies fully grasping the concepts of time and space. There is a right time and space to fulfill any dream and there is definitely not a time and space to do so. Calculating the fine line between the two is one's greatest mission. Thus, one must be both creative and rational to master the act of 'living'.
~ A philosophy of Karina Ochis

Your journey begins with reflection and with the purpose to create a vision. This is the stepping stone of your journey, as well as the cornerstone of your personal foundation. Visions are more than random dissipated thoughts about a lovely and vibrant future that may or may never come true. I challenge you to view a vision in a more profound way: a way of living that is based on concrete ideas which are rooted in elaborate thought processes. Most importantly, a clear vision allows you to remain steadfast against being impacted by external circumstances and by the non-beneficial ideas of other people that are beyond your control.

Look at your life. Envision where you want to go. Would it be helpful to lay out a course of action that grew into what you saw for your life? You can do this, and I help people reach this place and appreciate the hard work it takes. I have been on this journey. The wisdom I can offer for this essential process is to embrace your most creative and intimate side. After that, we apply pure logic to the process.

Step 1: Analysis
It takes a great deal of analysis to create a profound and compelling vision – not just a few days' time, but rather several weeks. You must understand what your current life situation and branding reflects. This is the moment when you face reality.

You must see things as they are—not worse and not better. Who are you? What do you like and dislike? What are your strengths and weaknesses? What are you willing to give up so you can achieve your dream, if you have a dream? The more in-depth you go, the better your analysis becomes.

Next, you must do something tough—analyze your past. What events marked the course of your life? What were your reactions? During this process, if my clients want to, I guide them to various psychological tests that help them to determine their personality type, the way that they learn (spatial, linguistic, or kinesthetic), how they work, etcetera.

You must know yourself in order to begin. When this is complete you begin analyzing your brand objectively. What do your hobbies, friends, clothes, and manner of speaking exhibit? What does the way you treat others say about you? How do you portray yourself with answering calls, conducting meetings, writing e-mails, and posting on social media? Encourage feedback from honest friends. Embrace this process, for it is essential to begin with factual information and interpretations of who you really are.

Step 2: The Conceptualization
What do you want in life? Your brand is a fusion of your business and your life. There is no separation of the two, so figuring out your life is a prerequisite.

To begin, read books and study many areas of interest to help you identify what truly resonates with you. To become elite, you must be fearless in learning as much as possible. When it comes to your psychological base and understanding, embrace time tested books such as: *The 7 Habits of Highly Effective People, Stairway to Success, Think and Grow Rich, The Social Animal, Thinking Fast and Slow, The Power of Habit, Secrets of Success*, etc.

Step 3: The Plan
Planning is complex, and it involves making calculations that only you can determine. It requires foresight at the right moments for developing your brand.

You need clear limits of what you can and cannot do. Awareness allows the opportunity to take advantage of every moment and includes:

- Envisioning exiting from situations you foresee as unfavorable
- Calculating risks of a situation prior to the opportunity
- Determining short-term focus strategies that enable stability and quick wins

Finally, review your plan monthly. There are wonderful planning tools on the market to choose from. An example is The RPM Method from Anthony Robbins, a results-focused, purpose-driven, massive action plan. Some of my clients research a plan management product that may be beneficial, or else we come up with an evaluation process that works for them, given their circumstances and objectives.

IMPLEMENTING YOUR ELITE BRAND

The right implementation involves creating an ensemble of yourself as a 'real person', your business, and your brand. Every part must be synchronized with the others.
~ A philosophy of Karina Ochis

Analysis is not enough and cannot attract success without proper implementation of the knowledge. Through collaborative efforts with clients, I help them do what is necessary to establish their elite brand. It may involve helping them with social skills, challenges, outward image, internal growth, and overall strategies for success. Everything must be constructed with willful intention.

Step 1: Construct Your "Offline" Brand
"Wannabe" is not an acceptable term for someone striving to become elite. There must be a shift away from it and toward "to be." It is a logical progression since the basis of your brand is "the real you." By this point, you have constructed a brand built on clear elite principles that will be present in everything you do.

Being natural is part of the basics of establishing this. Fake and trendy never come across as elite, and every trend is not meant for you to participate in. Actually, it will perish in front of a natural state of being. Be mindful that a healthy mind and a healthy body are one and the same. One must take care of his/her body in order to best take care of their mind.

Being elite and eloquent means finding styles, shapes, fabrics, and colors that work for you and be consistent with them throughout the process. Mostly, timeless, classic styles that do not date you will be of help. The authentic elite never forces anything. This person:

- Cautiously chooses the actions and activities they partake in, always performing actions completely and fully
- Is dedicated to developing their minds and reads broadly
- Understands that it is better to lose financially than to jeopardize their reputation
- Embraces that they are their biggest asset
- Recognizes their value and will not make long-term compromises for short-term gains
- Has clear daily habits, including morning and evening routines
- Moves with grace
- Exudes confidence
- Acts and is stress-free
- Gets enough rest

The offline brand also includes your mannerisms, hobbies, and your places of socialization. Determine where you want to be and research what you must do to create these opportunities. Start a club, go hiking, channel inner peace with meditation, join sports leagues, try race car driving, navigate a yacht, or even travel the world. Pursue your interests and the interests of those in the social circles you wish to enter.

If you desire globalization, you must first focus on becoming regionally recognized. You will need to learn strategies to gain expertise and recognition in your current domain. While establishing this presence, begin researching the cultures you wish to immerse in, so you understand them in great detail. This makes the integration process easier when it presents itself.

Step 2: Harnessing Human Capital
Your business must fit your personality. Only after you have cautiously chosen and implemented the basics in your domain can

you dedicate yourself to brand-building. You must look for people who share the same vision as you.

Visualize the team you need to create your results and find people who already did what you want to do. Analyze their process and progress and implement what is aligned with you. See if these people can become your mentors, coaches, or teachers. Embrace what they have to offer, as it is a powerful aid in your transition to an elite brand.

Step 3: Constructing the "Digital" Brand

Digital branding is where your business and personal identity merge. This means it is essential to be aware of how you represent yourself to the digital audience—always.

Your first action is challenging and often time consuming. You must edit all the existing information about you on the internet. If you cannot edit it, create a "crisis plan" in case unfavorable information ever gets out. This means that your PR and team must be aware of any potentially unfavorable images from your past so they can be prepared to act quickly in managing any events. Nobody accepts that certain pieces of information will hurt them, until they "get out" and do.

Next, share what you are doing. This is the soft branding process: a simple presentation website, a post related to your activity, a share from an influencer in your domain. This increases "value driven" content while decreasing what is less favorable or related to your past. The implementation of this can begin whilst you are constructing your business systems and harnessing your human capital. It is the prerequisite phase before the "brand boom", which is the moment you inform your digital audience what you are doing, including gaining a level of comfort in front of a camera through tests of what works for you and what does not. Your brand transformation should be apparent at this point.

Begin studying the manners of communication of influencers in your field and emulate what you can. Observe the language, style of debate, and various positions that emerge in those conversations to extract a direction for you to take. Prepare mood boards for your persona and scenarios: what will you support online? What topics do you talk about? What will interest your audience?

Prepare a personal logo, an elaborate website that contains your life story, and use professional photographs—this is a must. Keep in mind that you will constantly edit your online image but the core will remain the same.

As you rebuild your social media presence in the elite branded image, make sure your team has clear and precise instructions in regards to your real time posts, as they must be of the highest quality. This includes images and word choice, as well as message relayed. No photographs of you in altered states or in suspect situations. No rants that make it appear that you are unraveled or anything less than composed and graceful under fire. You have worked hard to establish your elite brand and it cannot be unrepresentative of your plans, goals, and persona.

Now you are exuding the energy of an individual with an elite brand and your natural existence within your environment is unavoidable to notice.

FIND YOUR ELITE BRAND

The formula for becoming elite can be achieved by anyone—in any circumstances—when they become dedicated to the mastery of it.
~ A philosophy of Karina Ochis

Your basic overview of establishing an elite brand is only the beginning of this journey. The process is intensive and represents a lifelong commitment to your own personal excellence. You are required to extract your best qualities and use them, as well as adjust the habits and patterns that do not serve your best interests. Establishing your elite brand is not easy work, it is challenging work that is made smoother by the use of a Brand Master. KO by Karina Ochis is the guide that will hold you accountable when necessary, take action when required, and learn what is involved in the intensive process of being assured and self-aware of your every move and action, and what that represents.

Only the individual who is willing to go through intense self-analysis that leads to significant implementation of change can become an elite brand. Everything from editing your social circles to your social media is involved. Implementations of precise strategies that are designed with a specific purpose in mind for your enrichment are always in motion. This new state of being never takes a break or a vacation, as it is a part of you. The rewards that come through these intensive efforts are notable, however, involving a new level of awareness that leads to success in all facets of your life. You will begin living in a constant state of high performance.

Treat this introduction not as a new chapter in your life, but as a new book. You now have a real means to start making your life a masterpiece. Whether you decide to undertake this process with the help of professionals, alone, or even at all, is up to you. However, you cannot use the "I do not know where to start" excuse anymore for not reaching your true potential.

About Karina

Karina Ochis is the CEO and Brand Master at KO by Karina Ochis, and Founder of Ana Karina Luxury Concept. Karina is a serial entrepreneur, investor, published author and concept strategist and speaker who travels the world in a relentless quest for life mastery and successful ventures whilst 'building her empire' and running several businesses.

KO by Karina Ochis, is the next-generation branding company. Through elite consulting and high-end digital services, clients are provided with luxury products for brand management. The team of devoted professionals collaborate in providing a complete and discreet service that is time-effective, quality and client-oriented. (www.kobykarinaochis.com).

Ana Karina Luxury Concept offers leading solutions and services for a superior lifestyle, aiming to one day revolutionize Romanian tourism. It comprises of elite business concepts, brands, and structures as well as an auxiliary luxury line of high-end merchandise.

The life of a serial entrepreneur always appealed to Karina. The visionary businesswoman with studies in cross-disciplines such as Politics, Marketing and E-commerce (London School of Economics), Karina naturally gravitated towards the intricate art of branding after envisioning her own pathway to success. Already a speaker, certified trainer and acclaimed artist, Karina entered the business world at only 19 years old with a 'bang' – being personally coached in business by JT Foxx (World's #1 Wealth Coach) and counselled by George Ross (Donald Trump's right hand man) who recognised her unique entrepreneurial flair. Collaborating with world authorities such as Lady Mone (UK's leading female entrepreneur) and Wayne Allyn Root (US vice-presidential candidate), she became the personal branding 'it girl', now running KO by Karina Ochis. She is currently the Producer and Host of Karina's Branding Biz. Club aired on YouTube, where she analyses famous personal brands.

Karina studied and finessed the art of branding, helping individuals create an elite brand—one that is true to them, larger than life, and results driven. She is currently writing *Welcome to the Elite* – the three-volume prophecy, comprising extensive cross-disciplinary studies on branding, interlinked with self-development, together with her forthcoming algorithms of creation and execution in real life.

Whilst branding herself, Karina adopted a complete mind and body transformation. The experience led Karina to found Ana Karina Luxury Concept inaugurated with Elite Life Beauty and Wellbeing Spa, in Karina's hometown (http://eliteliferesort.com/ and http://www.hotel-elite.ro/spa/), an urban escape that promotes a healthier lifestyle.

Karina wishes to develop Romanian tourism, the reason why she returned to her native country, whilst implementing her branding expertise and implementing successful ventures world-wide.

Karina, an international speaker, offers content on Branding, Marketing, Entrepreneurship, Lifestyle Design and Strategy. Living by her tagline -- 'redesigning success', Karina has been speaking in front of hundreds of professionals around the USA and Europe whilst mentoring a select network of unique individuals. A graduate from the prestigious Coach Training School of Anthony Robbins – World's Leading Life Coach, Karina coaches and consults at group and individual levels and is a constant catalyst for lasting change and self-development.

Contact Karina at:
- www.karinaochis.com
- email: karina@karinaochis.com.

CHAPTER 29

THE FENG SHUI OF "THINKING BIG"

BY DR. LINJIE CHOU

Throughout my career as a public relations strategist, I have had the privilege of meeting and working with some of the greatest leaders and extraordinary public figures all around the world, from Shanghai to Monaco, Geneva to Beverly Hills, and almost everywhere else in between. In working with this elite group of achievers, I have discovered that they possess specific qualities that make it possible for them to accomplish their goals. It's not their bank accounts and it's not luck. The main factor that sets these superstars and world figures apart from average folks is how they think. They understand the relationship between the 'idea' and 'reality' and how to bridge that gap to achieve success. So how do they think?

THEY THINK BIG

Thinking big is the key to success. This is true whether you are training to win an Olympic gold medal, auditioning for a major Hollywood role, or campaigning for a high-ranking political position. Thinking big is a frame of mind that is based on two fundamental conditions that must be present in order for you to be successful.

The first condition is visualizing success before it happens – picturing it and finding the right energy flow to carry the idea to reality. The second is location, location, location – ensuring you are in the right place and that your network is established and in place to help you achieve your goal. These are the two main principles that allow people who Think Big to succeed, while others simply believe it's all about 'luck' or 'being in the right place at the right time' and therefore never truly believe they can achieve what their heart desires.

What many don't realize is that the person who succeeds in winning the major role in a movie, or the political candidate who is elected to office, visualized their success and ensured that they were in the right place at the right time. They didn't sit back and wait for luck. They created their own reality by Thinking Big.

Feng Shui is an ancient Chinese philosophy that seeks to harmonize people with their environment. This is often adapted to suit a variety of applications, such as in the placement of furniture in a room to create the right energy flow. The same principle applies to Thinking Big – harmonizing one's dreams and goals with the right energy flow to make achieving success a reality. This is the Feng Shui of Thinking Big.

Principle One: Visualizing Success and Finding the Right Energy Flow

What distinguishes a highly successful individual from the average Joe? The successful individual believes that anything is possible provided he (or she) sets the right energy in motion, while the average Joe is only able to believe in what he (or she) can see or touch. The successful individual has dreams that are open to the challenges and moments of mystery. Dreams are related to reality, and all reality must first come from the creation of an initial idea. This is why dreaming big collects the height of energy to create the initial "thought" or blue print of the reality. The average Joe is skeptical of the possibilities that exist beyond their own backyard and therefore never truly follow their dreams and work towards achieving them.

Visualizing one's success is important – picturing yourself enjoying the success of reaching your goal is the first step to ever achieving that goal. This is the reason why many people who have accomplished great things in their lives are referred to as visionaries. They literally envision the success of their idea right from the beginning. Picturing the success in your mind is the first step to setting the right energy in motion – you are sending out the vision of success into the universe for the universe to set into motion as reality.

How do we put the right energy in motion?

We must understand energy to understand how we can use it to Think Big. In terms of physics, energy is something that an object possesses that can be transferred or converted into another form. Thinking Big involves taking one's idea, and with the right flow of energy, converting it into reality.

What does this mean? We have all heard the expression, "Think positive!" The truth is that thinking positive is the equivalent of sending out positive energy – and, as we know from physics, energy can be transferred or converted into another form. Therefore, sending out the right energy is likely to attract positive things and successes in your life.

The very nature of our universe is such that it records the amount of positive energy that you send out. The amount of positive energy that you send out will eventually come back to you – it's one of the laws of our universe. If you spend your time thinking of all the reasons that you can't possibly achieve your goals you are creating a negative reality that will block the positive energy flow. Negative thinking is the thought process of the average Joe. It needs to be eliminated to make way for a positive energy flow.

The speed of energy determines the speed at which you will achieve success. Your passion and the energy burning in your mind is what will propel you to reach the heights you desire. This is not some hocus-pocus theory. Major governments around the world are trying to accelerate their own national interests by researching and discovering metaphysical energy, through competitions in Hadron Collider machine construction.

Hadron Collider aims to find the vortex of atoms in their past, present, and future forms. By accelerating the speed of light, Hadron Collider hopes to find the height of energy. This may sound like science fiction, but the truth is that energy or invisible forces guide our very existence.

Thinking Big with this kind of focus purifies your energy.

If scientists and governments are able to realize that by focusing energy they can potentially reach new heights that may have unknown benefits to mankind and our planet and beyond, then individuals should realize that focusing energy can help them accomplish great things in their own lives as well.

Focusing energy within each of us, and using that energy to better our lives is not a new idea or philosophy. Ancient Chinese wisdom calls our vital life force energy the "Chi." Hindis call it the "Chakra." These ancient wisdoms have long known that energy determines our passions and souls. That's the true calling of our desire to make things happen. Every person has their own calling, and it doesn't necessarily correspond to their role in reality. Unfortunately, most people do not know how to use energy to discover and embrace their true calling.

Steve Jobs was one of the past century's most influential and accomplished visionaries and creative geniuses. His famous quote: "Making a dent in the universe" really signifies what energy means. Being successful is not merely striving for fame, and money and material success – it is being able to create a legacy. A legacy is what sets someone apart – creating a new reality – one that has the potential to carry on beyond the realm of what was once thought possible.

The word "legacy" is derived from the Latin word "Legotum," which literally translates to "I mean" or "I choose." Aiming to create a system or a solution that no one has done before in your industry, or offering services never dreamed of before, will set you apart from the crowd. This can be accomplished by focusing one's energy into a positive flow that will help create the reality you desire.

In terms of Thinking Big, setting the right energy in motion and finding the right energy flow must be accomplished in order to achieve success. But in order to obtain true success you must combine this first principle – visualizing success and finding the right energy flow – with the second principle: Location, location, location.

Principle Two: Location, Location, Location

Similar to what you were likely taught in your college foundational course Business 101, Thinking Big involves surrounding yourself with the right people, resources, and opportunities that will ensure your success. Being in the right location is critical – it puts you in the centre of the right people, resources, and opportunities that will allow you to set the right energy in motion to achieve your goals.

The right location for the goals of an actress is going to be very different from the right location for an archaeologist. Where you need to be is going to depend on the industry in which you desire success. For many this will require relocating to a new city, state, or even country.

While relocating can be scary, it is often necessary for success. It is a known fact that relocating is considered to be one of life's biggest stressors. New friends, new daily acquaintances, and a new home – all of these require some adjustment. But the relocation itself is small in comparison to the payoff.

Consider these following celebrities and other public figures that would have likely never succeeded in their fields if they had stayed in their hometowns and continued to 'dream' of making it big.

Jennifer Lawrence: She convinced her family that moving to Los Angeles from Kentucky when she was only 14 was necessary. Imagine what she would be doing if she had kept quiet and not followed her dream?

Taylor Swift: Although already writing songs and doing theatre in Pennsylvania, her family relocated to Tennessee to allow Taylor the opportunity to fulfil her dreams.

The Hemsworth brothers: Chris, Luke, and Liam Hemsworth were living in Australia when the family decided to move to the U.S. to follow their dreams of acting. It paid off for all three brothers.

Jerry Yang: He moved from Taipei, Taiwan, to attend Stanford, where he graduated in 1990. In 1995 he started Yahoo. His net worth when he stepped down was over $1.15 billion.

Vinod Dham: He moved from Pune, India to the U.S. in 1975 where he arrived with only $8 to his name. He graduated from university and worked for Intel, eventually inventing the company's first flash memory stick. He was CEO of Silicon Spice when it sold for $1.2 billion.

Elie Wiesel: He wrote with very minimal success about the Holocaust after surviving Auschwitz-Birkenau during World War II. He moved to

New York City – a major publishing capital – in 1956 and went on to publish more than 40 books about the Holocaust. He went on to win the Nobel Peace Prize.

What all of these successful people discovered was that their location connected them to the right energy base. Having the social contacts and networks of those with a similar wavelength is necessary – what attracts people is energy. Max Weber, a famous sociologist, once said: "Men are social animals."

We are all directly or subtly influenced by the people around us.

One of the top Chinese billionaires once told me: "If you hang out with ten successful people you are likely to be the eleventh." Mingling yourself into the right social network is therefore more about the support of energy rather than the opportunities. But with this support of energy also comes opportunities…

Successful people tend to have more big thoughts and are less skeptical of achieving the 'impossible": their energies are what can influence you. Success does not come easily – you have to be willing to step out of your comfort zone – this is something that all successful people share in common.

Nine-to-five folks on the other hand saturate their minds with questions of: "What if?" They don't see their life integrated with their work, while successful individuals see their work as their passion – and it is the passion that is integrated into their work and their lives. Settling on an average location negatively influences your attitude and your life because you are surrounded by those who cannot look beyond their nine-to-five existence.

The energy of many successful, positive-minded people can be felt in the air as you stroll down Sheikh Zayed Boulevard in Dubai or Century Avenue in Pudong, China. Even sitting down and having a cocktail inside Hotel du Paris in Monte Carlo, or sipping a cup of afternoon tea at Claridge's in London, you are touched by the positive attitude of the people around you. Often this will also lead into an engaging and mind-blowing conversation….

In essence, one can't be a true hero without a world class stage.

Location, location, location applies to much more than real estate. It is a mindset in the right location, surrounded by others with the right mindset and flow of energy. Being in the right location is what links you with the right people, resources, and opportunities that would otherwise not exist if you stayed in the wrong location.

This is the Feng Shui of Thinking Big. It is what sets the dreamers apart from the achievers. And these two principles are key to success.

If I had remained in Shanghai, I would not have built the career I have today working as a public relations strategist for some of the most successful and famous people in the world. It is my job to link my clients with the right contacts and decision makers in their fields, and it always amazes me to watch how these contacts and connections grow, often exceeding even my own expectations for success. It is a privilege to help people explore their dreams and set them on the path to help their dreams become their reality.

About Dr. Linjie

Dr. Linjie Chou Zanadu, award-winning public relation strategist, helps his clients explore their dreams in reality. He helps his clients to execute world class PR strategies and link them with the right contacts and decision makers in their respective fields around the world. Helping clients arrange from Royal purveyors to celebrity endorsements, from organising lavish balls in Europe to preparing the Premier Minister's private audience in the Asia-Pacific region, Dr. Linjie has unique solutions across all spectrums.

Brought up in a Shanghai merchant family, Linjie has travelled, studied and lived in more than a dozen of countries. From Hong Kong to Monte Carlo, from Beverly Hills to Cannes, Linjie's network expands from political lobbyists to Hollywood celebrities. He has been worked with public figures like His Royal Highness Prince Adel el Hashemite of Iraq, Pamela Anderson, Bertie Higgins, President Bai Koroma of Sierra Leone, and Gorbachev's family members. In May 2016, he received the Presidential Lifetime Achievement Award from the White House through volunteer service.

Linjie's career builds on his special talent in cross-cultural communication both academically and practically, his research has appeared in a dozen prestigious academic journals and he also is acting as guest professor at European New University - Kerkrade in the Netherlands, and Constantinian University of Rhode Island. Previously, he has given lectures at various management conferences and institutions of higher education. He has been the assistant to royalties and is currently advising on public relations for the International Civil Defence Organization in Geneva with more than 50 member nations around the world.

Linjie's commentary articles have also been appeared on the sites of NBC, FoxNews, *The Huffington Post*, *China Daily*, *Wall Street Select* and many other influential blogs.

- www.baronofxanadu.com
- https://www.facebook.com/linjiechouzanadu/

CHAPTER 30

SIX CONSIDERATIONS FOR A SUCCESSFUL BUSINESS

BY DR. MICHAEL GUEVARA

Blame it on Johnny Carson…and Marvin Hamlisch! Back around 1974, Marvin Hamlisch appeared on The Tonight Show and performed the hit piece from the recent Academy Award winning movie, "The Sting." I sat, mesmerized, as I watched Marvin perform Scott Joplin's ragtime piece, "The Entertainer." Immediately, I asked my parents if I could begin piano lessons!

Thus began my true love affair with music…and although I did not realize it at the time, my involvement within a specific niche in the music industry!

Fast forward approximately 30 years (2006), I found myself completing 20 years in the insurance industry, primarily in claims. During the last few years of my career in claims and private investigations (yes, I was a PI), I was assigned to investigate "large losses" for some major hotel/ motel chains and transportation companies.

During one of the last large loss claims I investigated, I had the opportunity to take my wife with me to the scene of an accident involving an 18-wheeler and a passenger sedan. With blood and brain matter still freshly present within the sedan, my wife and I hardly spoke a word as we drove the 2.5 hours back home after the investigation. Needless to say, we were still processing, in our own ways, what we had just seen. For almost 20 years, I had processed similar scenes and conducted similar investigations.

I mentioned we "hardly" spoke a word, but something my wife said, as only a wife can, rang crystal clear… "you need to quit that job." Having always been the main provider for my family, and greatly concerned with security, the thought of just leaving a comfortable job had never been a serious consideration. Until then. Yes, there does come a time when "enough is enough."

Throughout the days, weeks and months that followed, my wife's comment kept popping up in my mind. As I thought about her statement to me, the challenge always became, "What can I do that would allow me and my family to live at least as comfortably as I had in the recent past?" You see, although we were not "rich" by any means, my insurance job and my wife's job as an orthodontic technician had allowed us a comfortable lifestyle. Grossing about $85,000 a year between the two of us, we were at ease in that all of our bills could be met, and we could have food on the table. Nothing extravagant mind you, but at least content. Still, the question remained, "What could I do, outside of my current job, to support my family?"

Then it hit me; I had been staring at, and doing, this business for years now! I had been teaching piano, guitar and trumpet, although infrequently, since 1985. So, why not a school of music? Better yet, something that sounded even more professional, a "conservatory" of music that would provide true, high quality lessons by extremely talented music instructors! I certainly knew the pros and cons of teaching out of my home (and in my personal opinion, "in home" music lessons are not in the best interest of the student). My wife and I then began the lengthy process of discussing the merits of this possible business and conducting our due diligence.

To the absolute horror of my parents, my wife and I quit our corporate jobs on the same day…April 30, 2007. Approximately one month later (June 1, 2007, to be exact), with three instructors on staff and two registered students, we opened the doors to our first school of music, the Cinco Ranch Conservatory of Music LLC (now known as The Conservatory of Music at Cinco Ranch). Did we make the right choice for ourselves? Absolutely! We currently own two schools of music, have grown from 3 music instructors to over 35, and teach over 25,000 private music lessons a year! Between the years of 2010 – 2015, we averaged a 24.50% growth rate per year which, by any standard, is phenomenal, especially when one considers that a growth rate of 15% will have a business doubling in size in only 5 years!

Was our success easy to achieve? Well, no! We struggled as I believe most owners of music schools, and for that matter, any new business, do. We made wrong decisions. We struggled with the same fears and issues that you might be currently facing. We, too, wondered if we would "make it" in this business. Yes, we even cried quite a bit as we wondered what we had gotten ourselves into. Despite the struggles, we persevered. We learned from our mistakes. We continued to believe. And what I believe has separated us from many others, is that I set out to diligently study the ins and outs of all aspects of this industry. This overwhelming desire to learn why certain things worked and others did not is perhaps the most significant factor to our success! Yes, with God's grace and sheer determination, my wife and I have found wonderful success in this industry. You can too!

So, what are the tenets that we studied, implemented, etc., to help us reach our level of success? Let me briefly break them down for you.

1. YOUR MOTIVATION

I have observed that those who do best in this business are those individuals who have, as their primary motivating factors, a true love of music, who are genuinely interested in sharing their knowledge of music with others, and freedom of choice! To be truly successful in this business, you should have as your goal that of your student surpassing you…or your instructors…and you absolutely thrilled with that notion! You need to LOVE this business! Never accept mediocrity in any aspect of your business! Understand that once you diminish the standards upon which your business has hopefully been built, it will become increasingly easier to allow for less than your best in the future. Keep in the forefront of your business the goal of doing and providing your best, each and every day.

2. CAPITAL

We have all seen it before…a great idea, a wonderful location, passionate business owners and a talented staff, yet the business fails! With all these positive attributes, what could have caused the business to fail? All too often (and I say this based on personal experience, as my only prior business failure, back in the late 1990's, was due to this) the success or failure of a business can be traced to one tenet...CAPITAL! Yes, the source of funds to initiate, then perhaps more importantly, to continue the business, warrant very careful consideration!

3. LOCATION

Location, location, location...it's everything in business! Well, maybe not everything, but it is tremendously important. Get it right, and it will go a long way to helping your business become a success. Get it wrong and, well, you know, business is challenging enough already. Factors to consider when choosing a location are: Can you afford any potential build out of the location? Can you afford the rent? What is the proximity of not only your customers, but also of your competition? Is the area consistent with your image/brand? Will the location be able to sustain growth? These and other factors need to be considered when choosing your location.

4. BUSINESS PLAN

"If you don't know where you are going, then any road will get you there." I love that quote from Lewis Carroll! Stated another way, how do you know what is or needs to happen without a plan? Simply put, you don't! So, I believe that one of the biggest benefits of writing a business plan is that you commit your thoughts to paper, whereby you can better understand your business and "plan" specific courses of action to operate, and improve, your business. A well-written plan can also go a long way to help secure funding, help manage cash flow, and can even support a strategic exit from the business.

5. YOUR PROFESSIONAL AND BUSINESS TEAM

First, some clarification. Your professional team consists of your attorney, your accountant, your banker, and your commercial broker. Your business team consists of your employees and, perhaps, independent contractors. Choosing the right professional team members can ultimately "save" you a ton of money by being the experts in their field and, thereby, looking out for your best interests. Choosing the right business team members, on the other hand, can help you "make" money by providing the quality of service you desire, thereby keeping your clients happy. And happy clients usually continue to purchase your service!

6. MARKETING

Eventually, what will become one of, if not the most important facet of your business success, will be marketing. You know, the overall process by which you get clients through your doors. Much of our success has come from the diligent study of local marketing concepts, which include categories such as advertising, promotions, public relations and sales. Building your brand and brand awareness would be another facet of the marketing umbrella. Time spent learning how to "get known" will be a very worthwhile investment in your business!

These are just a few of the topics that we seriously considered and/or implemented, that have helped us to achieve our level of success!

Are we done growing? Absolutely not! I still have plans for additional growth within our current schools, for opening other locations, and perhaps even franchising. What gives me comfort, however, is in "knowing that I know" what it takes to succeed in this industry! With this knowledge in mind, I have no worries or fears that when it comes time to open our next school, it, too, will be a success!

Before ending this chapter, take a moment, close your eyes, and begin to imagine how different your life would be if you began to experience our kind of success in your music school business! Gone would be the days of endless frustrations due to a lack of growth, or not being able to crash through a certain ceiling, or worrying about cash flow, or not knowing where or how to effectively get more students. Instead, you would learn how to deal more effectively with parents and students... and instructors! You would learn how to create a more effective website for your business! You would learn of tools to help automate aspects of your business, where and how to effectively market, the importance of a business plan, the development of your professional and business teams, and establishing effective systems for management, administration/ clerical staff, and instructors, to name but a few topics.

You might be asking, "Well, if you learned all this on your own, couldn't I?" And the truth of the matter is that, yes, you certainly could. The question you then need to ask yourself is, are you willing to take nine years to learn what I have through your own trial and error...or would you rather cut down the learning curve, dramatically, of what it takes to succeed in this industry?

That is what I want to and can do for you! I want to short-cut this whole learning process for you and provide you with the knowledge, the tips and strategies that you will need to succeed in a music school business! So, whether you currently teach out of your home, have progressed to serious thought about opening a brick and mortar school of music, or you already have a school that simply isn't growing, isn't growing fast enough, or worse yet, is shrinking, I just want you to know that you are not alone and that there "is" light at the end of the tunnel!

A school of music is a fantastic business! The benefits of an education in music are many, and its impact can influence one, positively, for the remainder of their lives!

> *"Before anything else, a child should be taught music."*
> ~ Plato

Sound advice! Your wonderful future in this industry awaits! Let's begin!

About Dr. Michael

Affectionately known as the "Music Man of Cinco Ranch," Dr. Michael Guevara has been involved in the music business for more than 30 years. As a community servant, professional musician, arranger and composer, the main thrust in his daily life is to help people understand the importance of an education in music, and of fine arts in general.

Starting in 1985, in conjunction with his love of children and passion for music, Dr. Guevara began to teach the piano to children within his local community out of his parent's home. In that same year, Dr. Guevara also began to perform music professionally through a ministry he founded, "Golden Trumpet Ministries." In 1986, after receiving his BBA in Finance, Dr. Guevara moved to Houston to begin a career in insurance, but also continued to help children learn music and continued to perform professionally, as his schedule allowed.

In 2006, Dr. Michael Guevara and his wife (Berta Guevara) decided that corporate life was no longer an avenue they wished to pursue, and after much careful consideration, with their love of music and of children, they decided to open their first school of music. Consequently, on June 1, 2007, The Conservatory of Music at Cinco Ranch was officially opened. Focusing on slow but steady growth, Dr. Guevara has grown The Conservatory of Music (now with two locations), to be the most awarded schools of music in the Katy, TX area, inclusive of being the only Founding School of the Carnegie Hall Royal Conservatory Achievement Program in the entire greater Houston area.

In order to grow his schools of music, Dr. Guevara immersed himself in the study of all facets of marketing and business growth. The result? Dr. Guevara has developed a thriving music studio business! In fact, between the years of 2011 – 2015, his music studio business averaged a growth rate of over 20% a year! Dr. Guevara now wishes to share his business insights not only with others in the music studio business, but with other small business entrepreneurs as well. He is currently writing a book on this very specific subject, and will be helping others through personal coaching and through his new website, www.MusicStudioRescue.com

Dr. Guevara is a member of Beta Gamma Sigma and the Texas Music Educators Association, composed the music for the musical, *Invasion of the Potty Snatchers* by Houston playwright Jim Bain, and is also a speaker, business mentor and entrepreneur. Dr. Guevara is a founding member of the Katy Jazz Association and a member of the Katy Jazz Festival Committee. In his spare time, Dr. Guevara is an avid fisherman, having authored two digital books on fishing (*Flounder, The Basics* and *Bay Fishing*

Strategies Revealed) and enjoys playing golf and tennis.

You can connect with Dr. Guevara at:
- info@michaelguevara.com
- www.MichaelGuevara.com

Or if interested in the school of music business at:
- info@musicstudiorescue.com
- www.MusicStudioRescue.com

CHAPTER 31

SAY "NO" TO THE SAME OLD INTERVIEW

BY KURT HAUGAN

Being an Executive Recruiter with a niche means that I don't attempt to serve people in all careers, or even sectors of the field of expertise that I am in, which is large, commercial construction. I connect candidates and clients together for successful results for the building of hospitals, stadiums, and schools, just to name a few. These are the buildings that make up the landscape of a community.

To make these successful connections it requires a combination of attributes. Knowing my mission is essential. It's different for each client and each candidate. Success happens through understanding the purpose, focusing on the right results, and understanding the dynamics of human interaction. Through all of these efforts the value of an executive recruiter highlights itself and assists in giving you a successful outcome.

KNOW YOUR MISSION

For clients, the mission is to find the right candidate to fill a position. For candidates, their goal is to find a new career opportunity. For both, they have to understand that the process of doing this isn't a sprint. It's a marathon and by knowing your mission you can gain the endurance (patience to some) to succeed. Three things to help you do this include:

1. **Start with your eyes on the end-goal**. You need to have a clear picture of where you want to be. When you have this, you can put everything else into place.

2. **Be open to the different routes that lead to success.** Opportunities come at unexpected times, appealing horizontal career movements should also be considered.
3. **Plan and manage your career.** Don't just take a job. A job brings in money, but a career brings about fulfillment.

FOCUS ON THE RIGHT THINGS

When a candidate is seeking a new opportunity they must first identify and define what that looks like, exactly. Using a mentor for this is helpful, because they can ask you the tough and direct qualifying questions that an employer is likely to ask in an interview. It's more than just a role-playing opportunity, it is a chance to make sure you've thought things through. Here's what this process looks like:

Early in my career I was offered an opportunity to spend the day observing how a top recruiter ran his business. This guy was a rock star in the world of recruiting and I jumped at the chance. What I learned that day was shocking and it changed my career and my life dramatically!

When talking with prospective clients by phone he would start by saying "Even if you have worked with a recruiter before, you need to know that I work different than most and I want to discuss that with you right up front to make sure it makes sense for us to work together." He would then pose a dozen questions and requests for agreement to them. Only if they answered yes to all of them would he agree to take on their search. As you may guess, very few answered yes to everything. Coming from the traditional sales world where you worked to get as many yeses as you could, his approach blew my mind. Instead of trying to "rule them in" he was trying to "rule them out."

When he got off the phone, we discussed it. He explained, "I don't need everyone as a client nor could I properly serve everyone. I know the people I serve and I know recruiting. I know what produces the best results and I only need to find that one client today that recognizes my expertise and wants to work with me, my way. It's not that this is best for me, it is really best for them."

He concluded: "Kurt, if you needed brain surgery and the doctor asked you how you wanted to handle the operation, you would run away from him screaming! You would expect him to be the expert and to know how best to attain success. Recruiting is no different."

Enough said – I was a changed man from that point on. I now understood that while this approach may seem too direct to some, it really offers tremendous benefit to both the candidates and clients involved. Determine that there is a good fit and high likelihood of success right up front. If not, be honest that it won't work and respect other's time enough not to waste it.

Saying no is something that will serve you well. You have to get comfortable with doing this and eliminate the fear that you're letting your "best option" pass you by. It could backfire on you by allowing a wrong opportunity in. The power of no is necessary to achieve the great opportunities you really want in life.

In addition to saying "no" you must also:

- Ask, don't tell. Discuss solutions and obstacles; never assume.
- Invest in listening upfront. When we really listen we can learn a great deal.

I have a great example of how listening can make the difference that I want to share with you. A while back, I had a mentor who taught me a different way to do things in which I focused on a niche—not being everything to all people in my industry. I was a skeptic at first, but if you respect the man you respect the advice.

This guy walks in to meet with me and immediately says, "I need you to know that I don't have much respect for your profession—nothing personal. We've been burnt…so I'm cautious. I have some questions for you." What do you say to that? It was all I could do to not have my jaw hit the table when he proceeded to pull out 8 pages of handwritten questions.

But I was there for a purpose. I began my presentation, confident in my knowledge of my field. He kept interrupting mid-sentence and drilling me with question after question. Eventually, the interruptions subsided. As I spoke, he kept checking things off his long list and eventually I finished. It was time to ask for his business.

What happened shocked me…

I noticed the tension and scowl he came with was now replaced with a relaxed smile. He sighed and said, "Kurt, it's the damnedest thing. I had a bunch of questions for you, but you answered them all before I could even ask them. It was as if you could read my mind. I feel like you know us so well that I'm ready to transfer all of my accounts to you."

I just about fell on the floor. And you can believe that at that very moment, I became a believer and a practitioner of using niche expertise to my advantage.

In the example, if I would have not listened to understand their concerns and objections ahead of time the meeting would have failed. If I had not taken the time to become an expert in a specific niche, it would have failed too. As an executive recruiter, it is my professional responsibility to really know those that I serve. Their needs are an important part of the process that I go through.

RELATIONSHIP DYNAMICS

My candidates view me as their career agent and my clients understand that I am their trusted advisor. I truly believe one big reason for my success lies in how I look at the relationships that I help to create and cultivate.

I change peoples' lives as a result of the relationships I build. And life is constantly shifting. Candidates become clients. Clients become candidates. There is a tremendous potential for long-term relationships and networks that offer me inside knowledge about the market, companies, and individuals. What better person to use to your advantage for finding the right candidate, or finding the right career?

INVEST IN ONGOING LEARNING AND GROWTH

When we're stagnant in our growth, we lessen our value. Investments in ongoing learning and growth are necessary. You can do this in a variety of ways, which include your daily disciplines, as well as specific efforts. What I personally use and recommend to people is:

1. **Be open to change.** When we are flexible we are pliable. We can see the potential of different ideas than what we may have thought of. We might take a pass on them but we can be assured that we gave them thoughtful consideration, based on our goals.

2. **Put yourself in a position to say "no".** When you demonstrate mastery of the skills of your given position, you are often offered opportunities for advancement. You can always politely decline. However you always want the option to be yours.

3. **Mentor and train your replacement.** When you believe you're irreplaceable, you hinder your potential for advancement. Also, it's a sign of fear.

4. **Constantly assess yourself.** It's easy to correct and improve slowly and daily, as compared to only thinking about it once or twice a year. Are the actions you are taking indicative of the direction you want to go?

5. **Be coachable.** All professionals need a coach to help them, just like every pro athlete does. Take advantage of a mentor because there is so much to be gained—for both of you.

EXECUTIVE RECRUITERS SHOULD BRING YOU VALUE

The services that a proven, professional executive recruiter offers are high-value additions to both clients and candidates. I have experienced how the strategies that I use have positively impacted companies, thereby increasing their bottom line. For candidates, they find themselves receiving enriching, life-changing opportunities that help them reach their professional goals.

For candidates, the benefits of working with a recruiter include:

1. Gaining access to career opportunities that are not exposed to endless career sites and publications.
2. Gaining tremendous insight into the companies they represent, which is helpful in preparing you for an interview.
3. Confidentiality to protect you from backlash from your current employer.
4. Testing your marketability without putting your current job at risk.
5. Taking advantage of the recruiter's insight into market trends, both current and predicted future trends.
6. Having a relationship with someone who understands your long-term goals and can link you to opportunities to achieve them.

For clients, the benefits of using recruiting services include:

1. Gaining access to the best "hidden" candidates, the ones that are confidential and patient for the right opportunities.
2. Understanding that when top professionals seek out a career change, they are most likely to use the avenue of a recruiter to take action.
3. Recognizing that top talent can move fast. Establishing a relationship with a recruiter gives you a better chance of connecting with the talent first.
4. A high focus on the confidentiality of the process.
5. An ability to test the acceptance of employment offers, helping the company determine if they are competitive and appealing for the talents they seek.
6. Access to a ready-made pool of talent, which can make a company's growth and transition process faster and more fluid.

HOW I BRING THIS ALL TOGETHER

The niche group of clients that I serve are commercial general contractors, and the candidates that I serve are those who can fill specific upper-level roles within their organizations. The client and candidate are really two sides of the same coin. It's not uncommon for a candidate to later become a client as they climb the management ladder in their organization. Likewise, clients can become candidates when they are seeking a career change.

Through my years of experience, I have discovered that whether you are a client or a candidate, you are truly looking for the same things. Candidates look for roles that will:

- Excite them
- Motivate them to be challenged
- Grow their skills
- Offer them more responsibility
- Allow them to recognize that their contributions are appreciated
- Give them a sense of accomplishment
- Be rewarding for the long-term

To do these things you need to have attributes such as enthusiasm, ambition, complex problem-solving abilities, flexibility, and motivation. You must also have skills in working with others, teamwork, and leadership. All of these attributes just happen to align precisely with what clients want from a candidate. I offer the link that helps to position each side favorably, creating the ultimate win/win scenario.

ASK THE EXPERT

The number one question that clients ask me is how they can attract and retain top talent? The answer lies in guiding candidates with helpful, insightful answers to their big question, which is: how do I grow my career?

This is what a solid candidate will look like to an appealing client:

- The solid candidate will know how to market themselves to be an asset to the company they wish to work for. This involves understanding the importance of company branding. Candidates have the skills to know and cultivate a company culture and know the values that exist within it. It's a way of life, not just an impressive interview answer. The candidate knows that they are a walking advertisement for the company they work for, and can clearly explain in 90 seconds or less why they are proud to be a part of the entity.
- The solid candidate will be aware of their personal branding, which leads to strategic highlight of their attributes in their day-to-day endeavors, not just the interview. They are able to clearly explain in 90 seconds what their role is and accentuate the positives of their career.
- The solid candidate clearly knows their values and personality are an important attribute in their workplace. They accept that businesses hire individuals who have personality, are compatible with the workplace culture, and are willing participants in self-evaluation processes that help them with communication, effectiveness and style.

THREE QUESTIONS TO HELP YOU FIND THE RIGHT RECRUITER

Part of my ability to best serve my clients and candidates is to anticipate the questions and be prepared for all scenarios and possibilities. You should not accept less from a recruiter when you seek one out.

Here are three questions that you should ask and a potential recruiter should be able to easily answer:

1. *Are you an expert recruiter? (Don't just take "yes" for an answer, expect them to elaborate.) How long have you been a recruiter? Have you earned any professional designations?*
2. *Do you specialize in my industry or market? (Get the details!) Can you demonstrate formal knowledge of my industry?*
3. *How do you look out for me long-term? (A great chance to learn about repeat clients/candidates.) Do they talk about retention, not just placement?*

Whether you are a company looking for the best talent to grow your business or a skilled professional who is ready to grow and be challenged in a new career, you are a person who can benefit from the help of an executive recruiter. Connecting with the right people is necessary to achieve your goals and aspirations.

About Kurt

Kurt Haugan is an Executive Recruiter specializing in construction talent management. Since 1992, Kurt has spent his professional life assessing resources. He transitioned from managing financial assets to managing human talent when he saw that many companies and individuals were in need of a top-level talent resource. For businesses, they are able to take advantage of Kurt's talent and expertise to hire the right people—their greatest asset. For individuals who are looking for career changes, they have access to someone with the insight and know-how to help them prepare for the opportunities that will transform their professional life.

As the Founder of Haugan Group, Kurt leads a team of elite specialists in the field of construction recruitment. He works with individuals and businesses from across the United States, connecting the right talent with the right business. He uses the values and principles he believes in to create these successful introductions and connections. As a result, every executive search is thoroughly vetted so he has a full understanding of the needs of both the client and the candidate.

When it comes to recruitment expertise, there is a demand for a strong understanding of both the client's perspective and that of the candidate. Kurt is not a resume pusher, he is an elite level specialist. He is a Certified Personnel Specialist demonstrating his mastery of the federal laws and policies that govern the hiring and employment process as well as his adherence to ethics standards and commitment to ongoing professional education. As a Certified Retention Specialist, he has demonstrated mastery of engagement and retention practices because only through a long-term relationship can both employer and employee achieve their goals. Kurt earned his Construction Management Certificate in order to fully understand every aspect of the niche he serves in construction including materials, drawings and specifications, safety planning, cost estimating and project scheduling.

According to Kurt, "The key to creating successful partnerships between clients and candidates stems from knowing the right questions to ask. There is no better way to achieve successful, long-term results than to engage in this manner." Because of this, Kurt is able to offer services to highly-vetted candidates and clients.

Kurt was born in Nebraska, and currently resides in Scottsdale, Arizona with his wife Brandy and their four children. When he is not working, he likes to travel and enjoy all the adventures that a warm weather climate has to offer, including golfing and having a little fun racing sports cars. But when fall arrives, it's football time and you'll find him and his family cheering for the Denver Broncos and Nebraska Cornhuskers!

Believing strongly in being of service and giving back, Kurt is committed to helping children and is an advocate for animal welfare. Kurt's family has served many children through the foster care system and are supporters of the Arizona Friends of Foster Children Foundation. Kurt has also served as a volunteer Big Brother for Big Brothers/ Big Sisters of America and has taught as a volunteer for Junior Achievement USA. And for furry friends, Kurt's family has adopted several German Shepherd dogs through shelters over the years. They serve as volunteers at the Foothills Animal Rescue of Scottsdale and support Westside German Shepherd Rescue of Los Angeles.

CHAPTER 32

YOUR *ULTIMATE SECURE RETIREMENT*© IN 20 MINUTES A DAY

BY DR. FRED ROUSE, CFP

Have you ever noticed, nobody wants to work forever? There are more than several studies that show most people are actually unhappy with their job. Even more people would rather not work at all. If that's true, if that's really the case, then why are so many people still working?

It's not really a shocker of an answer, is it? You know. It's about the money. If we didn't need the money, would we do what we do? . . . Probably not.

Retirement is being able to do what you want, experience and maintain the lifestyle you want, without worrying about the money!

For most people, they'll ride a unicorn before they see that situation. I may not be able to get you a ride on a unicorn, but what if I could tell you with certainty that you could "retire", and not have to worry about having enough money to live the lifestyle you want and deserve? What if I could show you how do it in less than 20 minutes a day?

It really is possible. It is something you can learn, and it doesn't take a PhD in economics or a half a million dollars to start. It does involve looking at ourselves, at money, how we earn it and what we do with it differently than we have in the past.

I've been dealing with a wide range of problems and clients as a Certified Financial Planner for well over 20+ years. My clients' education ranges from High School drop outs to PhDs. Their incomes can range from 20K to mid-7 figures/year.

The people I see can generally be grouped into different categories based on their source(s) of income. Each group has their own unique situations that affect them, their decision making, their ability to make money and ultimately their retirement lifestyle.

HOW WE EARN MONEY

The W-2 Job:

Most people start out in this category. This can be anyone that works for someone else. Most people start working in their teens to early twenties, at least part-time in a W-2 job. *This is where you trade your time for their dollars.* This continues for a vast majority of people as they move from job to job throughout their lives. The money generally increases as you gain more job skills, however it's basically the same thing. You end up trading your time for more of their dollars. You may find yourself in this situation. It's relatively comfortable. You may not be happy with the job. But, it does provide a baseline of predictable income. At least as long as the company remains in operation in the area and permits you to have the job. You know that you'll never get "rich" working that "job" because there is also a "ceiling", an upper limit, to the amount of money you can earn.

There's nothing wrong with it. It's not your fault. No one has shown you there may be a better way where you could have more control over your time, life and money. Your ultimate retirement, if that's possible, is based on where your available money will come from – the pension and 401(k) plans that the companies you've worked for may have had in place, Social Security and whatever money you've saved and/or invested over the years (IRAs, CDs, Brokerage accounts). Even then, most of these people will need to work at least a part time job into their 70s just to survive, and then hope that nothing happens that will disturb their fragile finances.

Self-Employment:

There's another group of people that make money in a different way. These people may have started with a W-2 job somewhere in their history, but found they had a marketable skill or talent. Somewhere along the way, generally in their mid-30s to mid-40s, they got tired of working for someone else, and having someone else control their time and money so they started their own business. These people are "Self-Employed." Their businesses can vary dramatically.

They're the person standing on the corner selling flowers. They're also the carpenter, electrician or someone in any of the trades. A self-employed person could have a restaurant or a retail store of some type. There are even a number of "professionals" like Doctors, Lawyers, CPAs and a few Certified Financial Planners that are self-employed.

This is a stout group of people. There is no guaranteed base or floor of money for these people. *If they don't provide goods, services or advice that people are willing pay for, they don't get paid!* If they hire W-2 employees, they have the burden of making sure their employees are paid each week. They have fixed overhead and expenses they need to pay.

Some of these folks may have been downsized out of their job, and out of necessity, started a business. However, most of these people willingly took on the risk and traded their base floor of income for more control over their own lives. In removing the floor, they also generally remove the celling. If you take on more risk, you would expect a potentially higher reward.

The average self-employed person makes more money than the average W-2 employee. They also generally put in considerably more time in the background than most employees ever see or understand.

Their ultimate retirement, if that's possible, is based on where their money will come from, whatever pension and 401(k) plans that they have funded over the years, Social Security and whatever money they've saved and/or invested in IRAs, CDs, and Brokerage accounts. They'll have one other source of income too, the sale of their business, even if they sell it to their kids through several creative wealth transfer techniques. These folks generally have a very comfortable retirement and get to enjoy the fruits of their labor for all the additional hours they put in behind the scenes.

There's a third group of people, another way to make money that doesn't come to mind immediately. It's a more select group, only because they have a different set of skills.

Trading:
When I talk about Traders, I'm not talking about the folks who opened up a trading account at the bank and get all those wonderful "Trading Tools," "research" and free online apps. I'm also not talking about the boiler room of salespeople like in the movie, *The Wolf of Wall Street.*

When I talk about Traders, I'm talking about professional traders that make their living from trading, whatever it is they trade.

Professional traders are truly a different group of people. They're generally at least 40 years old. Most started with a W-2 or commission-based job at some point. They acquired a unique skill set and tend to be exceptionally independent and in control of their own time and lives.

Traders are like the above self-employed on steroids. They have no guaranteed base of income. Because of the field they've chosen there is nothing that comes close to resembling a ceiling on their income. They have no need for employees, no inventory to buy and sell. Their business doesn't require any real estate to maintain and there are no retail hours to keep.

These professional traders make more than W-2 employees and most all self-employed people combined.

They generally do it in just a fraction of the time. These Traders are independent and lead an extraordinary lifestyle. You wouldn't routinely run into these people at your local cocktail party, and if you did, you wouldn't notice them. These people don't tout what they do. They're not interested in impressing anybody. They're content with their own accomplishments and their lifestyle, which most would envy.

Their ultimate retirement is considerably different than what you would think. They lead their life as though they were retired. They may own Real Estate that they don't see. And have brokerage accounts that they don't watch. They have enough money to have a full-time property management company for the Real Estate and a broker that manages a portion of their money that they've set aside for the kids/grandkids. The

Real Estate, partnerships and brokerage accounts were just a place to put some of their excess money. Why, because the work day for a professional trader, when they decide to work, is an hour or two a day. Their lifestyle IS the Ultimate Secure Retirement© of which most people dream.

The Biggest Problem:

The biggest problem is that most people don't realize there's a problem! People are greatly influenced by the people they associate with, the books they read and the experiences they have in their lifetime. The vast majority of people working a W-2 job are surrounded by other people that are working a W-2 job. Their parents and relatives work a W-2 job. It's all they know. The manufacturing base, union jobs and lifelong employment with one employer have been on a decline since the mid-70s, so most of the decent pensions are gone.

If you're self-employed, you know it's harder and harder to cover the expenses and crank a reasonable amount of money out of that business without putting in 70+ hours a week.

If you're a W-2 wage earner or self-employed you know that things happen. Life happens: work – whatever that may be, trying to spend time with the family, the car breaks down, the kids in school, a trip to the ER, a bad back or other health problems, a wedding, a funeral, it all takes time, on what seems to be a daily basis. There's only so much time. But you knew that it was important to put some money away. You've been doing it for years. You've put some money into a 401(k) and an IRA. You have "some" money off to the side so you think it's doing OK and you'll think about retirement "later" you say to yourself.

The Alarm Went Off:

You do that for a while and then one day you wake up and you're 50 years old. If that day hasn't happened yet…it will. Now it's time to take an objective look at your life. *You realize that by the best measure, half of your life is gone!* The first half went OK but do you really want a repeat of the preceding 20 years for the rest of your life? You've been working for more than a while and you'd like to do the mystical "retirement" thing while you're young enough to enjoy it. But when?

Right about now you start thinking:
- Do I have "enough" money to retire?
- Can I maintain my current lifestyle?

- How much will I have to start cutting back?
- Can or will I have to at least work part time?
- Is that going to be enough then?
- How long can I physically do it?
- How long do I want to do it?
- Who's going to hire me at that age?
- What happens if I have health problems?

Yes. All these questions come up and then some. But, they are really inconvenient questions. You're busy with life. You'll just put a little more money to the side and that should take care of things and you put off answering the questions. You'll just think about it later. At age 55 or so, the same awakening comes to you. Only now you're a bit more concerned and you spend some time consciously "thinking" about your situation. It's been lingering in the back of your mind since you were 50.

When age 60 hits you, you know it's time to get serious. You start to actually answer those questions and you realize that *even if you had a million dollars working for you (and you probably don't), you're still likely to run out of money before you run out of life.* About now you start to go into panic mode and start getting depressed. That would be the routine end of things for most people.

The Light Went On:
However, you're not most people. That's why you're here. That's why we're both here. So HOW do you get "there"?

That W-2 job, a questionable pension and even more questionable Social Security are NOT going to get you there. The self-employed person has a better chance if you can live through the extra hours and stress. *But chances are you're still going to have to cut back on your lifestyle and that's not your idea of a secure retirement.*

What about the Trader? They're almost retired when they're working. Can you do that too? The really interesting thing is that not one of them came out of the womb being able to do what they do. Most Traders actually had a W-2 job at one point. So, what happened from birth to where they are now? What makes this select group able to pull in an extraordinary amount of money almost at will, and lead a lifestyle while they're working that most of the rest of us would consider a great retirement? The professional Traders have honed their skills over time by reading for hours about trading techniques and the underlying things that they trade. They've studied under mentors. They've taken what they've learned, tested and refined their individual trading systems. Trading IS their business and they treat it that way. It's not uncommon for these people to have over a million dollars a year in trading profits.

Yes, almost everyone knows someone, who knows someone, who has lost money trading. "They" tell you that it's one of the riskiest things you can do. For people trying to trade from an app on their phone or that have taken a weekend trading course, it is. For the professional trader, it's just a solid business model that produces a predictable income. You don't have the years, connections, desire, mindset or time to develop the skills to be a professional trader?

What about a semi-professional trader?

The good news is, with the right training, those "job skills" can be acquired. You can work a W-2 job and/or be self-employed AND learn the easy way to acquire skills to become a semi-professional trader on a part time basis *and make an extra $50K to $300K a year or more well into your retirement.*

That means you can continue your W-2 job or self-employment, whatever that may be, control your life, and get the maximum impact for your money in as little as 10-20 minutes a day after the markets close. You can lead an iconic life with a skill set you can carry into retirement for yourself, and share with your spouse and children for their financial security as well.

That's exactly HOW you get YOUR Ultimate Secure Retirement in 20 Minutes a Day.

My recent quest is to show people a new way to fast track their income and achieve their Ultimate Secure Retirement at a young enough age to enjoy it. . .

WHAT ARE YOU WAITING FOR?

About Dr. Fred

Dr. Fred Rouse, CFP (aka: The REAL Money Doctor & Quiet Trader) started as the son of a blue-collar carpet installer in South Philadelphia. His entrepreneurial spirit soon emerged as he started painting handrails at age 10. After five years in the US Coast Guard at the tail end of the Vietnam War and ten years as a Registered Respiratory Therapist working the critical care units of an inner-city hospital, he thought there had to be a better way and started his in-depth study of money and people.

Becoming a Certified Financial Planner® was not enough for him. He went on to graduate studies and now holds a PhD in Taxation, a Doctorate in Business Administration and even did a year in law school just for some additional background.

The Real Money Doctor's College Student's Money Guide is Dr. Rouse's book to give high school seniors and college students short, practical, usable lessons, and insights into situations that most young people find themselves while making their first attempt at true independence.

In 2015, he teamed up with Jack Canfield (*Chicken Soup for the Soul* fame) to write the international best seller, *The Soul of Success*. Dr. Rouse is now a top Certified Financial Planner®, Money Expert and International Best-Selling Author who has received several national awards for his writing and money expertise.

He works with select individuals and a variety of small businesses that earn in excess of seven figures a year – to improve their lives, cut taxes, make money, protect their assets and help them gain the personal time to enjoy the iconic lifestyle they want and deserve.

He's developed *The REAL Money Doctor's Business Rx, 6 Essentials for a Healthy Business to Make Money* with the legendary Brian Tracy that helps aspiring as well as seasoned entrepreneurs take control of their business, cut their taxes and make more money while still having time to enjoy a personal life.

Dr. Rouse also helps serious people that are 50 and older with a simple blueprint to find 63% more money for their Ultimate Secure Retirement© in less than 20 minutes a day, even if they have zero business or investment experience – so they can be financial independent and retire at an age young enough to enjoy it.

Dr. Rouse and his work have been featured on FOX News, ABC, NBC, CBS, CNN,

CNBC, A&E, BRAVO, *USA Today*, *Forbes*, *Wall Street Business*, *Hollywood Live*, *The Money Show*, *Investing Daily* and more.

His passion for helping is shared through his books, courses, special reports and webinars through his website. If you would like to learn more about Dr. Rouse and how he can help you and or your business, please contact him directly at his website: DrFredRouse.com.

CHAPTER 33

WHY GO OUT LOOKING FOR HAPPINESS WHEN YOU CAN CREATE IT FOR YOURSELF?

BY ELLA RIVKIN

Challenging moments can lead us to our greatest breakthroughs.

Sometimes the moments in life where we meet the greatest obstacles and endure the toughest challenges can lead us to breakthrough moments that turn our lives around. This is what happened to me few years ago. I had worked very hard all my life, went to college, had a family with two beautiful children, a caring husband, and a large house. To my friends I appeared to have it all, but suddenly I felt that something was missing. Being successful didn't bring me the happiness that I thought it would.

Success without happiness is meaningless.

I became increasingly nervous and wasn't myself physically or emotionally. I was going to bed early and sleeping late the next morning – something I had never done. I tried everything to get myself recharged and rejuvenated and to start my day with energy, but nothing was working. It kept getting worse and worse and my energy was completely depleted. Searching for an answer, I went to my doctor and learned that I had an iron deficiency, which would explain my lack of energy. But could this alone have caused such a drastic change in me? It didn't seem likely.

With my crumbling health, also came a crumbling marriage. My husband and I had reached a point where we were thinking that enough was enough. I had no desire to work on my marriage, nor did I have a desire to work on my career.

I was searching for some kind of escape.

My friends suggested I take a vacation, and I agreed that I should. In the past vacations had helped me become rested, clear my mind, and recharge myself for the "amazing" life that I was fortunate to have. However, a vacation did not clear my mind nor heal me at all.

The day before we were supposed to return home, my husband and I went for a bike ride. We were approaching a bridge as it started to rain. It became very slippery. I lost control of the bike and crashed onto the metal surface of the bridge. My whole body was terribly bruised and I had a shattered elbow and a broken arm and wrist. I also hit my head pretty hard, but thanks to the helmet I was wearing I had no serious head injuries. After seven hours of surgery, I ended up with a metal plate in my arm, and the doctor told me that I would have no movement in my fingers in my left hand. My hand would be paralyzed!

Like many people in tough situations, I was "forced" to revaluate my life. In an instant everything had changed. Time was all I had as I was lying in the hospital recovering from my surgery. That's when it suddenly came to me. What I had thought of as a "forced" re-evaluation turned out to be a gift to me, delivered under the harsh circumstances of that accident. Before that I would have blamed the entire mess on my husband for choosing the wrong path. But I didn't.

What was going on inside of my mind as lay there? Constantly working for success, thinking if I had a god job, I would be happy; if a had a car and a house – I would be happy; if I had more money - I would be happy. But even though I had all of this and my oldest daughter was graduating from high school, I realized that time had passed by and I had not fully enjoyed any of it.

I started thinking about my life, the changes I would need to make,
and what would truly bring me happiness.

A few weeks later, I was in a store waiting for my daughter to buy something, when out of nowhere, I noticed a book titled, *Heal My Body* by Louise Hay. The book is about the mental causes of physical illnesses and metaphysical ways to overcome illnesses. I'm not sure why I was drawn to this book, but there it was and it demanded my full attention.

As I began browsing through the book, I almost immediately stumbled upon the pages that referred to my situation. Once I started reading it and exploring the meaning of my body's message, things became much clearer to me. According to Hay, my bodily injury signified that I had to change my life's direction. While that's easy to say, the real question was how to do something like that?

As I started to search for the deeper meaning of my life, a wonderful life coach I had been working with, Len May, introduced me to various personal development books, seminars, and workshops. I started to discover more interesting things about my body, my soul, and my life – the most important of which was:

We are often so caught up in day-to-day things that we forget to stop, to breathe, or even to enjoy the moment we are in.

I realized that since I was thirteen years old, I had been focused only on achieving more and more success. Everything else had been put on hold; my happiness, time to enjoy with the ones I love, and most important, time for myself. I was exhausted. It was as if I'd been running a twenty-seven year marathon and suddenly was at the finish line. But what was next? I had no idea.

Finding our path in life is always easier when we create clarity for ourselves.

It took a tremendous amount of time and energy to overcome my injury. While focusing on getting back to my usual activities, I had the full support of my family and the help of a wonderful physical therapist, Eduard Reiter. I started to see improvements in my arm function. The "impossible" suddenly became possible and the word "never" was expunged from my vocabulary. The changes we started to see were so exciting that within six months I was able to recover almost the full function of my hand and arm.

I began spending more quality time with my family. I started swimming, running, and biking again. I started feeling less stress and experiencing more positive emotions. My energy was returning and I felt like myself again. I kept on learning, expanding my knowledge, awareness, and growth. I realized that my transformation was a work in progress and would continue to evolve and perhaps never be finished. I noticed that I had gained a lot of wisdom and had a tremendous wealth of knowledge that I could share with other people. I created a workshop coaching a group of women to help them improve their health, transform their bodies, expand their minds, and redesign their lives to bring them greater happiness and success, much as I had done with myself.

You can have an extraordinary life by seeking constant improvement in the following five areas:

1. Nourishing your soul:

The connection we have with ourselves is a reflection
of how we connect with others to create a successful life.

Think back to a time when you were first in love. Everything was exciting, you were floating on air, colors were vivid, and you forgot about food and were high on life. You believed in what you were doing and felt inspired and confident. Discover what feeds your soul now and how to get joy and satisfaction back into your life. Meditate, spend time with those you love, find time for yourself, develop hobbies, and most importantly, find the things you believe in most passionately. Don't forget to breathe. You body can't function without oxygen. Love yourself and be excited about your potential.

2. Rebooting your health and transforming your body:

Without good health we have nothing.

You need to reboot your health and learn how to create a healthy life style. Try to implement one healthy alternative at a time and replace bad habits with good ones. For example, drink more water instead of soda, herbal tea instead of coffee, and cook home meals instead of fast foods. Listen to the signs your body is giving you. Our bodies require physical, emotional, and spiritual balance to be at their best. If you work out and improve your physical well-being, your capacity to maximize your health, energy, and vitality will be limitless.

The same is true for your emotional and spiritual life. Find ways to connect with the sources that help you achieve this. Determine what works for you physically: exercising, swimming, biking, dancing, doing yoga, or just walking, as our body requires consistent movement in our daily routine. To sustain yourself emotionally and spiritually you may listen to a beautiful piece of music, read an inspirational piece of writing, or quietly meditate. These will lead you to self-discovery and optimum performance in your daily life.

3. Expanding your mind:

*Fear and false limitations can destroy
opportunities and future success*

It's important to overcome old ways of thinking that inhibit you and keep you doing the same things over and over again while producing no new results. You may feel as if you are stuck in a rut and are not making any progress. *Instead of complaining and giving up, you can begin to see every problem as an opportunity to learn and grow.* Having an open mind will give you new insights and eventually greater wisdom, which will allow you to have more success and abundance in your life. Try not to say "No!" to things that you don't fully understand yet. Avoid putting off doing what you are most afraid of because fear leads to procrastination, negativity, and a feeling of hopelessness. By taking action you can conquer your fears, solve your problems, and educate yourself. You don't always have to do this by yourself; you can rely on a mentor or a coach as well as others who have expertise that will help you.

Occasionally, the best opportunities come your way when you are least expecting them. By expanding your mind and being open to new experiences, you will be better able to recognize these opportunities. Be open to them, accept them, explore them, embrace them, and finally act upon them. This will lead you to greater success in your personal life as well as in your business and professional life.

4. Developing financial skills:

Developing money management skills
will help you live the life you really want to have.

The key to being financially healthy is to make sure you are spending and saving money wisely. You need to begin with a strong desire to be financially successful. You need to establish financial goals and then develop a plan to reach these goals and have the discipline to stick to it rigorously. You want to establish priorities in your spending so that you are not buying things that you don't need. Take time to account for all of your income and then create a spending plan based on what you need to maintain yourself. Find ways to spend less money by, for example, cooking more of your meals at home rather than eating out. Have fewer credit cards and use them less often so that you are not buying things based on emotion and whim, thus running up debt.

Develop a savings plan by contributing a certain amount of your income to a retirement plan and into a savings account each month. Review your spending and savings plans each month and see where you can make adjustments to spend less and save more. If you need help with this, reach out to a financial professional for their expertise.

5. Designing your life:

If you want to live a truly extraordinary life,
make sure that you live it on your own terms.

Do you want to end up living someone else's idea of what they think your life should be? If not, it's essential to know exactly what you want your life to be. You need to discover what really makes you happy, what gives you fulfillment, what your real purpose in life is. You need to get in touch with your innermost self. Then you will develop the clarity and focus that allows you to move forward. You will need to create a vision of what you would like your life to become and then make a personal commitment to take the steps that are necessary to achieve this.

Ultimately, you need to realize that within each of us is a person burning with desires and ideas that are must to be brought to existence. This inner life is what drives us and gives us the determination to fully participate in life and make the most out of the one life we have been given. Let's make the most of our lives!

About Ella

Ella Rivkin is the founder and CEO of ERPS Group, Inc., a business that reflects her heart and determination. In addition, ERPS is also a wonderful companion to her additional work as a life, business, health, and fitness coach, where she has the honor of offering her 20+ years of business expertise coupled with her strategic advisory background to clients. This makes her a unique asset to a number of businesses in a variety of niches and industries. Through her coaching, she offers her proven expertise to entrepreneurs and individuals, helping them to make their dreams come true through consultations and personal aid to assist in business start-up. In addition to this high level coaching, she assists with the intricate details involved in business planning, insurance and payroll services, tax preparation, and daily business operations.

Ella's life experiences have provided her with some of the greatest inspiration, motivation, and education one could have in their life. Born in Moscow, Russia, Ella was raised by someone she says is "one of the strongest and most determined women on earth"—her mother. In 1989, when the Soviet Union was going through vast political reforms, Ella's mother emigrated with her two small children to the US in search of a better future. Although small, Ella was inspired by her mother's determination, especially since she only had $300.00 to her name. But she was committed, a quality that Ella greatly admires to this day. All these experiences inspire her work, relationships with others, and her desire to help people recognize opportunity and achieve success.

Through the ERPS Group Foundation established by Ella, she has created a way to give back to the community; especially elderly people and children in need. The focal point of this organization is to help teenagers and adults find purpose in their life, attain financial freedom, and overall happiness and comfort in life. This inspires Ella to continuously seek out new and efficient ways to share her knowledge with others. This is busy work…and rewarding work. Now, she's also excited to be a co-author with renowned author Brian Tracy in the book *Cracking the Code for Success*; something she has certainly done!

Today, Ella never forgets her blessings in both her personal triumphs and professional pursuits. In addition, she is thankful for her opportunity to be here in America, a country that has offered her so much. Through helping others find their happiness and purpose, she is constantly reminded of what a great gift those two things are. In her free time, Ella cherishes spending time with her two daughters, teaching them about the spirit of service to others, and also enjoys reading anything that promotes personal development. She loves being creative in the kitchen and always delights in sporting activities such as biking, swimming, and running.

CHAPTER 34

AGELESS, NON-INVASIVE
EXCITING TRENDS FOR THE ANTI-AGING AND WEIGHT-LOSS MARKETS

BY DR. MICHAEL RENZULLI

*We all **crave** a desire to look and feel great,*
without having to juggle a long recovery time to do so.

In today's reality, TV-infused instant gratification and vanity-based culture, the consumer is highly drawn to high-quality, looks-based aesthetic, as well as health and well-being services that are focused on enhancing their lives in some way, based on what the individual perceives to be of value to them, or for their life. A substantial increase in procedures to help in anti-aging, weight loss and wellness exists today. Let's face it, our society has become obsessed with our wellbeing and looks, plus our physical, emotional, sensual, and sexual needs. Few things offer a greater way to achieve this than non-invasive aesthetic and life-enhancing procedures. They inspire greater confidence in the individual. As a result—the demand for state-of-the-art facilities to address these needs is surging with no end in sight. The catch is... consumers are *less* willing to choose archaic invasive techniques over the non-invasive procedures that allow quicker recovery *with* exceptional results.

We sent a man to the moon in 1969. Today we can completely, non-invasively shrink your body's fat cells, take a decade or more off your face, or tighten, tone and rejuvenate your female parts! Non-invasively. ~ Dr. Michael Renzulli

The face of weight loss and cosmetic procedures is changing, rapidly. In this high demand, fast-paced, instant gratification world we want it all; however, we are less willing to take any more risk than necessary. This means that non-invasive procedures are a sure winner. The caveat—consumers who want these procedures still demand and expect (rightfully so) to receive it from top notch professionals who are highly reputable and positively viewed via online feedback and referrals from friends. Fortunately, the pool of amazing talent for owning and operating a non-invasive weight loss and/or aesthetic practice is large for four reasons:

- The changes in rapidly declining insurance reimbursement have lead to healthcare professionals, such as doctors and nurses looking for rapid cash services. Other professionals do, as well.
- Spa and beauty-based businesses looking for an additional revenue stream that offers the services those clients want today. Why send them somewhere else when you can service them? They love you already, and even more than that, they know you are professional and passionate about serving them!
- It's a logical add-on service for the traditional plastic surgeon to incorporate into their practice.
- Intelligent entrepreneurs who are looking for smart business choices are able to access, own, and operate the explosively-growing weight loss arena, utilizing cutting-edge technology and procedures. They find this type of business very appealing because they are able to tap into the massive market and receive the training they need to participate actively in changing others lives for the better.

With this excess of highly-qualified individuals at the consumers' disposal, especially doctors and medical professionals, consumers can gain peace of mind.

ELITE MEDICAL EXPERTS ARE SEGUEING INTO THE NON-INVASIVE AESTHETIC MARKET ALL THE TIME

When the Affordable Care Act was implemented, it turned the face of medicine on its ear. Along with that potential for everyone to have access to "affordable healthcare" came enough of a financial burden to the medical field that one of two things took place:

1. Those who would have been the "best of the best" in the medical field chose to go into another profession, in lieu of wanting to avoid being increasingly mentally, emotionally, and physically consumed with the daily insurance fight. Doing all of that just to give your practice a chance and pay the bills takes away from the heart of what they love to do.

Or

2. Doctors have made the tough and deliberate decision to sell off their practices to the large medical facilities that are better equipped to deal with the bureaucracy. They didn't go to school all of that time because they love paperwork. They did because they love people. The result of this initiative is that the doctor is no longer the owner of the practice, just a paid employee.

I am in a unique position, one in which I have both exceptional insight and sympathy for both doctors and their patients—because assuredly, everyone suffers when doctors and medical professionals are discontent. Doctors suffer because the reason they went into medicine is stifled, and their creative ability to heal is taken away by what insurance companies "will" and "will not" allow. Patients suffer because they no longer feel like they have rapport with their doctors or that their health needs are being met. In times long ago—ones that I can barely remember as a child—families had one doctor for nearly their entire lives. If the doctor retired, they built rapport with their replacement. Sadly, this is no longer the case.

For me, I no longer saw the value in practicing primary care medicine the way I had been. No one was more shocked than me, either. Nothing is worse than looking into a patient's eyes and telling them that you can't help them—simply because some policy, procedure, or guideline won't allow it or their insurance doesn't cover it. Most people don't even have the disposable income to justify paying for what is best for them on their own, resulting in them just dealing with their lessened wellbeing because there is no other option. Non-invasive aesthetic procedures offer an intelligent, viable option, and they are affordable—either through financing geared toward these improvements or cash. This is why so many people love this market.

In today's world, individuals are more likely to address what they can do medically on their own in order to feel better and live better. Strangely, more so than what they did before "healthcare reform."

This is where I come in. I offer professionals access to the equipment that allows them to enter into the non-invasive aesthetic and life-enhancing market. Our providers are fully trained and ready to be that source of value and inspiration to clients.

IT'S A REVOLUTION FOR THOSE WHO WANT TO LOOK AS GREAT AS THEY FEEL

A better lifestyle and a personal commitment to one's own wellbeing is the motivation for most people who look to these procedures to give them a boost in confidence or physical appearance. Their lifestyles are important to them and whether they just want something "because they do" or it will benefit them in some other way, they want the service from a professional and caring provider. When they are done, they are uplifted, and as a result, they are not opposed to a little outward uplifting in the way of a non-invasive procedure. And with access to trusted and respected professionals to administer these services, it has become a way for doctors to reconnect to the people part of their profession. By helping people find or restore their confidence, you will find few things that feel better than that. I'm blessed to be the one who provides them the equipment and turnkey training to do this.

As the only North American distributor and trainer for LipoTechnology™, I get to connect entrepreneurs with the equipment that helps them open up their own aesthetic-focused practice. These business-savvy people are filled with expertise and knowledge for helping others and are excited to offer cutting-edge, state-of-the-art procedures that people want. This client pool consists of both men and women, as well.

THE APPEAL OF AESTHETICS

People in today's world are willing to invest more of their
disposable income in feeling better about themselves.

Within a matter of five years, I have segued over into the business of aesthetics from my family medical practice. The opportunity for success *if* you have the right processes in place, has been revolutionary for many people—life changers through this new and dynamic career opportunity. Creating the culture in which to help people bring out the best in their lives through helping entrepreneurs take business initiatives inspires me to keep going and offer perspective and expertise that supersedes what others can realistically offer.

The stories that people have shared with me about their life's changes, as policies, regulations, and laws have changed, are both heart touching and emotional. Whether it's the person who is just looking for a solid business opportunity to grow with or the one whose life and livelihood have been shaken by forced changes beyond their control, they see a way to add value to the world through aesthetic services.

Attributes that I've brought to my position are unique in this industry. I understand medical needs and knowledge from being a doctor who has both owned a practice and enjoyed success in that role. However, I also understand the heart and soul of entrepreneurs and those who are ready to shake things up with big, bold moves designed for good. The anti-aging and weight loss markets are ideal for this, as they are all about moving forward in a dynamic, personally-empowering way.

PEOPLES' LIVES ARE CHANGING FOR THE BETTER BECAUSE OF NON-INVASIVE AESTHETIC PRACTICES

Through a commitment to remaining above and beyond all others who offer similar equipment to clients, I have really gone forth in an effort to blaze a new and innovative trail to help business start-ups succeed, keeping in mind the importance of helping them to establish a stellar reputation for their service offerings.

- Due to my reputation and proven results in this market, I can help business people who are serious about going into non-invasive aesthetic practices with the BEST and EASIEST financing options available. Financers know that people who work with me are good investments for them.

- Knowing that having the equipment is not enough, I am deeply involved in the training on all the equipment, ensuring that the purchaser and their employees understand all the nuances of it thoroughly.

- Furthermore, I offer extensive training on connecting with consumers. When any person is considering undergoing a non-invasive aesthetic procedure, they are most often nervous and full of questions, a bit unsure—albeit still excited. Making sure that a true and caring provider/client relationship is intact is an important part of their success.

My own personal growth is important to these things, as well. Therefore I invest extensive time into improvements and educations in my own life so I can take these concepts and the knowledge to my clients. It's a group effort that leads to this success. Just "selling" equipment and then being done with it is never an option. Too much changes too quickly, and new innovations are always works-in-progress and new releases. Through me remaining on top of this and connected, my clients remain leaders who are trained professionals in offering these procedures in the market long before most others. In fact, I am even in the process of finalizing the invention of a piece of equipment that is geared toward the largest growing trend – bringing to market a completely non-invasive procedure that dramatically heightens a woman's ability to experience intimacy and even incontinence! That's an advantage I have, I can see what improvements can be made to existing technologies more easily, and I have the resources and knowledge to take effective action.

There has never been a better time to participate in the rising trend of non-invasive aesthetic procedures. Anti-aging and weight loss techniques are in the spotlight right now and that light is only becoming much brighter. People who want to help others and create opportunities for themselves gravitate toward this type of practice because it just makes sense, first and foremost, and it is also lucrative if you do it right. Is it for everyone? No. However, maybe it's for you. I believe in helping people do the right thing for themselves, their families, and the people they care about. Perhaps you won't be surprised to recognize this is a smart, good, right thing to do. Let's start a conversation.

About Dr. Mike

Dr. Michael Renzulli is a Naturopathic Physician with a compelling message that lends well to the motivational speaking circuit, where he is a sought-out international presenter and lecturer. He conducts many of these informative sessions through ongoing live seminars and trainings that inspire, motivate, and tap into the hearts of people, helping them to bring out their best potential. Dr. Renzulli says, "I espouse the practices that can help others inherently improve their professional, financial, and personal lives."

In addition, Dr. Renzulli is a Weight Loss and Aesthetic Practice Trainer and the exclusive distributor in North America for Lipo Technology™, a company that makes advanced non-invasive body contouring and slimming technology. With the rising trends in people proactively bringing out the best within themselves, he works closely with business owners who want to create an opportunity that is based in helping others be their best.

Dr. Renzulli is honored to co-author an authentic best seller with internationally acclaimed self and business development guru, Brian Tracy. Their book entitled *Cracking the Code to Success* promises to be a road map to personal and business success for both the seasoned and beginner alike.

Among Renzulli's mentors is the late Jim Rohn, a source of inspiration where he learned: "The secret to life is to come up with a way to add the most value—you must find a way to do more for others than anybody else is doing. Happiness and success in life are not the result of what we have, but rather how we live and what we give." He teaches people to tap into the God-given greatness within themselves and allow it to become expressed in everything they do. Other personal inspirational sources that Dr. Renzulli cites include John Grinder, Peter Guber, Tony Robbins, Grant Cardone, and Marshall Sylver.

Charlotte, NC is where Dr. Renzulli currently calls home. He has three college age daughters and two international show level Standard white poodles, Sydney and Remy.

You can reach Dr. Renzulli at:
- 212-518-8484 or
- DrMike@LipoTechnology.com.

CHAPTER 35

THE WEIGHT IS OVER!

BY CYNDIE KNORR

The formula for Success is:
A few simple disciplines practiced every day!
~ Jim Rohn

Many successful entrepreneurs and business people will admit that they can achieve any goal that they set for themselves in their careers but for some reason they can't seem to apply this same determination to losing weight and keeping it off.

Many people decide that they desperately want to lose weight by a certain date or special occasion (their upcoming High School Reunion, a tropical vacation or wedding). They know exactly how much weight they want to lose, by when, and they decide how they are going to do it. That's great! The motivation is high, and the weight comes off! They reach their 'goal' and feel amazing. But what happens after this event is over? It's always the same story! They gain it all right back.

When setting weight loss goals, it's better to be specific as to your ideal weight, but be happy with any and all progress in the right direction. Don't be too hard on yourself for minor setbacks. Considering that it took you many years to put on that weight, be patient with your body, and be happy with yourself for making an effort toward improving your health.

Growing up, I watched my mother struggle with her weight, constantly yoyo dieting and fasting for up to 40 days in a row. She said "they did

337

it in the Bible," so it must be alright for you. Mom developed diabetes when she was 40, and by her 50's she was almost completely blind and had extremely poor circulation. She would often fall asleep with her feet right next to an electric heater trying to warm them up, and awaken to discover third degree burns on the soles of her feet.

For years, dad administered her peritoneal dialysis treatments at home on our farm. Mom eventually refused to eat and spent her last days in the hospital. Her muscles continued to wither away. There was hardly anything left of her.

One day when I was visiting her, she asked me to help her change position. She clasped her arms around my neck and I was able to lift her by the knees and help her turn over. I said "Mom! You're literally skin and bones!" She sounded so pleased to hear this and said, "Thank you!" with a big smile.

This is the last memory that I have of my mother.

She struggled her entire life to become 'skinny' and had finally achieved her goal.

When our family got together for my father's funeral many years later, I learned for the first time that my older sister had been on Diabetes medication for the past 10 years. My older brother was also a diabetic and the neuropathy in his lower legs was so bad he could hardly walk.

I thought to myself, "I'm NEXT!" This was the turning point for me. I am the third of six kids and I decided right then that I would take control of my health.

At 220 lbs, I could feel rolls on the back of my scalp when I tipped my head up, and had trouble applying my own toe nail polish. My gut was in the way and bending was difficult. I hated shopping for clothes and didn't enjoy going out because I had nothing to wear that felt comfortable or looked good on me.

As a Goal Getter Coach, I help people achieve remarkable goals in their lives. The two main components to accomplishing goals are Mindset and Actions. Over the following year, I implemented these Goal Getting techniques to 'release' over 70 pounds, with the added confidence that this time it is gone for good.

Here's what I did, in four main stages. Much of it may seem like 'common sense', but there is a big difference between knowing what you should do and actually doing it!

1) Determination:

Decide that you are ready to make a change!

Realize that "quick fixes" do not produce lasting results. I have relatives who had gastric bypass surgery and lost 100 lbs, but did not keep it off because they hadn't changed their mindset or habits.

Extensive research proves that crash diets and yoyo dieting are harmful to your health. Every time you lose 'weight' on one of these diets, you lose muscle as well as fat. Unless you're doing resistance or weight training to build muscle (which many dieting people aren't), when you regain the weight you usually gain back mostly FAT. So, your percentage of body fat increases, and you become physically weaker every time you regain the weight you lost.

2) Awareness:

Accept the fact that 'You are where you ARE.'

The actions that you have and have not taken in the past have resulted in your current weight. Also, know that where you will be one month or one year from now is up to you, starting now!

Growing up, I developed numerous unhealthy eating habits. As kids in a large family, we ate very quickly and reached for more food before we were done. We always had to "finish what was on our plate." On the rare occasion when we would eat out at a restaurant, it was usually a buffet. The food was inexpensive, there was a lot of variety and we would stuff ourselves as full as possible!

Then when I had my own kids and we were always rushing to

get them from one activity to another, the frantic eating tradition continued and our kids learned unhealthy eating habits as well! It takes time and considerable effort to reverse these.

Start a journal to keep track of your progress. This step is crucial! Writing everything down is the most powerful way to become aware of what you're doing. It doesn't matter if you use paper, your phone, or an app. Use whatever method works best for you.

Date everything. Record your starting weight and your body measurements.

Write down every single thing you eat and drink and how much of each. Note the time of day, what you were thinking about, how you were feeling, who you were with, what you were doing, what just happened in the previous few minutes, were you hungry, craving something, and how did you feel after eating?

You will quickly notice if you are eating because you're bored or frustrated, or eating at a particular time of day just out of habit. You only need to keep this food journal for one to two weeks. By then, you will become aware of your eating habits! The more specific details you record, the more transformative this exercise will be for you.

Weigh yourself: either once a week on Wednesday mornings, or every morning as soon as you wake up, or once a month. Do whatever feels right and works for you!

Make a point of not eating while you are doing something else, like watching TV, driving, reading, etc. Take your time eating, and really taste the food! Listen to your body and stop eating when you feel like you've had enough. These are simple Mindfulness Exercises that will have a huge impact on what and how much you end up consuming.

3) Mindset:

**There's a 'huge difference' (bad pun intended!)
between people who say, "I can't have that!"
vs. people who say, "I don't eat that!"**

One focuses on deprivation and the other on personal power and choosing to make healthy eating a priority. One will struggle, and work desperately hard at losing weight but unfortunately will not keep it off. The other will demonstrate healthy eating habits, and will eat without regrets. One feels powerlessness, and the other feels complete control.

When it comes to losing weight, do you focus on the pain, how hard it will be, and what you will need to give up? Do you make excuses like these: My entire family is obese. It must be in my genes. My thyroid doesn't work properly. I've tried losing weight and it doesn't work for me. I hate exercising.

Or do you focus on the long-term gain? I want to live longer and be healthy. I'll have more energy to play with my kids (or grandkids). It is wonderful to enjoy shopping for clothes, and look and feel amazing! Optimism is the magic formula for success. Picture yourself already at your ideal weight and immerse yourself in how great that will feel!

Change your focus from thinking, and discussing with others, how much you hate your body, how you can never lose weight, how gross you feel, how you wish things were different, and how you can't stop thinking about food. Instead focus on loving your body and what's going right in your life.

Choose to eat foods that fuel your body with nutrition and that make you feel good in the long term. Short term gratification is gone only moments after swallowing the last bite of empty calories.

Obstacles and setbacks are inevitable. Even with the greatest intentions, mindfulness and awareness, you will have days when you fall back into your old unhealthy habits. Don't give up! Wishing it was happening 'faster' or that you had "lost more by now" is futile and destructive thinking. Be genuinely happy with the progress you are making.

4) Take Action!

Move your body! Create healthy habits.

I made a conscious decision that my health would become a top priority each day! I used to say that I didn't "have time to exercise." The truth is that there is always time for exercise once you make it a priority. Just make a decision to fit it in.

The amount of time you spend exercising is not as important as creating the habit of getting moving every day! If you don't feel like it, then just go for a short 10 or 15-minute walk. Missing one day makes it more likely that you will miss a week and eventually get completely off track. Each time you stop, it becomes harder to get started again.

Think of ways that will make it easier for you to take action. Line up a partner to go to the gym with you and keep each other accountable. If you genuinely don't like exercising, get creative and make it fun!

Plan "Walking Meetings" with clients or for catching up with friends!

Multitasking has been scientifically proven to be ineffective (and often dangerous). Exercising, however, is one task to which I love to "pair" another activity and accomplish two things at once. This also makes the time seem to pass more quickly. While engaged in simple repetitive exercises such as walking, running on a treadmill, or riding a stationary bike, you can listen to online programs, podcasts, or audible books, watch TV, or catch up on phone calls with family and friends.

Increase your NEAT (Non-Exercise Activity Thermogenesis). This is the regular moving around you do every day. Standing burns more calories than sitting. You could get yourself a 'standing desk'. Make a conscious effort to take the stairs instead of the elevator. Park a farther distance away from the entrance. Take your dog for a walk. Track your daily 'steps'.

Aim for 7 to 8 hours of sleep each night. Your body needs this time to rejuvenate.

Find ways to lower your stress. Cut down (and eventually eliminate) the amount of sugar you put in your coffee or tea. Drink lemon water instead of soda. Increase the number of glasses of water you drink each day.

There are so many small things you could do that will have an immense long term benefit. Record your progress. Enjoy the process and reward yourself often.

Out of all of these suggestions, what are you committed to doing that will take you in the direction of improved health and lasting weight loss? Decide to do something, starting today. Keep it simple and achievable. Take action on one or two small changes. These will become your new habits when you do them daily. You will gradually develop additional healthy habits over time.

A year from now you will look back on this moment and be amazed at how much better you look and feel because of these simple daily actions you took to improve your life!

About Cyndie

Cyndie Knorr is a multi-passionate entrepreneur. Besides being a Coach, Speaker, and Trainer, she is also a Professional Portrait Photographer. Her favorite subjects to photograph are families, kids, and business portraits of people who don't like having their pictures taken and hate the way they look in photos. A beautiful portrait captures a person's unique personality and character. Cyndie has a way of making people feel comfortable, and knows how to pose and light them in the most flattering way.

Her background in photography naturally lends itself to her desire to help her Coaching clients see themselves in the 'best light', and FOCUS on what's important in their lives!

As the "Goal Getter Coach" she helps people get unstuck, out of overwhelm, achieve the results they want, and finally discover true Happiness in their lives! She motivates those around her to live into their best selves, to grow, and stretch beyond the complacency of their comfort zones. This is where the magic happens!

She is down to earth, compassionate, and loves to have fun, plus at the same time has a straight forward, no-excuses approach which inspires people and brings out the high achiever in them.

Cyndie has the philosophy that Success is inevitable for anyone who chooses to put in the effort. With a positive mindset, inspired actions, patience, and unwavering determination, there are no limits to the human potential.

There is no such thing as 'Failure'; instead just consider it 'Feedback'!

She has an unquenchable thirst for studying the concepts of Habits, Productivity, High Achievement, Success, Neuroscience and how our minds work, Motivation, Persuasion, Sales, Positive Psychology, and Confidence. She keeps up with the current thought leaders and shares these insights with her coaching clients and the students in her courses.

Cyndie is a Speaker, and also leads private workshops and retreats on her "Goal Getter", and "Confidence" courses. These have recently been developed into on-line courses.

She is married, has three grown children, and lives in Saskatchewan, Canada.

Cyndie is a proud supporter of Habitat for Humanity, both financially as well as physically helping out during the Women Build days! Habitat for Humanity's vision is a world where everyone has a decent place to live. Their mission is to put God's love into action by bringing people together to build homes, communities, and hope.

You can connect with Cyndie:
- via email at: Cyndie.Knorr@CynergyCoaching.life
- www.CynergyCoaching.life
- www.facebook.com/CynergyCoaching
- www.Original-Cyn-Photography.ca
- www.facebook.com/OriginalCynPhotography

CHAPTER 36

THE VALUE OF EXECUTION WITH YOUR ONE BIG IDEA

BY GARY ABRAHAM

It's important to keep going and learn from failures, because most people give in before they get the wealth they deserve and desire.

There are two types of people attempting to become entrepreneurs. The first are those who try and fail, but don't bother to find out why. They choose to surrender. The second is those who have stories of failures that have compelled them to their stories of success. I get it, as I had a great many years of failing before finally succeeding.

When I began my entrepreneurial endeavors, I was eager, opening up business after business, hoping to find the right road. They all failed for various reasons, and eventually I took it upon myself to find out why. It was only when I understood this, that I was able to embrace this aphorism:

Treat nothing as a failure, but everything as a learning experience.

When I finally acknowledged this, things got better, quickly. Despite being resistant at times, I tried. Then something significant happened to jar me at just the "right time".

One night I came home from a night out with the boys and when I got there, my mother-in-law was waiting for me. Gulp. "When are you going to make a proper husband for my daughter and get yourself a proper job and start bringing in some income?" she asked. There was no acceptable answer either than, "Right now." It really got me thinking, and it resonated with me, and I'm forever grateful.

There was only one way that I could adjust, and that was by getting a life coach and becoming a master at that which I was seeking. You see, entrepreneurialism is often a lonely process and you need to have someone reliable to hold you accountable. No excuses—just execution and action.

As I went through this, I recognized that somewhere along the way, my dreams and aspirations were stolen from me. I wanted them back! Becoming aware of this, lead to another helpful aphorism:

Don't steal your children's dreams. Tell them they can be, do, and achieve what they desire.

When a child dreams of becoming that ballerina or star athlete, allow them to believe. Help guide them on a route to see if it can happen. It's their commitment to make, not yours. Let them develop their resilience muscle and a drive to pursue their dreams. Remember this: our minds are programmed early in life—between the ages of one and seven. During this time, we learn most of what we know today. Right or wrong doesn't matter; our parents don't intentionally teach us wrong, of course. They teach us what they know, not necessarily what we need.

Through me focusing on what I needed and avoiding abandoning successful ideas prematurely, my life began to transition and I found that one big idea that opened up a world of opportunity for me. My business, RentShield Direct, Ltd., flourished and I sold it five years later. I could finally say, "I did it!" But then I thought, now what? Once you get a taste of this type of success, you are linked into a formula that you can repeat. You've lived it once and you can do it again! This is why today I invest in helping other entrepreneurs move past quitting and onto success. I have been on both sides of the coin—the pitfalls and triumphs alike.

THINK FROM A PLACE OF EMPOWERMENT

*It's not you against the world, it's you getting your world
to work with you.*

It's important to know that most people want you to fail. Not consciously, of course, but rather on a subconscious level. They want you to be in the same position they are in, and to not outgrow or outshine them. If you surpass them, it frightens them and stifles you in their eyes. Not a favorable feeling, obviously. By understanding this you can begin transitioning to surroundings that enhance your desires for success. It involves creating a team to make the experience favorable, as well as surrounding yourself with individuals you can rely on.

You don't have to go it alone, you just have to go about it properly. Be passionate about what you wish to create, because if you're' not, you aren't focused in the right area. The people you surround yourself with should uplift you and help promote that message. It's not about the destination, it's about the journey.

We can all build a wealthy life while having fun. Wealth is much more than money alone, it's a state of mind about everything around you— family, friends, business, connections. Entrepreneurs never retire; they continuously reinvest, never knowing the end—just the potential that exists from where they are.

Start by thinking about your perception of failure, because this impacts how we give ourselves permission to learn and grow in our pursuits. For example, baseball players can be in the hall of fame despite not making the "big hit" 7 out of 10 times. For them, succeeding 3 out of 10 times is great— exceptional in fact. Why not view your own failures this same way?

Next, you have to train yourself to see what it's like to be "wealthy". And by wealth, I mean more than just money, I mean everything in life. There is so much information out there in publications to extract from. It may sound hard, but it doesn't have to be hard.

Remember, making your first million will be the hardest. After that, things become significantly easier because you're wiser and more self-assured. People who desire to take their ideas to a higher financial level don't surrender their dream too early. It's like a baby learning to walk. When they fall, we don't say, "That's it. They're not meant to be a walker." We keep coaxing them to continue on, step-by-step, until they walk.

Everything you do is habit forming. If it was easy to be successful, we'd all be successful.

12 STEPS TO FINANCIAL FREEDOM

Understand that wealth and a prosperous life is out there for you—for everybody. You just have to grab it.

Fifteen years ago, I began a journey to bring in a continuous flow of wealth for myself and others. To do this, I had to take significant steps. Some were hard, but it didn't matter. I'd honed in on my passion that would propel me towards my purpose. I know it can do the same for you.

Realize that everything is linked together so you can take greater strides. Our physical actions lead to our mental acumen, which is all a part of having overall health of the body, mind, and soul. We are like the Formula 1 race car – no matter how finely tuned we are, if we put the wrong fuel in our engines, we are going to run into problems.

Most of us do not grasp the exact power our mind holds. It's our greatest currency, actually. They say we only use about 5% of our conscious mind and 95% is subconscious. By taking steps to make even 1% more of our mind based in conscious thought, we become 25% more "switched on" than most people. I've used my coaching to really study my mind to see how I can get the best impact from that extra 1%.

This 1% gives you the edge and helps keep the road to your dreams so wide; as long as you keep moving forward you are sure to reach your destiny. Along the road to my destiny, I developed 12 strategies that gave me the edge to mastering my mind. I believe they can be of value to you, as well.

Here is my list:

1. Choose to pursue things that you can have fun doing and are passionate about.

No other route works, and I can guarantee you that discipline is actually enjoyable if you're passionate about the subject. Discipline is also long term. It reminds you that your efforts are not about the destination, but rather the journey. If you ever reach your destination, you have not aimed high enough.

2. Choose the people you associate with.

If you want to experience success you need to invest your time around people who will help with that. If you share your vision with someone and they respond with a, "Why would you do that?". . . it's time to re-evaluate the company you keep.

3. Teamwork builds the dream work.

True synergy occurs when you have multiple people conspiring to succeed. This is where the magic happens and people come together to create results that move you forward. Think of a chess match, you'd be foolish to play the game with just a King. So why play your business ventures on your own? Don't be frightened to surround yourself with people who have more skill sets than you. The one true skill set you require to propel the team to success is Leadership. You will have heard the saying, "If you help people get what they want you will surely get what you want".

4. Goal setting.

It's important to create goals that stretch you and allow you to dream big. If you want to be a billionaire, put it out there. If you reach 10% of the goal, "Hey, you're doing okay!" Through working with my coach, I learnt how to really make these goals real and tangible. Visit your goals regularly and re-set them at least every six months.

5. Know your values.

Never compromise your values. By staying true to your values the universe transpires to help you. If challenging situations arise, you can always walk away knowing that your values are intact.

6. You cannot think about what you don't want without thinking about it.

The human mind doesn't process negative thoughts immediately and we must be mindful of our internal dialogue because of this. Our minds are like a computer and negative thoughts feeding our mind lead to negative outcomes. On a subconscious level, we'll believe we are a failure and that transcends to our conscious mind. Likewise, positive thoughts do give us positive outcomes!

7. Train your mind for more empowering thoughts.

Place yourself in a brilliant mindset where you are always motivated toward what you want, and not away from the things you don't want. For example: instead of saying, "I need to lose weight, I'm overweight", which immediately causes your mind to think of those negative words associated with such a sentence, choose to say something to your mind that takes you to a place you want to be. "I am going to lead a more healthy and fantastic life".

8. Expectations rule your outcome.

What we expect can be different than what we want. When I began being coached and setting goals, I also began expecting everyone to come up to a higher level. I was already living in a successful state of mind. To do this, I began living the lifestyle I envisioned in my mind because I knew that would lead to tangible results. This was so powerful.

9. Don't underestimate cause and effect.

This Universal Truth is best explained by an example. I had a friend who went to America to learn a new management system. He was quite stoked about its potential for his life and when I caught up with him a year later and asked how it was going, he told me that he was thinking of quitting—it wasn't working out. After a few hours of talking one thing was clear: he blamed everyone and everything else for the failure. Not a single thought of his involvement in it. I listened and then went bold, suggesting why it wasn't working—he had programmed himself to have everything transpire against him. I love a good challenge and this situation had one in it. I offered to coach him to see what we could do to turn things around. The results were almost instant and in less than six months went from a position of failure to bringing in a six-figure salary into his business. Much better than quitting, right? Be self-aware and take accountability, always.

10. Both problems and solutions come from our imagination.

Everything stems from our mind and when we understand this, problems can be good stimulators for creative solutions. It all links together, as our minds can solve anything we want them to; we just have to get the right help and coaching to learn the techniques.

11. Hone in on the flashlight of your focus.

What do you focus on? Think of your mind as an internet search engine, knowing that what you punch in is what you get out.You wouldn't go online and type in "crap" or "loser" because that's exactly what you'd get back—all sorts of information to teach you about those things. Make sure your mind's search engine is helping you find out all things positive and beneficial. Why search for something you do not want?

12. The joy is in the journey not the destination.

When I sold my business at the age of 47 I thought, what am I going to do now? I sat down with my coach and began creating new goals new challenges. I knew that it was my time to give back and help other entrepreneurs. That was my next journey and it meant that there would never be an "end", but a series of beginnings and journeys that fulfilled me. Play the game of life at 100% because understand, how we do one thing is how we do everything.

TODAY IS YOUR DAY

Your outcome is a product of your thoughts and actions.

When I talk to people about moving past the failures and toward the successes of being an entrepreneur, I always do two things. I give people a copy of the book, The Alchemist by Paulo Coelho, which is the first book I read on my path to wealth, and also a printed million-pound note, which is exactly what was given to me at one of my first Leadership seminars. On that note it reads: "What's the value of one big idea?"

To determine the value of the big idea you have to fill in the lines, much like I did. Put down what you want as a reminder to claim it and live it. Carry it with you everywhere as a physical reminder, as well as a reminder of the fusion of action and mind that is required to achieve it. By doing this, you are making a difference that takes you from failure to success. You are the true essence of an entrepreneur.

About Gary

Gary Abraham, a serial entrepreneur and a leading authority on personal empowerment and mastering the mind, helps other budding entrepreneurs and companies break through their own challenges and boundaries to achieve wealth and power. He gives eye-opening insights into the road to wealth and why some people run out of fuel on the way. He provides techniques and tools to expand the road so wide, that as long as you are prepared to take action you will undoubtedly move forward towards a rich and prosperous life – fulfilling your own life's purpose while having fun on the journey to design your destiny.

Gary lives in Teignmouth, Devon with his wife, Vicky and two sons, Ross and Max. To dispel the myth that wealth is just for the privileged few, he left school at 16 with four "Grade C" passes and a disillusioned Careers Officer telling him, "A life in the Services is as much as you can hope for." So, after a brief spell in the Royal Navy, where he learnt his life skills, he embarked on his entrepreneurial journey to which he knew he was always destined. After many failed businesses, which he now knows were not failures but lessons on the road to success, he realised that to become the best at something you've got to make it a study. If you want to be happy, you study happiness, if you want wealth and all it brings you've got to study. That is exactly what he did. He got himself a life coach and became a master of his own mind with some astonishing results. In November 2006, he set up a company, Rentshield Direct Ltd. and less than 5 years later, sold it for a seven-figure fee.

Gary now spends his time doing what he wants, not what others want him to do, and is free to enjoy his family and help others overcome the obstacles on the road to a prosperous and wealthy life.

Gary is a graduate of The Christopher Howard Training and is a master practitioner and trainer of Nero-linguistic programming and advanced neurological repatterning, a certified performance consultant and master results coach, as well as being a Master in Ericksonian hypnosis.

You can contact Gary at:
- gary.abraham64@gmail.com
- www.linkedin.com/in/gary-Abraham-489347a5
- www.twitter.com/garyabraham6
- www.facebook.com/garyabraham

CHAPTER 37

WORK HARD AND BELIEVE IN YOURSELF

BY CAMILO GUTIERREZ

My grandfather taught me what it means to work hard and believe in myself. I found my childhood passion of baseball in my neighborhood at the age of six. I'd play all day, sun-up to sun-down. The game blew my mind and changed my life. I was obsessed. Starting from my childhood – baseball became my positive outlet for my challenging home life. Gramps supported my love for baseball, but also provided me with my mentality. He gave me a constant desire for self-improvement. When I wasn't playing, I was training. He imprinted me with self-confidence. Everything Gramps said I eagerly listened to. His coaching led to a weightlifting and strength program. Even at this age, I loved working on myself.

Anything my grandfather suggested, I was willing to try. I have always been hungry for self-improvement. I would weight lift with him every day for years in his garage. My mother was experiencing her own challenges, but my grandfather was my guiding light. He would give me chores, and reward me for my hard work. More than just assigned chores, he urged me to challenge myself. I remember trying to rake leaves on all of his rental properties, just how I'd watched him do. I couldn't finish the lawns, I was young and I was exhausted quickly. Even though I couldn't finish the task – I gave it my best effort. I wasn't rewarded with the bike I asked for from Gramps but I knew I tried my best; and that was enough for me to feel successful.

Sometimes he would take me to work with him—he was a salesman.

I remember sitting on the couch next to him, hearing him convince people they deserved something better. He made people feel good about themselves, that's why he was successful. It was in these moments, during the ins and outs of every day that his positive mentality made an everlasting impression on me. He was constantly speaking about the freedom and benefits of owning his own business. He taught me how to believe in the power of positive thinking.

My grandfather had his own battles, as he struggled with alcohol during his younger years. He gave up drinking as soon as I was born, and he helped raise me and the rest of his grandchildren, as his addiction had prevented him from raising his own children. He wasn't capable of making a strong emotional connection with his children during his struggle with alcoholism, but once he became a Gramps, he put a lot of his effort into helping raise us to become successful, happy people. I couldn't understand his struggle until I went through it myself. I was on a promising path in collegiate baseball in Texas.

Unfortunately, my girlfriend of the time was struggling back home, so I returned home, I came home to a painful relationship that quickly failed. In a flash, I had stopped pursuing my first love of baseball. I felt lost, and defeated. I gave in to the harmful, easy, negative side of my brain. I didn't understand what addiction was. I didn't realize how powerful it could be. I was lost, and worse yet, I felt trapped. Soon my alcoholism and my demons made me want to give up.

Somewhere in the pain and addiction I lost a major part of myself: my positive and hard-working attitude. I lost the part of me that craved self-improvement. It vanished, and I came to a point where I couldn't understand how I could want to help other people so much, and yet I wasn't able to help myself. How could I ask for someone else to lead a healthy lifestyle, to keep their mentality positive and to push themselves when I didn't even want to be alive? I realized then I needed to ask for help. I needed to ask for help for myself and for my future. If I wanted to continue to be a weight lifter, if I wanted to be a successful personal trainer, if I wanted to follow my passion and succeed in the goals I set for myself, then I needed to get help.

I've been sober for four years now. During my bout with alcoholism, I absorbed so much pain it was unbelievable. I felt so defeated, so worthless and it was terrifying. It is humbling now to reflect and realize how much our bodies and our minds can tolerate. It is our personal job to help heal ourselves. Staying active keeps your mindset in check, pushes you to perform your best, and keeps your confidence boosted. Life is a new challenge, post-addiction. I have the choice, and I am blessed with the ability to give myself new challenges. I set new goals for myself, create positive changes, and I feel accomplished when I complete one. My life now is challenging, because I choose for it to be. I challenge myself to lift heavy weights, and to eat healthy foods for fuel. I am happy to work hard, with the confidence that my life will never be as hard as it was under the rain cloud of addiction.

Hard work can be a tough concept for people to grasp. If a person isn't shown what it means to work hard, or what the benefits are from working hard, they'll likely never understand its importance, until it's too late. They may find themselves lost or stuck in situations hard work wouldn't allow. Mental strength is hard work. Having the capability to concentrate and to make yourself believe you can do anything, is a constant fight. Don't get me wrong, the word 'fight' isn't negative. Fighting for something you wholeheartedly desire is invigorating. Taking control of your thoughts and putting them into action, even when it's difficult, that requires strength. The challenges you present for yourself to overcome are often the most rewarding to see achieved.

People tend to have this notion of mental strength as being akin to an athlete's physical strength. As if mental strength is only used in big competitions and extreme moments of desperation. When you're willing to face what's coming next, no matter how difficult the climb, that's mental strength. Mental strength can and should be developed in every person's life. To be mentally strong is to be willing to be uncomfortable, to be willing to push yourself outside of your comfort zone, to test your limits, to start a task knowing the outcome won't be perfect, but willing to train to get there. To be mentally strong means to be confident in yourself and the work you put in towards your goal.

Obviously, we can't always be mentally tough. We all have different hurdles. For some of us those hurdles are caused by a challenging home life. Others have addiction issues. For many, and probably all of us, there are self-confidence hurdles—something like an abusive relationship or our own destructive habits that wreak havoc on our mental strength.

Being told you aren't good enough by any person or your own negative voice, your mind can convince you that you're not worthy of success. It'll tell you you'll never achieve it anyway. It's easy to give in to the monster inside your mind. It's easy to bow down to the negative aspects of your situation and succumb to a negative life.

Mental strength is a hard skill to train. Mental strength takes twice as much work to create as your negative self-talk, but it is worth the price a thousand-fold. Once you can listen to the positive and powerful part of your brain you will succeed. You'll succeed in any and every part of your life. Your mental strength will naturally gear you towards positive change. You will be able to see what you want and have the courage to chase after it. You will be willing to be uncomfortable. You will have the confidence to try new things. You will want to change for the better, all the time. You won't care what anyone else thinks. You won't listen to anyone's negative comments. Your mental strength shields you from your negative mental monsters.

Your mental strength drowns out anyone else's unnecessary comments. Once you have built yourself up, your path becomes clear. The only roadblocks you'll find then are the ones you set up for yourself. The roadblocks you choose to overcome to better yourself. Becoming mentally strong means giving yourself the best jumpstart you can imagine. It means you are doing everything in your power to set yourself up for success. This positive motivating part of your brain propels you forward in everything, every day.

I couldn't find this part of me for a long time. All I could hear was my negative self-talk, and all I could see were my failures. I found myself again through fitness. Throughout my recovery my mentality completely changed. Weightlifting brought me back my self-confidence. It helps me focus daily on the positive changes I'm making in my life, and the lives of the people around me. When I'm in the gym, my negative attitude doesn't exist. It's impossible for me to do anything but focus on pushing myself to be my best. When all your energy is focused on trying your hardest, any negative outcome can always be seen in a positive light. That may sound contradictory, but think about it. If something doesn't happen the way I expect it, when I'm giving it my all, that's not a failure. If I miss a lift but I'm giving it my maximum effort, that doesn't mean I'm weak. That means I'm working towards getting stronger. That means

I'm pushing myself harder and eventually if I continue to work hard, I'll make that lift easily and continue to build confidence.

This is my passion. I am blessed to be able to push myself in my gym every day. I am blessed to have the ability to coach my friends and clients to better themselves. This is my reward for my mental strength. My mentality has given me the gift of pursuing my passion. Often times when people are struggling they can't see ahead. It's hard to imagine a positive light at the end of a negative tunnel. People are unwilling to put in the effort it takes to get there. I was lucky enough to have been taught the value of my efforts. If I didn't have such a positive force in my life as my Gramps, maybe I wouldn't have found my strength. It took courage for me to get help. I wanted to stop the negative voices in my head. I wanted to fight back. I found my mental strength through my struggle.

I am surrounded by good people who found their mental strength through their struggles. My career and my passion is pushing people to get the most out of their work out. I believe fitness is the key to a positive attitude and great work ethic. I learned at a very young age how important it is to feel good about ourselves and how important it is to push others towards their own confidence. I love motivating people to believe in themselves. I thrive on seeing people at my gym working hard and pushing past their limits. When we push ourselves and see our success, we build our confidence. Every time we take a step forward, we are creating positive momentum within ourselves. This momentum is the driving force that empowers us to achieve our goals. To me, there is no unrealistic goal. If you are willing to work hard, to be uncomfortable, to believe in yourself, nothing can stop you.

Nutrition and fitness are vital to maintaining healthy thought patterns. People can be embarrassed by their fitness level or their weight, but if they're willing to put in the time and effort, they will succeed. Before starting a fitness journey you'll often hear people comparing themselves to an elite level athlete with frustration. People will complain they aren't as fit or as strong as someone who's been training for five years. You cannot fear trying something on the basis that you will not compare to someone else. You have to be willing to be uncomfortable! You have to be willing to try something new, and to work to be at their level. That's how they did it—hard work. No one starts any task at an elite level. Everyone starts somewhere; your job is to be willing to put in the hard work. Your job is to be patient and never give up.

You will succeed. Mental strength does not equal physical strength! You cannot succeed in the gym or in your life if you don't have mental strength. You can be physically capable of doing a thousand push-ups, but if you don't believe in yourself, you can't. You probably wouldn't even try. There's no argument. If you don't believe in yourself, you will never succeed. You have to build both, together, in order to be able to use either. Your mental strength and your physical strength rely on each other to keep you motivated. The two are vital to maintaining each other. When I'm having a rough day, I go to the gym to fix my mindset. When I'm going to lift a heavy weight, I turn to my ability to focus and believe in myself. You cannot have one without the other.

Deciding to work on yourself is never an easy task. You have to have the courage to admit your faults. You have to be willing to work hard. Whether it's in your fitness or in your nutrition, you have to change. When you change for yourself, you are changing for the better. There is no recipe book for everybody. There's no diet that's going to work for everyone. There's no magical workout that fits every single person. Growing means experimenting. Experimenting with our fitness kick-starts our momentum. This momentum propels us forward. If you're doing it correctly you're not always going straight, but you're always moving forward. As a trainer, I want to encourage as many people as I can to work out. As we maintain our bodies, we also maintain our minds.

Mental strength can be revolutionary. Changing the way you think about yourself will change your life. Through your mental strength you will find success. It's important to remember that life is meant to challenge you. Our paths aren't always easy, or straight. Often we climb treacherous emotional mountains, or we make ourselves jump through hoops. There comes a point where you have to realize you are the only person who can overcome your struggle. I can tell you this, with the connections I've cultivated and the strength it finally took to make personal life changes, I was able to experience my best self!

I've proven myself to be who I've always wanted to be: giving, encouraging, strong and kind. To be able to continuously work toward those goals earnestly and to use my mental strength to help myself and the people around me succeed – that's what I wanted for myself; that's what I started for myself!

About Camilo

Camilo Gutierrez lives in Sacramento, California. Through his recovery from addiction, Camilo found his beautiful wife, Maria. He often refers to her as his cornerstone for life and love. They live together with their three cats: the one-eyed Puma, Super Mario, and BearBear. He owns and operates his gym Midtown Strength and Conditioning. He is a personal trainer, strength coach, and incredibly enthusiastic entrepreneur.

During his youth he played baseball in the Sacramento area, most notably for Sacramento City College. Camilo has a unique athletic background in the fact that he's so dynamic. Starting with excelling in collegiate baseball, growing into a competitive bodybuilder, power lifter, CrossFit athlete, and finding an everlasting passion for Olympic weight lifting. His knowledge in all different types of fitness helps him train all different levels of athletes.

Camilo has a giving nature, and one of his life goals is to help others grow in every aspect they desire. He has accomplished the goal of helping ten of his former coaches start up their own businesses. He achieved this goal by encouraging these coaches in his gym, and from leading by example every day. He has been a keynote speaker at National Strength and Conditioning Association seminars. He frequently holds weightlifting seminars for any and all to come and learn the basics from a Masters level athlete.

Camilo holds the honor of being inducted into C.K. McClatchy's Hall of Fame, his hometown high school – for his excellence in baseball. Camilo himself has been taught by some of the best weightlifting coaches in the country: Dave Spitz, Jim Schmitz, Paul Doherty, Chip Conrad, and countless others. Camilo's work ethic was greatly influenced from his baseball coach, Jerry Weinstein. Over the past ten years at his gym he has helped coach over 3,000 members. He is continually learning and growing his mental strength through listening to motivational speakers everyday: Brian Tracy, Napoleon Hill, Les Brown, and Tony Robbins – his ideals have had a profound effect on Camilo and his work ethic.

You can find Camilo online everywhere:
- MidtownStrength@gmail.com
- Facebook: Midtown Strength and Conditioning
- Instagram: MidtownMilo
- WordPress: StrengthSessions.Me

CHAPTER 38

CRACKING THE CODE TO INVESTMENT SUCCESS
ENJOY A SMARTER, MORE SECURE RETIREMENT WITH THE RIGHT INVESTMENT STRATEGIES

BY ANDREW A. ARONS

When it comes to investing for retirement, people have a wide range of goals—to live a comfortable lifestyle, to travel the world, to provide for their children and grandchildren, etc. Regardless of the particular dreams you have for your retirement years, your primary investment goal should be to avoid outliving your money. With life expectancies getting longer all the time, meeting this goal has become more of a challenge than ever before.

If you're living longer, then your money needs to last longer; which means your investments will need to generate more income over a longer period of time, and more than they did in your parents' and grandparents' day. That makes how you choose to invest your assets for the long-term a crucial decision that can have a dramatic effect on your overall success. Invest wisely, and you will likely have the assets to enjoy some version of the retirement you dream about. Make a mistake, and your golden years may be marked by more sacrifice and struggle than you ever anticipated.

There's a lot at stake—which is why most people don't make these decisions on their own. Instead, they turn to professional financial advisors who present them with a range of options and help them make crucial decisions about where and how to invest their money. These advisors generally fall into two camps: those with an active money management strategy, and those with a passive money management strategy. Oftentimes, the advisor you choose may well determine the strategy options you're offered, without you knowing all the choices at your disposal.

ACTIVE VS. PASSIVE—THE PROS AND CONS

Active money managers are constantly watching the markets and reacting to them, buying and selling as indexes rise and fall. Their goal is usually to outperform a specific benchmark index and therefore "beat the market," so they tend to attract investors who are willing to take bigger risks in the hopes of reaping bigger rewards. When it comes to U.S. stocks, however, the reality is that only 33% of active money managers actually beat the S&P index[1] (though the ones who do sometimes secure a windfall for their clients).

Passive money managers employ what's commonly referred to as a "buy and hold" strategy. They invest their clients' assets in a mix of stocks and bonds selected to meet their needs and then basically leave them alone, trusting that, since the market historically goes up over time, their clients' investments will remain secure while earning them money over the long term. Passive advisors rely primarily, and often exclusively, on what's called **strategic asset allocation**. They determine a client's risk tolerance (what percentage of their assets they can afford to "play with" compared to how much must remain secure), and allocate their assets to higher-risk stocks and lower-risk bonds accordingly—most commonly a 60-40 split between the two. They then sit back and essentially let the market do what it's going to do.

If your money is invested passively, you probably trust that it's fairly safe and secure. What you may not realize, however, is that you could be missing out on some significant opportunities, and even be putting your future at risk.

1. Adam Shell, "66% of fund managers can't match S&P results," *USA Today*, March 14th, 2016

First, let's look at a missed opportunity. If you had your money invested solely in the S&P 400 Mid-Cap Index for the past 35 years, you would have earned about 13.5% on your investment over that time period. However, if your advisor used the strategies that our firm uses, you would have earned an impressive 17.3% on that same investment.[2] This seemingly small percentage difference is actually quite significant because of compounding—the difference is three times the return in dollar amount.

What's even more significant are the risks that come with this supposedly safe and conservative passive investment strategy. Let's say that during the crash of 2008, your portfolio went down 40% (the S&P actually went down 39.6%). In order to recover what you lost and break even again, you would need to earn back 67% of the post-crash value of your portfolio. That could take you 8 to 10 years. I don't know about you, but most of my clients don't have 8 to 10 years to recover from a downturn.

Finally, there's another hidden hazard on the horizon for clients of financial advisors who stick solely with strategic asset allocation. As you get older, most financial advisors will likely advocate moving more of your money from higher-risk stocks into lower-risk bonds. Right now, interest rates are historically low, but they're beginning to climb higher. And when interest rates go up, the bond market goes down. Meaning that, while you think any money you have invested in the bond market is at a low risk, it's actually in more danger than you think.

So, where can you find that sweet spot between risk and security that cracks the investment code and maximizes your investments—so you're provided with an income that lasts as long as you do?

The solution is to utilize a mix of both passive and active strategies. That means you need to work with a financial advisor who understands all of the options available and can tailor a customized plan for your specific financial needs and goals.

UNDERSTANDING THE RANGE OF STRATEGIC OPTIONS

Because my firm, Synergy Advisory Management Group, typically

2. Alpha Mid-Cap Brochure, Page 6, http://www.alphaim.net/mid_cap_power_index _brochure.pdf

works with people in and nearing retirement, we employ a full range of investment strategies to maximize our clients' results over a shorter time horizon. One thing that sets us apart from most of our competitors is the fact that we look at everything that's out there and, instead of relying upon only one or two set strategies, we create a custom plan for each of our clients that is designed to help them achieve their goals. So, in addition to a baseline approach of strategic asset allocation, we employ some combination of the following:

1. Tactical Investing

Tactical investing generally refers to short-term deviations from an overall investment plan designed to take advantage of specific opportunities. At our firm, however, it refers to something a little different—investing according to market patterns that have existed for long periods of time. Tactical investing isn't "playing the market" or even trying to time the market, it's simply looking at seasonal patterns that have existed for decades and using them to our clients' advantage.

Here's one amazing example: Every year from 1950 through 2015, during the months between November and May, the market delivered an average return of 7.4% during this particular six-month period.[3] We call it the "Power Zone"—a time when, year after year, the market usually experiences the vast majority of its gains. The other six months of the year, from May 1 through October 31, have proven to be an investors' "Dead Zone," delivering an average return of just 0.4% over that same 65-year period.

So, for the half of the year that the market is in the Dead Zone, we react accordingly. We may take a client's money (especially if that client is a retiree and needs to minimize their risk) out of the market and keep it in cash. Sometimes, if there's a sector that has been through a major downturn, like the oil industry at this writing, we might "buy cheap" and invest in that sector to take advantage of the opportunity that downturn presents. This kind of flexibility allows our clients to benefit from conditions that a typically passive financial advisor would likely overlook.

3. Alpha Mid-Cap Brochure, Page 3, http://www.alphaim.net/mid_cap_power_index_ brochure.pdf

2. Constant-Weighting Asset Allocation

A **constant weighting approach** is a more active investment strategy that involves reacting to shifts in the value of assets in a client's portfolio and making changes accordingly in order to retain its original mix of assets. To simplify all that jargon, it's basically a "buy low, sell high" strategy, where we buy more of an asset for our client when the price drops, and sell it when the price goes up. While there is no universal rule as to when this type of rebalancing should take place, most financial advisors make a move when an asset class either gains or loses more than 5% of its original value. This helps our clients maintain stability in their portfolios.

3. Dynamic Asset Allocation

Like constant weighting allocation, **dynamic asset allocation** is also an active investment strategy. In this case, we continually adjust a client's mix of assets as the economy fluctuates and the market rises and falls. However, this strategy is basically the opposite of constant weighting allocation—when the price of an asset is falling, we sell it in order to avoid any further losses, and when the price of an asset is rising, we buy it with the idea that it will continue to grow. This allows clients to take advantage of overall market trends. (Note: Because this strategy is the opposite of constant weighting allocation, they cannot be employed at the same time.)

4. Insured Asset Allocation

When utilizing **insured asset allocation**, we establish a portfolio for a client that is not allowed to drop below a certain, predetermined value. For example, if a client's portfolio has a base value of $500k, as long as that portfolio receives a return above its base, we exercise active management strategies in hopes of continuing to increase its value. However, should the value of that portfolio ever drop back down to 500k, we then invest that base value in risk-free assets to protect the client's initial investment.

5. Integrated Asset Allocation

Employing a combination of strategic asset allocation mixed with one or more of these other strategies is what's known as **integrated asset allocation**. This is our overall approach to investing at Synergy Advisory Management Group—we take into account each client's economic expectations as well as their risk when establishing the right asset mix for them. This individualized approach is aimed at producing the best possible result for each client's specific wants and needs.

CHOOSING THE RIGHT FINANCIAL ADVISOR

The right investment strategy for you will depend on several factors, including your goals, your age, your tolerance for risk and market expectations. Finding the right financial advisor to implement those strategies on your behalf could be more important than the strategies themselves. Many advisors never move beyond a basic strategic asset allocation philosophy. Others don't really consider factors such as seasonal market patterns like the Power Zone and Dead Zone, which can impact investments in a profound way.

If you're looking for an overall investment approach that is more customized to your particular needs than a basic 'buy and hold' approach, something that takes advantage of opportunities while also minimizing risk, you should look for an advisor who understands all the different investing strategies and knows how to maximize them in order to help meet your specific long-term goals.

So how do you find that kind of financial advisor?

The first step is to gain knowledge about all the different strategies I've briefly discussed in this chapter, so you can begin to understand what you want and don't want—and what you do and don't feel comfortable with. Not every advisor knows or uses all of these strategies, instead relying on what's comfortable and familiar to them. Working with an advisor who doesn't fully take advantage of all the options out there means you could end up in a situation where you don't get the results you're after—and never even understand why.

Before you meet with an advisor, do your research. Look them up on Google and LinkedIn and use the Financial Industry Regulatory Authority's (FINRA) BrokerCheck to make sure there are no ethical or legal violations on their record. When you do meet with an advisor, don't hesitate to ask them to describe their investment approach, and how they would go about determining the best course of action for you. If their philosophy or approach doesn't resonate with you, try someone else.

Remember, you may not be able to control what happens in the market, but you can certainly control who helps navigate that market for you. It's the smartest way to ensure your retirement "nest egg" is as abundant as possible.

[Disclaimer:
- Securities offered through: Nationwide Planning Associates, Inc. Member FINRA and SIPC.
- Advisory Services offered through: NPA Asset Management, LLC, a registered investment advisor.
- Synergy Advisory Management Group, LLC is not affiliated with Nationwide Planning Associates, Inc.]

About Andrew

Fascinated during childhood by the financial markets, Andrew Arons' early interest flourished into a career spanning more than two decades. Andrew earned a BA from Emory University, and is a Registered Financial Consultant, Registered Financial Planner, National Ethics Association member, and a Series 7, 63, & 65 licensed securities and insurance professional.

Specializing in retirement planning and wealth management, Andrew founded Synergy Advisory Management Group, LLC., an independent financial services firm. As indicated by its name, Synergy employs a holistic team-based approach to financial planning, and utilizes strategic alliances to help each client achieve their individualized vision of retirement.

Well known as a financial educator, Andrew offers seminars for individuals, human resource managers and Fortune 500 companies, and teaches retirement planning courses at local colleges and university-sponsored programs. An experienced financial professional, Andrew has received many accolades and appeared on CNBC, Fox Business News, CNN, financial news radio shows, and has been featured in *New Jersey Monthly, Newsweek, U.S. News and World Report, The Street.com*, and the *New York Times*.

Andrew lives in River Vale, New Jersey with his wife and two children. He enjoys tennis, travel, and coaching his kids' softball, baseball, basketball and flag football teams.

If you're interested in learning more about your investment options, his contact information is:
- 1-888-503-4001
- aarons@nationwideplanning.com.

CHAPTER 39

HAVE HOPE! EVERYONE GETS A SECOND CHANCE

BY ADRIAN DRAGOMAN

When l decided to co-author a book about success, I realized it was going to be a challenge. In the last few years, I read many books, attended seminars, completed online training programs and studied hard to learn how to improve my organizational skills and time management, as well as to learn how to succeed in every area of my life. To make a long story short, I wanted "to be successful" – not just as a businessman in Romania, but in all areas of my life. As a result of my research and learning spree, I realized there is an abundance of great authors with valuable information, principles, strategies and clever techniques that made me say to myself, "Adi, what can you tell people about success that hasn't been already said. Then I realized! I can talk about success and be original. . . Why not tell my own story by sharing my own experiences with others?

I was born in Transylvania, the central part of Romania, East Europe, under communism. When I was 18 years old, the revolution took place and we became "democratic." It was a new beginning; instantly everything changed dramatically, most people had no experience in many areas. Many communist factories closed down and many people were willing to make a living and open small business. So was my family. At the time, we were living close to a corner street. Our side of our house was next to big buildings with small apartments; crowded with people. It didn't take long for my dear father, Florean, to realize our house is wonderfully located in a "hot spot," so he decided to build a small store right there by the sidewalk. Mostly the people walked and used public transportation. The bus station was across the street from our house which made it a gold mine!

My father's decision to open a family-based business placed me in a position to learn business from the ground level! Small retail stores like the one my family opened became popular at that time, and people could buy foods, drinks, cigarettes, candies, a few hygiene products, even fast food products and fresh coffee: all of this merchandise in a ten-square-meter building! The selling process was going through a small window and there was one door for access and supplying. Our little place became very popular, so we were selling big time; moving goods out, getting money in. We were putting the money in a big flat drawer, and in the afternoons we had to empty the drawer twice because of all the cash coming in! The salesperson had to have an assistant to help pick the goods from the stock faster. It was only a matter of time before my father decided to invest more and rent new locations.

At the first location, behind the store, we had a garden area. In a short time, instead of having fresh tomatoes, onions, and other vegetables, we built a warehouse and an office. We bought a truck to supply and deliver the products to our other stores, but more than that, we became a wholesaler to other retailers like us. We bought the products in order to resell. We become an important supplier for the entire county.

My parents had two sons and I was the younger. At that time, I was just a teenager. Starting this new business and expanding it wasn't easy. We had no experience before this and had to learn a lot! But somebody had to do inventories at all locations, calculate prices, do all legal forms, go to the bank, learn how to use the computer and many other activities. My father decided he was too old to learn all that. My brother chose to be the supplier and driver of truck. I had no choice and missed the fun that most teenagers enjoy.

All good so far, but step-by-step, things started to slow down. The Romanian economy, as a young democratic country, was unstable and vulnerable. Inflation rates started to go up rapidly. With the same money we were buying less and less products each time. We were making profits only in theory. The wholesale supplying business we started had its own problems. Retailers were having problems paying us; therefore, we had challenges paying our bills. In a short time, we had to close store after store and then the warehouse, and finally the first store by our house; the one that we called our "gold mine." We still had customers, but our debt was growing to the point we had to file bankruptcy.

While working in my family business, I learned many things that were very useful for me in the long run. After the bankruptcy, I tried a couple more business on my own but they didn't work out, so I started working as a salesman for a few years. My life wasn't so bright anymore. I become unhappy and depressed. I lost hope. Then I decided to ask God for help for the first time in my life. I heard about Him but didn't know Him. It wasn't too long before I got His answer. I met a wonderful family of people who came from America as missionaries. We become best friends and our family become one. My first trip to visit the United States was a miracle, since getting a tourist visa at that time was difficult. I had no wife or kids or obligations. The US Embassy looks at visitors' background that they trusted would return to their homeland.

At the time I went to the embassy to apply for my visa, it was two weeks after the terrorist attack on the twin towers on 09.11.2001. I was in a long line of people waiting for my turn for the visa interview. While waiting, I was observing people in front of me, and I saw that most people's applications were denied. I become agitated and thought I didn't have a chance. I was feeling desperate. Suddenly, I was overwhelmed with a heavenly peace. I felt something supernatural. My turn came. I was asked if I can speak English and I said, "yes, I think I do." The man in front of me started asking me many questions about what I do, what I have, but I had to answer, "no" to everything he asked. I guess he thought I didn't understand him and called a translator. My answers were still "no" to most of his questions. One of his final questions was, "Mr. Dragoman when would you like to go to the United States?" My answer surprised both people in front of me. "Now" I said, "I have a family of friends that I will travel with and they are waiting for me to go to the airport." He gave me a three months visa! It was an amazing trip discovering a new world. My heart changed my spirits, and I was no longer unhappy or insecure. My first Sunday in the USA, I was invited to attend a local church. During the service something happened to me, I was very touched and put my life in God's hands.

After returning to Romania, I started a new job in a company as a manager. Today, I own 50% of the business. After this, I opened my own company and I started building homes with a small crew of workers and selling the homes one by one. I branched out and start building for other companies – investor homes and apartment buildings. My company grew bigger and stronger every year and I opened two more business. This time around, I had a strong desire to learn, to do things better and not to fail anymore.

I questioned myself, what happened the first time, when I was running my family businesses? I had done my best and the reasons for our failure were due to a very unstable economy. I was a victim of my country's economic system. My answer to this question is different today, "Absolutely yes, it's my fault too!" Yes, it was an unstable economy, but is today any better? We have an economic crisis, politics that change along with governments, changing laws, and more competition. The rules of the game are changing and we need to be prepared and know what we doing. And before we get to know what we are doing, sometimes we must fail; maybe several times. For many of us, that is the way to learn.

A few years ago, someone invited me to a free business seminar that was taking place in my hometown. The best Romanian business coach, Lorand Soares Szasz, conducted it. It was amazing; all the information was so clear and valuable! I was so inspired and motivated! It was like discovering a new world again! I continued to go to many events and seminars. I bought books and downloaded information that I could use. Lorand start inviting other international speakers. That's how I met Brian Tracy. I loved his materials. I started reading his books and watched his videos on YouTube, and all materials I was able to get. I found out that, "YOU HAVE TO LEARN BEFORE YOU EARN!"

I would like to share with you the seven principles on what I think makes a successful person.

1. **Do your best to become a positive person.** It is so important to always expect the best in life. Negative people focus on negative things and waste energy without getting anywhere. They blame others for all their problems, they may think they were born into the wrong family or the wrong country, and consider it is someone else's fault for all their problems. They complain all the time about everything that happens to them, and consider themselves

victims of circumstances. Positive people expect the best and take responsibility. If you consider yourself a winner and know what you want in life, you will use your energy to move in the right direction. It will give you positive energy and self-confidence. It is true in life that we have ups and downs, but when that happens, you must work to get back on your feet and keep going. The more we practice a positive attitude, positive things will happen to us.

2. **Be open-minded.** Self-confidence is great, but don't take it to a level where you consider yourself smarter than everyone else! If you think your way is the best and only way, then, you are wrong, and don't try to control everything around you. No matter how much experience we have, there is always more to learn. Everything is constantly changing and evolving! Being open-minded will allow you to grow. If you are open to new ideas you will be able to learn new ways of becoming a better person, a better family member, a better employee and a better businessperson. Your life, health and opportunities will get better and better, in a progressive way.

3. **Have faith!** Even if this is number 3 on my list, it is actually the most important principle to become successful! There are many doctrines and religions in this world, and there are so many things to be told about the supernatural. Many people believe in many different ways and some call themselves atheists. People call God different names in various cultures. There is much discussion and disagreement on this subject. Who is wrong? Who is right? It is impossible to study every religious specialist in the world. Doing this will not help you. There is a more efficient way. Make it between you and God; nobody else in-between. Don't know if He is real? Call Him! It is that simple! And it is the essence of life. What you will discover is the key of all keys to success! That's all that ever matters!

4. **Study all you can about other successful people and learn from them!** This is good news! Access to information today is easier than ever. In order to become successful, you don't necessarily need to reinvent the wheel. There are many books to read on every subject in which you want to become successful. Find the best in your profession, in your field and don't stop learning. The more you know, the better you become and as an result, it will grow your income. Always use part of your money to reinvest in yourself.

5. Set goals. Plan your life in advance. Meditate on what you want to accomplish. What are the most important things for you to achieve in order to become successful? What really matters? Setting your most important goals will guide you there like a road map. It is important to know where you are today and what is your final destination. Writing them down, planning and working everyday on your goals is the vehicle that takes you down the road to your final destination.

6. Stay focused. It happens many times. You choose a path to work diligently to get to your goals, but then discover that taking a different direction is more attractive. Information is good, but that can be a problem too. We can be flooded with information and all the activities that go with that. Then we start complaining about not having enough time, and we act like a fireman on a mission; running to put out fires that never end. It is important to set your goals, but then you need to continue to focus and have clarity in using the right information and doing the right activities. Stay focused again and again!

7. Don't stop learning. You may learn and work hard to become one of the best in your field. You may spend thousands of hours studying and reading books. Then you start to apply everything you know – succeeding and failing many times – until you have learned what matters. Let's say, you did everything you needed to do to become successful and now you are a success, an authority or expert at what you do. The present is great! But don't consider the present good enough to cover your future. Things are changing faster today than ever before. Today's best computer is tomorrow's number two device.

Always stay connected, learn new things that are good for you and read again the old principles that made a difference in your life! And what can I say, if not everything is working for you and you still struggle, then go to principle number 3: *Have faith* – everyone can have another chance! Don't stop! The best will come if you keep doing your part.

To your success!!!

About Adrian

Adrian I. Dragoman is a successful businessman in Romania. His company, Harris Enterprise has been awarded the title of "Number 1 Local Business" by the Chamber of Commerce of Sibiu. In 2015, his company was in third place for building, buying and selling real estate products by the National Council For Small And Medium Private Business of Romania.

By 2012, he was CEO, and 50% owner of Stabil SRL, which is a sales and rental company for construction equipment. Since 2012, he started Harris Enterprise SRL, a construction company and real estate business. He is also part owner of Sara Residence SRL, a real estate developer and investor company and part owner of Inteltipo SRL, a typography and publishing business.

In the USA, he is owner of Grizzly Homes Inc., in Texas, and is builder of tornado and strong wind-proof homes.

In his personal life, Adrian Dragoman enjoys spending quality time with his wife and daughter. He has a strong desire to improve people's life and to build great relationships. His belief is, "with people for people." This is a concept that offers fair values in all facets of life that include, but are not limited to, family, employees, business partners and society. He encourages others to seek personal development and to help and encourage others by paying it forward, and lead prosperous lives.

You can contact Adrian at:
- Mobile Phone number +40 741254070
- Business adi@harris-enterprise.ro

CHAPTER 40

THE '10-POWERS' TACTIC LADDER TO METEORIC SUCCESS

BY MOHAMED BADAWY

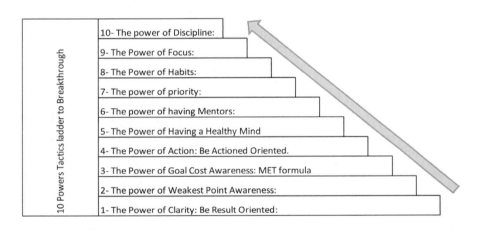

It's impossible to live without failing at something, unless you live so cautiously that you might as well not have lived at all, in which case, you fail by default.
~ J. K. Rowling, Harvard Commencement Address, 2008

My story started since 2004. I've graduated from Engineering School, barely out of a mediocre Egyptian university, and rifled through this book I had especially gotten for this twice-daily two-hour commute. My "career" as a maintenance engineer had already kicked off in a public plant modelling bargain-basement products, spartan work setting and low wages which should've been okay; except that Mr. Ambitious and

– according to others, not realistically so – loathed the bog-standard, unprogressive and dull as a dishwasher job. I needed to go great guns.

With a sore bottom I grew accustomed to, I reached in time for the warm welcome I was supposed to give this American expert who was visiting the factory for a major maintenance issue.

A lifetime of that isn't exactly what I called fulfilling. It was in fact antithetical to my notion of life. I was sick of living *the life* vicariously. I needed to get out of this hell hole, but without a lead, it seemed an endless nosedive to oblivion. Only a year later did I find the missing piece in the puzzle; a mentor. It only took a 144-page book to turn his life around. Man! That Brian Tracy is something. *Eat the Frog* galvanized the dude. I became indoctrinated; dogmatic. Being successful and realizing one's dreams was uncertain no more, it is no moot point; it is a natural phenomenon, a fact, a given. Of the many quotes that resonated with me, this was my all-time favorite: "It doesn't matter where you are coming from. All that matters is where you are going." It's a quote I will remain reciting for years.

Under Brian Tracy's indirect mentorship, I build a stepladder with my ultimate goal on top. I would take it one step at a time. It was only common sense that I didn't try to high jump over the top right away. The second step of my 'sure-fire' construct was to get a respectable job that pays. "Like it or not, money is freedom," I thought. But to land such an opportunity, I needed some self-investment. I needed to pump up my 'D' in English to an 'A' and then get some technical fine-tuning; that was the first step, basic and stereotypical, as it may seem. Well, it took me a year, there I was in a big multinational corporation in Bahrain. Then it kind of snowballed. A bigger job in Qatar followed, then I tie the knot, got a place of my own and BAM! – I get a Master's in Project Management from Roehampton, UK.

Mr. Project Manager now is in Dubai working for a major-league British company. I would think I would take an intermission. I take a few self/career development courses in the US instead, and end up becoming an international speaker and now, evidently, an author.

In the upcoming pages, I will be sharing the powerful tactics that helped me up to the top of the ladder.

THE '10-POWERS' TACTIC TO METEORIC SUCCESS

1. The Power of Clarity, "Be result-oriented":

Everybody is equally gifted when it comes to the energy they have within, except that – just like with money – some are foolish with spending their fortunes, others are a bit more providential. Most people squander their energy for nada. They work hard but in all the wrong directions, they wear themselves out for achieving less and less.

97% of people do not have a clear set of written goals or a mission statement. Commitment to paper is a key. Not Surprising. They work for the remaining 3% who have that clarity of purpose and subsequently a clear idea of how their wealth of energy should be channeled.

Clarity is the key to prompt success. The clearer your purpose, the faster you achieve it.

When you are clear about what you want, your line of thoughts is going to shrink to a fraction of its length as you look for the easiest, most productive way to achievement. Your learning-curve will spike and you will get more done in much less time, so will your productivity be doubled, tripled, quadrupled. In turn, your worth shoots up at the same rates. You start gaining control of your life. Moreover, when you are result-oriented, viz., clear about your objectives, you get to enjoy what matters. You don't need to give up your social life, your friends and family or enjoying your favorite pastime to be accomplished.

2. The Power of Awareness of Your Major Weakness

Question: What holds you back? Why are you stuck where you don't want to be?
Answer: It's your major weakness – simple, eh?
If you overcome your weakness, you will move up a step or two on the ladder. More often than not, a greatest weakness is the turning point, after which you become irreversibly and invariably dead set on taking up new challenges; with much less prohibitive shortcomings.

I told you about my once most repressive weakness - the English language. I spent around a full year just breaking my anglo-glossophobia. But once I did it, my life metamorphosed. Now, the world really is my oyster. I have taken a Master's from the UK, and another one from the USA; I became a project manager in a British company, an international speaker and author. That was the product of a year's work. It was no picnic, I tell you. But it paid off big time. I have a better life, live in a better house, drive a better car and I'm not worried about money; I 'liaise' with white-collar higher-ups (remember the factory incident?), all out of beating a single point of weakness; in this case, picking up one new skill.

3. The Power of Goal-Cost Awareness: "MET formula"

> *The good life is expensive. There is another way to live*
> *that doesn't cost as much, but it isn't good.*
> ~ Spanish Distillers

Every goal has its damages. You pay, it's yours. You don't pay, forget it. People out there fail to achieve their goals, because they're at a loss to figure out the costs. I developed the MET formula for myself when I first started working out the investment that my goal demanded. It really does simplify the estimation. So, before setting out on any endeavor, figure out how much its worth using the MET formula.

$$Goal\ Cost = M+E+T$$

(where M= Money; E= Effort; T= Time)

Here's a script for the MET formula, if you are any bit as mathematically-challenged as I am:

"In order to achieve my goal ......, I have to sacrifice $ ...... and make an effort ...... for ...... months/years."
Fill in the script for any goal and you will come to know exactly what the goal costs. In doing so, you will be manifesting the law of attraction. Circumstances will then work in your favor and you will likely achieve that goal faster that you ever thought possible.

4. The Power of Action

You need to shake a leg if things should go down! Most people have dreams but for many, this is as good as it gets; just a bunch of castles in Spain. Sure it sounds fancy, yet it's a fantasy. Some people shrink away until they get guarantees. Well, let me warn you. In the real world, there's no such thing as a guarantee, period. These fellas like it in their comfort zones, they're not in for that bit of effort we talked about. Well, guess what? They never get to have so much as a stone slab in Spain.

On the other hand, successful people make it happen. They set goals, prepare action plans and they get moving. They very well know that nothing will happen unless they shake it and are equally aware of the pain involved. After all, who likes giving up their security blanket? Should you make good, you won't even remember that any pain was involved. Even if you don't do so well, you learn something and then it won't be as painful again. Odds are you'll make the grade next time. But you need to speed up the rhythm; define the goal, plan out your moves and get cracking.

In time, you will grow addicted to exploring the outskirts of your comfort zone. It becomes exciting as long as it's new; because you now know that success starts at the threshold of the unconventional. That's when you know you're about to enjoy phenomenal success.

5. The Power of a Healthy Mind

What is a healthy mind? A healthy mind is a cognizant mind which is free from negative feelings and bad experiences; alive with positivity and focused on improvement.

The mind can be focused on only one thought at a time to maintain a healthy awareness and fill up with positivity.

Winners always focus on the here and now, because they realize that the future depends on what they do today. The healthy mind innately chooses desirable thoughts and feelings which colors your aura, energizes and peps you up. A healthy mind renders you aware. Awareness paves the way for creativity and creativity is the backdrop for productivity. The more you accomplish, the more you will love to move and learn, and the better achiever you become. On the flip side, the majority fall into the trap of reflecting on the past; re-calculating misguided decisions, picturing a different course of action for things that've gone the wrong way and lamenting how it all panned out. The past is gone; you cannot change it. Stop waiting for a comeback. You can't begin a new chapter if you keep re-reading the old ones.

6. The Power of Having Mentors

Mentors are an essential element of any story with a happy ending. A true mentor would save you years - even decades - of hard work. They're a godparent without the hassle; your guide on your free tour of life. A Mentor helps remove road blocks, draws out your route on the map, and is with you when the going gets tough.

If I go on about mentors, ten 700-page books sound about the decent space needed in which I may be able to give a somewhat fair picture of mentorship. However, for the purposes of this chapter, I think it's safe to say that I'm bursting at the seams with emotion as I write this. Just by a stroke of luck, I found my mentor and it turned out to be the best thing that's ever happened to my career as a human being. I grew hopped up on everything that was Brian Tracy. I read his every book, signed up for every one of his courses – those I knew of.

Mentors take you under their wings, that's what they do; they're anything but selfish. Thanks to my mentor, my career as an international trainer and consultant kicked off, and get a load of this, I'm a co-author in his book.

If you don't have your own mentor, go find them NOW.

7. The Power of Prioritizing

Most people like to start off easy, to warm up, ending up doing low-value tasks which have minimal impact on their goals. Again, that stems from fear of exiting the comfort zone. Some get naively sucked into others' agendas or out of solicitude, they are not aware that this is at their own expense. Now, that won't work. You need to put first things first and here's what you should do:

a. Always start with your own agenda, reserve the highest of your energies for yourself.
b. Start with the tasks that are more likely to seriously impact your goals (stop starting off easy).
c. Reduce distractions by setting boundaries and putting yourself first.
d. Always plan one day ahead.

8. The Power of Habits

Greater than 40% of our daily decisions are impulsively-practiced habits; these are the habits acquired during the first nine years of life. You follow a pattern without realizing it. This is really scary – 40%.

We all grow up practicing different negative behavioral patterns, and our subconscious becomes sadly programmed to stick to what has become a routine. If you are to change a deeply-engraved habit, it requires some serious effort on your part. You will put your back into it before it's corrected. In order to change a negative behavioral pattern, you should:

a. Be more aware of what you're doing. Ask yourself why you're doing it? And if it's worthwhile?
b. Do a pre-emptive strike; foreclose your habit-trigger.
c. Just avert your focus; deliberately get yourself busy.
d. Force in a new routine. It will become a pattern in time.
e. Create a reward system; fool your subconscious into loving the new thing.

9. The Power of Focus

Things don't get done without focus. If you want your child to get straight As, you tell them to focus. If you're working to a deadline and your friends pop by, you'd say, I need to focus. A picture is best when it's in focus. Whatever your focus is set on, it booms. I would say this is probably the most important one of the ten. You need it to pull off the rest.

When an idea is the object of your focus, it gets the best of you. You will be the epitome of this idea; a magnet pulling all that serves your end to it. So what can we do to sharpen the focus?

a. Believe that curiosity really killed the cat. Resist the temptation to engage in what is of little relevance to what matters.
b. Identify your grail and have it as clear as day.
c. According to some lexicons, distraction is one antonym for focus. All sources of distraction are a no-no.
d. Put yourself, your goals and what matters to you, first.
e. Develop a routine in which you give your heart and soul to the tasks.

10. The Power of Discipline

Without discipline, chances are you will never see your dream through, you may as well drop it. Thousands of dreamers don't like getting out of their shells when the very essence of discipline is breaking it. Discipline is perseverance; it is the maintenance of your dream-in-progress. You need it to make it.

To get things done, you have to get emotionally attached. *Don't let a morning slip by without offering your subconscious the dream for breakfast.* Visualize that you have realized your goal, savor the triumph of achievement as if you have it. When your senses taste the engendered fervor, every bit of you will then exist for the fulfillment of your dream; this gratification, this urgency, this need is the very drive for becoming disciplined. It does not come overnight though. The closer you are to realizing your dream, the more disciplined you become. The good news here is that once disciplined, always disciplined; no matter what you're doing, you have the discipline it takes to win big.

When you wake up every morning to re-commence working on what you want, when it becomes a daily routine against all pressures of life, all distractions, then you know you have the discipline to see it through, and you will.

About Mohamed

Mohamed Badawy helps his clients to set, and achieve their personal and business goals in the easiest, fastest and SMARTEST way ever. He is an expert in the training and development of individuals and organizations. He is the Middle East's Leading Super Performance Coach.

Mohamed speaks to corporate and public audiences on the subjects of Personal and Professional Development, including the executives and staff of many of the Middle East's largest corporations. His professional talks and seminars on Superb Performance for Management Level include Change Management, Crisis Management, Effective Practical Business and Marketing plans, Communication, Negotiate with Power, Triple Productivity and Triple Income, Time Management, Master your Life as well as Workshop to Manage Complex Projects, Workshop for Risk Project Management and Effective Leadership.

Mohamed Badawy has an MBA and is a graduate of Crisis Management of Brian Tracy Inc. (USA). He has his Masters of Project Management from a University in the UK. Mohamed Badawy is also a multi-best-selling author – including the best-selling *Cracking the Code to Success*, which he co-authored with Brian Tracy.

He has been helping the largest corporations in the Middle East on two continents (Africa and Asia), and in five countries (Egypt, Bahrain, KSA, Qatar and the UAE). His practical experience and education level assist him in providing effective Life and Business coaching for Management level – in order to achieve their personal and business goals faster than they ever thought. Mohamed assists corporations' top management leaders to work at high performance levels in order to be role models for their staff, which enhances the organization's performance accordingly.

Contact Trainer Mohamed Badawy at:
- me@mohamedbadawyint.com
- www.facebook.com/trainermohamedbadawy/
- http://www.youtube.com/c/TrainerMohamedBadawyInternational
- http://engmohamedbadawy.blogspot.ae/

CHAPTER 41

THE POWER OF THOUGHT
MASTER UNIVERSAL ALIGNMENT TO ATTRACT SUCCESS

BY VICTORIA LEDAY

There are many meanings to the power of thought. In this chapter, I will reveal to you how our mindset is tied to our emotions, speech, and behavior. You will also learn how to align with the Universe to create the life you desire. The first thing to do to recreate yourself is to not just think positive, but to understand how your brain was created. There are two main parts, *our conscious mind* and *our subconscious mind*. The conscious mind is our logical thinking – everything we take in from our five senses. Our subconscious mind stores our memories delivered by our consciousness to create behavior or habit. The main attribute of our subconscious mind is our programming. What many people don't know is we are programmed from birth.

There are two types of programming, what we take in from our media, television, environment etc., and what we are told by our parents or any other authority we are required to listen to growing up. This type of programming is put in our subconscious, and if it's not healthy, it's the very thing that holds us back from accomplishing everything we set forth. It's that voice that brings up negative thoughts and the things we were taught that we find out later were not healthy for us. This is where limiting beliefs are born and where doubt or fear of success creep in. If you feel like you take one step forward and three steps back, your subconscious is not aligned with the Universe to create the successful life you are reaching for.

These challenges are called **success blockers**, which come from our subconscious due to our thought patterns. If you are truly seeking success, you have to be willing to reprogram and recreate yourself. The first step to creating the life path you seek is to **F.E.A.R.** – **F**ace **E**verything **A**nd **R**ise. I say this because there are several steps you must take to recreate yourself and align with the Universe to attract everything you desire. Below are the stumbling blocks that hold us back with a solution to eliminate doubt and self-sabotage.

Step 1: Negative Thinking

This type of behavior comes from your subconscious and is not healthy. For example, maybe growing up, those closest to you told you everything you couldn't do. Well, have you ever heard the saying, if you want something different you have to do something you've never done before? The fact of the matter is: *you cannot allow your past to create your future with negative thinking.* If you really want to create a path to success, it's time to get comfortable getting uncomfortable, and do things you've never done before and be okay with it. *This is a part of reprogramming yourself for success.*

Step 2: Unforgiveness

In order to align with the Universe, you have to operate in love. All of us have been hurt and in most cases, it's by those closest to us. We are all familiar with this pain but this is what keeps us thinking negative, which creates negative behavior and a negative outcome.

You have to do three things to align yourself in this step

1. forgive
2. operate in love
3. see the best in that person

Forgiveness gives you freedom and the ability to love unconditionally. Living free emotionally and mentally aligns your desire to become successful to the Universe and puts you on your journey to a new life. Before going to step 3, I would like you to do an extra step.

Assignment:

- Please take out a sheet of paper and draw a line straight down the middle.
- On the left side, write the bad events that took place in your life going back to your childhood. On the right side write who was responsible for that event even if you were responsible. This exercise will reveal toxic relationships in your life as well as self-sabotage.

Forgiveness stops negative vibrations from going out to the Universe preventing you from operating at your full potential. My advice to you is to take your results, forgive those individuals with love, and forgive yourself to eliminate self-doubt and guilt.

Step 3: Not Changing your Routine

Remember you are aiming for success so your comfort zone is obsolete. For example, wake up early in the morning and work out. The wealthy live healthy lifestyles but also mindful of programming, so they watch less television and replace it with reading. It would be wise to make time daily to read about material that enhances the growth of your mind, body, and spirit. This is a huge part of aligning yourself to the Universe to unlock your full potential without limit.

In addition, create a 'to do' list and hold yourself accountable to complete each task. Lastly, set monthly goals for yourself and break it down to tasks you are doing weekly and daily to accomplish your outcome. What we put into ourselves will reprogram your thought process and is a big part of eliminating limiting beliefs to acquire success.

Step 4: Self-Sabotage

The way self-sabotage is born is by what is stored in our memories. We reflect on bad experiences growing up with the things we saw and heard in our programming including television and other media. These memories are stored up to be used so when a situation or opportunity arises we react.

We either act out in anger due to the situation or reject life-changing opportunities with skepticism. This type of behavior prevents your ability to attract wealth and have healthy loving relationships with others.

The best way to end self-sabotage is with forgiveness and letting go of the past. The best way to let go of the past is to view your life and situations outside of yourself. If you learn how to see life situations from a higher power, you will not see failure in your life. Changing your perception and self changes your environment and ends self-sabotage.

Step 5: Being Ungrateful

There is a huge difference between just enduring where we are and being truly grateful for where you are in life right now. When a person is complaining and always reaching for more from a negative perspective, they will always hit a wall. This type of thinking is why some people aim for success just to prove someone close to them wrong. The result of this is a life where everything goes south, and the power of how you think has taken over subconsciously and you have attracted nothing but misery to your life. This can all be turned around by two simple things, developing a quiet mind and being grateful.

A quiet mind will teach you how to appreciate life and develop gratitude. You will also learn how to view people and situations you face differently. The way to develop a quiet mind is to meditate. When you meditate you ignite a vibration in you that communicates to the Universe that you want a new view, peace, and happiness. When you start to see things from a higher level, you will be grateful for every single thing people take advantage of everyday. If you show gratitude, the Universe will manifest what you desire and more. This is the key to having a healthy subconscious and reprogramming yourself to acquire the abundant life you deserve.

Step 6: No Faith

A lot of people aiming for success create their own hold backs.

Where do these hold backs come from? Well, your thoughts for example, like, "Am I good enough? What if I don't make it? What would my family think if I quit my job to start a business? I don't have the capital so I can't." Do any of these statements sound familiar?

Do you know what else this creates? . . . procrastination, doubt, and excuses. The result of this is you just endure, which means you let everyone outside of yourself tell you what you can and can't do in life. You cannot allow anyone or anything to create your identity. You have the power to create your own identity to accomplish and attract every single thing you want, including success.

Step 7: No Fight

In your re-programming journey to your new self, you will discover how to fight. You are probably wondering who am I fighting? The answer is yourself. Remember the subconscious mind can be used to hold you back or create a life of prosperity.

As entrepreneurs reaching for a life of abundance, it requires work and part of the work that needs to be done is fighting yourself on a daily basis. You have to fight negative thoughts and any past memories that create doubt and fear about moving forward. When you have fight in you, your attitude is of a conqueror, one that doesn't back down, one that is focused, always ready, and will not let anyone or anything stop them from taking all the steps required to get the life they know they deserve.

Now remember I stated it is more than taking steps to think positive. I brought up alignment but how does a person align themselves to the Universe to send out the right signals to manifest their desires? The biggest misconception is the teaching to look outside of self to get approval for what you want. The truth is, the very thing you are looking for is already inside of you. We have all been given special gifts and talents to do our part in the world we live in. There is a power inside of us that, if just tapped into any and everything we want in life, is right at our fingertips.

A lot of people do not know the power to manifest is within us and it starts with your thoughts. Now the way to align yourself is quite simple. You have to make sure your thoughts, emotions, and speech are all in harmony with what you desire. Your thoughts have to be positive and not be in conflict with your subconscious. You have to feel the emotion you would feel as if it already happened and you have to speak as if it has already occurred. This requires operating your faith muscles to do the work required to prepare for it to manifest. When your thoughts, emotions, and speech come together for one desire with hard work, before you know it, manifestation takes place.

There is an amazing amount of power in our thought process, and when working in this way, there is a vibration that is sent to the Universe to obey it. This also applies to looking at it from a negative perspective. If you think, feel, and speak bad things, you will manifest a negative outcome. On another note, if you want success but it's not aligned with your feelings or speech, you manifest a delay. This happens because your emotions or speech do not match what you think you should have. *The Universe is designed to do one thing, give you what you align yourself to. All you have to do to communicate effectively is make sure everything lines up so the vibration you put out activates the Law of Attraction to manifest what you desire and more.*

In closing, there are two more words that can help you achieve all of these steps to create the life you want, **emotional intelligence**. *Emotional Intelligence is the source of self-control.* Normally, a person who lacks emotional intelligence is not where they want to be in life. You can master emotional intelligence by gaining self-control. You can master self-control by taking the seven steps which will lead to you evolving into a creator of your success. *Taking this seriously, you will not only crack the code to success, but learn to live an abundant lifestyle.*

Let me be the first to Congratulate you!

About Victoria

Victoria LeDay, NLP, LWP started working at age 14. At the age of 18, while working for a loan officer, she realized she wanted more. After studying and researching more about the industry, she decided to start her own Real Estate Investing business, offering high-end homes to self-employed families that couldn't qualify for traditional financing. Victoria LeDay developed a niche and as it evolved, unleashed the entrepreneurial spirit within her. Since May 1996, she has owned, operated, and sold several businesses, as well as helped others build their businesses in various industries. She has also mastered starting a company with very little to no capital while maintaining a good work-life balance. She has conquered the good, the bad, and the ugly in starting and operating a business while having to face daily challenges in everyday life as a mother, wife, and business woman.

Victoria has taken her past challenges and used them to create a successful life and future with education, professional alliances, faith, and helping others achieve their personal and business goals. Her passion for people led her to receive a degree in Psychology, study psychotherapy, and became a Certified NLP and Law of Attraction Wealth Practitioner – specializing in helping women entrepreneurs find balance, identify purpose, create freedom, and unlock their full potential to attract and receive every single thing they want in all areas of their lives. Victoria has mastered operating at her full potential through the Law of Attraction. She has a mission to teach women strategies and techniques to attract abundant living, so her clients launch more successful businesses with balance and peace while on their journey to greatness.

Victoria LeDay knows what to expect, and most importantly, how to empower each one of her clients to position themselves to achieve any goal they desire. She is committed to her clients moving forward and growing in their life – mentally, emotionally, physically, spiritually, and financially. These are *The Five Wealths*. Take her direction, and she will get you there.

For more information, please connect with Victoria below:
- Website: www.shiftyourdestinynow.net
- Email: vleday@shiftyourdestinynow.net
- Facebook: https://m.facebook.com/shiftyourdestinynow/
- LinkedIn: https://www.linkedin.com/in/victoria-leday-48a9a112

CHAPTER 42

HOW SMART MONEY WORKS IN THE 21ST CENTURY

BY WILLIAM FEGGINS

❖ Generation Millennial: Born 1979 – 1996
❖ Generation X: Born 1965 – 1978
❖ Baby Boomer: Born 1946 – 1964

In my early 20s, as I started finding my way in adulthood and the "working world," I wondered how entertainers and athletes went bankrupt very shortly into their career. According to a 2009 *Sports Illustrated* story, as many as 60 percent of U.S. professional basketball players faced bankruptcy or serious financial hardships within just a few years of retiring.[1] Why didn't they save their money? Why did they purchase multiple exotic cars and houses, throw lavish parties and assume that the corporation that they worked for had their best interest in terms of an income strategy for retirement? Lack of financial education, lack of business ownership and full trust into the idea that the corporation will take care of all their short-term and long-term financial needs were the root causes for frivolous spending, and ultimately, financial demise.

In 2008, I built the Divine Insurance, for the purpose of teaching financial literacy across America to prospective clients and insurance agents so that they could live a better, tax-free life, and help others become financially-free and prepared for retirement. As I always tell my clients, "Our money must make money all the time." I noticed that the biggest challenge people in my community face is to understand

HOW money works. Only 14 percent of Americans are confident they will have enough money to live comfortably in retirement.[2] Independent, economic development is the key to community revitalization and political success in a capitalist society. Those with the most money are the same individuals who can make political decisions and have access to elected officials in their community. In addition, a community with ample economic opportunity reduces other societal ills (for example, crime, drug use, etc.), because individuals have the means to support themselves/families and the time to engage in a more productive activity.

Financially speaking, there are three places to store/accumulate our wealth: Banks, Wall Street or Insurance Companies. We've been led to believe over the past two to three decades that Wall Street is the mecca of wealth. Wall Street manufactures and markets only benefit Wall Street 100% of the time, providing no guarantees against loss to the small investor. They have the "too big to fail" mindset. This is hardly a recipe for long-term financial success. In fact, it's a no-win situation for small investors, no matter what the scenario or best intentions Wall Street might have, because small investors ultimately absorb all risk and incur all losses when Wall Street gambles with their money. Furthermore, if Wall Street firms ever need bailing out when things get too reckless, our tax money will be used to get them back on their feet.

For 401(k) and IRA owners, the government provides the illusion of safety by regulating the securities industry under the guise of offering oversight and "protection" through agencies like the Securities Exchange Commission (SEC) and Financial Industry Regulatory Authority (FINRA). Safe Money must be shared with individuals who are relying on a 401(k) or any government qualified account for that matter to create a secure retirement income.

Sidenote: Government retirement accounts like 401(k)s/IRAs will produce government intended results – more income taxes! So you get the double whammy of qualified retirement investing: no protection against loss (thank you Wall Street) and Uncle Sam digging in your pocket for every retirement dollar when you hang up your golden spurs to retire off into the sunset. In this particular case, two negatives certainly do not make a positive! For those who might point out that a Roth IRA will produce tax-free income, please remember the contribution and income limitations put on these government retirement accounts and the fact that your investment options are directed right back towards the Wall Street casino.

Financial Literacy in American has been a virulent undercurrent in our society for the last one hundred years. In various forms, it insinuates itself into all aspects of our lives. It is time for serious dialogue and a change in financial strategies moving forward. Although skeptical at first, I am now a firm believer that an Index Universal Life insurance product is a far superior vehicle to a government sponsored plan, e.g., 401(k), 403(b), and 457(b) to secure one's retirement income. A person can get stock market-like returns with no stock market risk. The Index Universal Life insurance policies do not have exposure to tax risk or stock market risk as all 401(k) plans that are in the market do. Most people saving for retirement make the mistake of focusing on accumulation rather than distribution. Distribution is what pays the retiree the money that he lives on.

Most Americans believe that we have a retirement crisis in this country. Most workers (about 58 percent), including 66 percent of both Millennials and Generation X and 46 percent of Baby Boomers, expect their primary source of income in retirement to be self-funded through retirement accounts or other savings and investments. Generation X (52 percent) is most likely to cite retirement accounts such as 401(k)s, 403(b)s, or IRAs. Almost 36 percent of Baby Boomers will cite Social Security, up from 26 percent in 2007. Not only are there major risks in the traditional retirement approach and social security, but what many people don't realize is that the amount of money they're saving for retirement is secondary to where they are actually saving/investing their money. The three biggest obstacles most Americans are unaware of are: inflation, taxes and Wall Street fees in retirement plans that eat up as much as 2/3 of retirement income before actual retirement.

While most public, private and union plans are moving out of the old retirement package of the gold watch, lifetime employer pension, and social security, most consumers are stuck with a Wall Street retirement plan that is threatening their financial security. Social Security may not be a reliable source of income in the near future. According to a recent government report, a shortfall of the trust funds that support Social Security is approaching – as it stands, it is predicted that funds will run out by 2033, three years earlier than expected. If these funds are exhausted, the program would only receive enough in payroll taxes to pay partial benefits.[3]

Whichever vehicle has the best distribution is where a person needs to put their money. The Index Universal Life insurance trounces a 401(k) or similar plan by paying out 2 to 3 times more net hard cash during a person's retirement years. That is the strength of an Index Universal Life insurance. If you care about your finances, your friends and your family, then pass along this book and share it with everyone you know. I know it is meant to provide hope and solutions about how to make a serious change in retirement strategies. We have been misled by others for so long, and no one has taken the time to properly educate us on truly safe and profitable alternatives, so we can avoid taxes and the pitfalls of our shaky economy. Although taxes rarely excite anyone, those with an entrepreneurial spirit or true interest in the security of their future will be excited to learn about Tax-Free Wealth.

Own your future. Own your happiness. Own your success.

References

- According to a 2009 *Sports Illustrated* story, as many as 60 percent of U.S. professional basketball players faced bankruptcy or serious financial hardships within just a few years of retiring.

- People are living longer. U.S. Life expectancy is increasing, and, as of 2010, it was 78.7 years of age. [1]

- Just 14 percent of Americans are confident they will have enough money to live comfortably in retirement. [2]

- Social Security may not be a reliable source of income in the near future. According to a recent government report, a shortfall of the trust funds that support Social Security is approaching – as it stands, it is predicted that funds will run out by 2033, three years earlier than expected. If these funds are exhausted, the program would only receive enough in payroll taxes to pay partial benefits. [3]

Footnotes
1. "National Vital Statistics Reports;" Volume 61, Number 4; Sherry L. Murphy, B.S.; Jiaquan Xu, M.D.; and Kenneth D. Kochanek, M.A.; Division of Vital Statistics; Centers for Disease Control and Prevention; May 8, 2013.
2. "The 2012 Retirement Confidence Survey: Job Insecurity, Debt Weigh on Retirement Confidence, Savings;" Ruth Helman, Mathew Greenwald & Associates, and Craig Copeland and Jack VanDerhei, Employee Benefits Research Institute; March 2012.
3. 2012 OASDI Trustees Report, officially called "The 2012 Annual Report of the Board of Trustees of the Federal Old-Age and Survivors Insurance and Federal Disability Insurance Trust Funds."

About William

William Logan Feggins is the Founder, President, and CEO of Divine Insurance Group. In 2008, William recognized the need for private retirement planning and financial literacy. William's mission to provide financial literacy and college planning services across the United States and to promote quality of life via college and retirement solutions fueled the incorporation of Divine Insurance Group. Under his leadership, Divine has become an Independent Marketing Organization specializing in various insurance and retirement services for Millennials, Generation X and Baby Boomers. He is also co-founder of the Certified Final Expense Advisor Association, the first designation in the country that provides funeral planning education for insurance agents.

William is equipped with over 10 years of experience in working with major corporations, non-profits, colleges, universities and government entities to oversee outreach program activities. In addition to building a successful enterprise, he has had the honor of visiting the White House, the United States Congress and the floor of the New York Stock Exchange, along with accepting a prestigious award at the United Nations in New York. In recognition of his award at the UN, Divine's logo, along with the companies of other distinguished entrepreneurs, appeared on the main board of the NASDAQ situated in Times Square in New York City. As an Empact Showcase honoree, Mr. Feggins was invited to the UN's headquarters in New York to deliver a speech on the importance of business ownership, private retirement planning and economic development in the 21st century.

William, a national speaker, has won several business awards and appeared on multiple news outlets. He wrote articles in many business magazines, conducted multiple radio show interviews around the country and trained hundreds of insurance agents throughout his tenure.

You can connect with William at:
- Info@divineinsurancegroup.com
- www.Divineinsurancegroup.com
- www.linkedin.com/in/divineinsurancegroup

CHAPTER 43

COACHING THE CODES TO SUCCESS

BY YOGENDRASING GIRASE

INTRODUCTION

Success is not a destination; it is a continuous incremental process towards our dream. Success comes with the zeal and zest (exuberance) accompanied with passion. I personally believe that there is nothing more exciting and satisfying than earning in the very field you have lived, are living for and dreaming for.

As a coaching Professional for the last 16 years, over 10,000 Engineering Students have been trained under my institute. During these years, I asked them about their dreams, future plans, careers and perspectives, and I was shocked to know that there were only a few students who could answer me about their plans and perceptions. Most of them were willing to settle with secured jobs. I was concerned about them because what I believe is the exact opposite of what they believe. They think that securing jobs would secure their lives, which is hardly acceptable.

Jobs do not provide security. These job lovers will fall in the rat race and ultimately live an insecure life. That's what I personally feel.

I wonder why nobody aspires to be an entrepreneur. . . Nobody wants financial freedom at their early ages. . . Nobody wants to take advantage of ever-growing opportunities around the entire globe that were not even possible before. This is the main reason to start writing, promoting and trying to spread this message worldwide.

So, here we get you a clear pathway to focus and fulfill all your dreams through the *'Dreamers World Workshop'*. In this workshop, we cover all those things which are necessary to "Crack the Codes to Success."

We conduct workshops on the following topics:

1) Fear
2) Procrastination
3) The Power of the Subconscious Mind
4) Happiness
5) Leadership

Fear and procrastination are two major stumbling blocks in the path of success.

FEAR

Fear is the major stumbling block on the journey to success. We all have fear of something – depending on our past painful experiences, which hold us back. What is Fear? Fear is an emotion experienced in anticipation of some specific pain or danger (usually accompanied by desire to flee or fight). Fear exists simply because we are not living in the reality of life. We are living in our minds. Our fear is always concerned with what's going to happen next.

Actually, nothing has happened yet, but we assume that something may happen tomorrow, and people always suffer through this phase. It means our fear is always about that which does not exist. It means it is absolutely imaginary. This is insanity. People suffer from fear simply because they are not rooted in reality; they are always rooted in their minds. Your mind has two parts, one is memory and the other is imagination. Both of them are in one way imaginary, because both of them don't exist right now. They are lost in our imagination, that's the basis of our fear. If they would be rooted in reality, there would be no fear.

What does fear do? It puts limits around us. It is because of fear that we build boundaries all the time. By raising boundaries around us we may live a safe life, but we can't live life to its fullest, which we deserve.

Here I want to ask you a simple question, whether you have come to experience life or to avoid life. If you have come to experience life, one thing that is very useful is intensity. If you do not have intensity, you will experience a stingy life. If you live your life with fear in order to protect yourself, ultimately your intensity will go down. It will eventually affect your ability to experience life. However, you are most likely to waste your opportunities and capabilities that you have as you are unable to do anything fantastic and delightful. As long as you are fearful, you will remain apart from the sense of abundance.

In our *Dreamers World Workshop*, we train you how to deal with this FEAR, and how you can use it effectively to accomplish your dreams.

PROCRASTINATION

Procrastination is another big stumbling block on the journey to success. It affects the overall performance of an individual. (Procrastination means delaying or postponing something.)

There are so many people who postpone their important activities until they become urgent and sometimes for no reason. Procrastination becomes a habit and they believe that they are helpless. My suggestion to all procrastinators is: "Stop procrastinating! Act now!" Avoiding procrastination is the only way to stop it.

Part of us is not in favor of our success. Another part of us wants a restful, relaxed life – it avoids taking risk.

If we plan something which is very important to us, we should be able to plan it properly and successfully. But at the time of its execution, part of us resists taking action, part of us distracts our focus, and we are ultimately caught in the trap of procrastination.

Why do we procrastinate?

During my graduations, I was going through the arduous phases of procrastination. Procrastination almost became my habit. I had paid great attention to it and suddenly, after 3-4 years (almost after completing graduation), I realized my mistake. Thereafter, I fixed my faults and was able to find a solution for the same.

Reasons why we procrastinate:

- Reason 1- Lack of commitment
- Reason 2- Fear of commencing the task
- Reason 3- Lack of prioritizing the activity
- Reason 4- Lack of knowledge about the task
- Reason 5- Laziness

Procrastination is the thief of time.
~ Edward Young

In our *Dreamers World Workshop*, we train you how to overcome Procrastination.

THE JOURNEY OF WINNING SPERM

In science (biology), we learn that after mating (sexual intercourse) about 250-300 million sperm are deposited by the man. These sperm swim upwards within the tract to meet with the ovum. Of the over 250 million that are deposited, only 400-500 actually reach the site. Others get tired on the way because it is no small race, while out of the 400 that manage to reach the egg, only one fertilizes it, and in this case the winning one is none other than YOU!

Have you ever thought about this?

- You ran a race without your eyes and you won!
- You ran without a formal education and you won!
- You ran without a certificate and you won!
- You ran without help and you won!

Then, what happens to you now? What makes you think that you will lose now? Now, you have a certificate. Now you have a plan, a dream and vision.

You didn't give up on day one, you can't give up now. Giving up is not in your DNA. It doesn't matter what you see now; always remember that you won from the womb. You are a different breed. You are born to win. Believe in yourself. Believe in your abilities.

Explore your capacities to get things done. Maximize and stretch your performance. Do things together for the long term. Check your efficiency and accountability from time to time. Always remember that you are THE WINNING SPERM.

THE POWER OF THE SUBCONSCIOUS MIND

In our day-to-day life, we come across different types of people. There are lots of poor people and a lot fewer rich people. If you see this through your mental eyes, you will be shocked to know that you behold the power house of infinity within you, which you can use miraculously to attract anything and everything that you need in your life – excellence, glory, joy and abundance.

Your subconscious mind has an ability to bring more happiness, more wealth, more health, more joy, and more fun. The key to do this is learning to contact and release this hidden power.

This is not something that you have to acquire; you already possess it. The only thing is that you have to know how to use it. You need to understand this power so that you can use it in all aspects of your life. This is something which is not controlled by anybody else, but only by you. Once you start believing and using this power, miracles will start to happen in your life and your environment.

RE-SHAPE YOUR THINKING

When you're more aware of the way you think, you have the power to act accordingly. This is so because, at this stage, you realize you have to make the best of all positive situations for your upliftment and re-shape the negative ones. The goal is to think positively, regardless of the situation, and make a conscious effort to see the opportunities instead of obstacles.

COME UP WITH IDEAS

Yes! One idea can change your life. So, whenever ideas are flowing through your mind, keep writing them on paper so that later you can develop them through a working plan. Ideas are like water bubbles, they come up and vanish immediately. A few years ago we never knew that we would be able to see each other via communication devices, but today's technology has made it possible. So, initially, it was an idea that we could make possible some day; then people started working on that idea and eventually it became possible today.

This is how an idea can bring a drastic change into your life. Here, I would like to share an interesting real story to help you understand how manifesting and implementing ideas can change fantasy to reality.

One of my students, Mr. Pankaj Wadnere, an average student, took six years to complete his 4-year program. He is an IT guy and completed his Master's in the USA. Then, he was able to find his first job in the IT sector. Now, I knew he had the passion to start a business, and after a long period (nine years), he started his own USA-based company, Austere Technologies, Inc. (www.austere.us) – with the help of his wife and his friends. As he was continuously observing and learning market strategies, he finally emerged as a successful businessman and I'm very sure that he can raise his business to even greater heights.

THE POWER OF IMAGINATION

"I have a great power of imagination." – Once you start using this affirmation, immediately you start imagining things you want in your life. This is my personal experience. I would like to share my experience of imagination.

I signed a book contract with international speaker Mr. Gerry Robert. And from the next day, I started imagining that I'm addressing around 2,000 to 3,000 foreigners in a big auditorium, and once I started walking towards the stage they started clapping. I have felt that feeling. I have written on paper that I'm an International speaker and I will never stop until I make it! It's possible! No one can stop me. I will make it happen. And you won't believe the event came within that month. I remember I was in Mumbai wandering in the mall, and received one Facebook notification that Gerry has invited his authors to Singapore to speak on the stage in front of around 2,000 to 2,500 people.

And I experienced the same thing which I imagined. I addressed 2,000 to 2,500 people at the Singapore event.

In our *Dreamers World Workshop,* we will train you in different imagination and visualization techniques to use the power of your subconscious mind at its highest level.

HAPPINESS

It sounds great when we read the word *Happiness.* It feels awesome when we experience happiness. One can define happiness in different terms based on personal experience and expectations of life. Happiness is something we can feel by doing certain things in certain ways. And that's why we are continuously searching for these certain things and those certain ways throughout our life. But I feel that happiness is within us. Happiness is in this moment. We have to discover all those practices through which we can find different ways of being happy. I feel happy when I help someone in all the ways I can. I feel happy when I share my knowledge with the people around me, and I feel very happy by learning from them as well. Everyone is special and blessed with some miraculous powers. The only thing is that you have to unleash that power.

We live a very short life, so let us try to make it worth living. Be generous to others. Take care of as many people as you can. We were born with nothing in our hands and leave this world with empty hands. So, isn't it a good notion to donate some part of your earnings for the upliftment of the society? Try to share with those who cannot produce for themselves, it will give you immense happiness. Happiness is the spiritual experience of living every minute with love, grace and gratitude.

Happiness is "the progressive achievement of a worthy ideal or goal." When you are working progressively or step-by-step towards something that is important, you generate a continuous feeling of success and achievement within yourself. You feel more positive and motivated. You feel more in control of your own life. You feel happier and more content. You feel like a winner, and you soon develop the psychological momentum that enables you to overcome obstacles and plough through adversity as you move towards achieving the most significant goals of your life.

LEADERSHIP

*Educationists should build the capacities of the spirit of inquiry,
creativity, entrepreneurial and moral leadership among students
and become their role model.*
~ Dr. A.P.J. Abdul Kalam

1. A strong leader develops an Action Plan:
It is a habit of a strong leader to develop an action plan and pass it on to his subordinates to achieve their goals. A strong leader has follow up sessions to meet short-term goals, and a perfect checklist to check off whether all the activities are as per the plan.

2. A strong leader takes Responsibility for His Decisions:
At times, when an organization has to undertake important decisions to cope up with rising critical situations, it looks for someone with strong leadership to handle this onerous task. Yes, a strong leader is solely responsible for any decision, keeping in mind the previous, present and future consequences. A strong leader empowers employees to make decisions within their responsibilities. A strong leader measures and rewards their results and not their activities.

3. A strong leader takes Responsibility for Communication:
Good communication in an organization is the X-factor of an organization's success. A strong leader takes responsibility for communication and successfully sharing the organization's vision to achieve short-term as well as long-term goals. They make the communications clear, concise and easy to understand. They think and say "WE" and not "I".

4. A strong leader focuses on Opportunities, NOT on Problems:
A strong leader allows employees to try and fail. He knows that their success relies on their Entrepreneurship. He/she always focuses on the opportunity rather worrying about the problem. They create new possibilities to solve problems. They believe in themselves.

Successful people . . .
1. Take the responsibility.
2. Think to resolve problems.
3. Sense opportunities.

4. Live for their dream.

5. Live in the present moment.

6. Do things they like the most.

7. Know what they want and how it shall be attained!

8. Spread happiness all around.

9. Motivate and inspire others.

10. Lead from the front.

About Yogi

Yogendrasing Girase is the Founder of Dreamers World Smart Solutions, LLP, a company specializing in the professional training and helping individuals in personal and business development. Yogendrasing Girase is an author, inspirational and motivational speaker, professional coach and entrepreneur. He believes in consistently providing impeccable service to his attendees. He conducts his workshop "DREAMERS WORLD" worldwide to guide youngsters to start their business early. Through his workshop, he speaks on topics like Fear, Procrastination, Power of the Subconscious Mind, Happiness, Leadership, Motivational Speaking and Positive Thinking. His company also focuses on the training essentials for adopting and manipulating Renewable Energy Sources like solar energy. Yogendrasing Girase is a graduate in Mechanical Engineering and has accomplished his Master's in Thermal Engineering.

Yogi is a true inspiration! He leads his life on his own standards and that motivates his loved ones and people around him to achieve pedestal positions. Personally and professionally, he sticks to his credo and doesn't let anyone or anything throw him off course. He lives life in the fast lane and everyone admires him for that. He started his coaching/training career at the age of 19, when he was just in his second year of college. He knows all the ups and down of a career. He started from nothing and has been able to convert his earnings into seven figures. Everyone admires his confidence as he can train anyone to crack the codes to success.

Yogi's Mission is to help anyone and everyone attain their highest potential and create and live the life of their dreams. He has a simple step-by-step action plan to build your dream. Through his seminars, he can assist you in making your dreams come true. He helps you to move forward to achieve your dream. He is passionate about encouraging individuals to start their businesses at the inception, so they can achieve financial freedom in the early stages of their lives. His personal philosophy involves attaining wealth in order to help others.

Yogi is an author of an upcoming book, *BUILD YOUR DREAM, NOT SOMEONE ELSE'S!* This book talks about how to achieve financial freedom in the early stages of your life. He has presold 1000 copies of this book.

Yogi has his own Academy, the PERFECT ACADEMY, where he has trained over 10,000 engineering students and thousands of other students since 2000. He has personal experience in coaching and training over 17 years in his own institution, PERFECT ACADEMY, a coaching institute which coaches technical subjects.

Yogi is an International Speaker, and has shared the stage with some top speakers like Gerry Robert and Jean-Guy Francoeur in Singapore.

CHAPTER 44

SUCCESS IS INEVITABLE

BY VELKO TUHCHIEV

Everything starts with YOU: who you are, and your identity!

When we are born, we start with no identity of our own. In early childhood and in the teenage years, 100% of our belief system is designed and based on the knowledge we have gained and adopted from our parents, other family members and teachers.

We accept these values, beliefs and "truths," rarely questioning them at that time. As we age, we begin expanding our social circle and have different friends. We often go through life defending the beliefs we had programmed in from the beginning, although some of the things stuck in our subconscious are ridiculous. But we tend to defend them passionately.

As we continue to grow and face different challenges and see many other models of behaviors, belief systems, and values, we often find conflicts. We can find new things that match more closely with our personalities, but conflict with our belief systems. We then find ourselves with identity crises.

These are good for us. It's a moment of truth and the real moment of personal growth that every human who wants to live truly free must go through. We can finally start questioning things with no fear. We realize we've been copying other people's behavior. We're trying to live our life based on social approval. It is when we start to explore new choices, lifestyles, friends, cultures and belief systems that we enter the new search for who we truly are.

An identity crisis could happen at almost any age. It's never too embarrassing or too late for us to take that journey. Ultimately this is our most important mission in life.

Think about it. Everything starts with loving yourself. All problems and limiting beliefs like "I'm not good enough," or lack of self-love, or the belief that life is dangerous – all these negative messages are false. They are stuck in our belief systems from years ago, maybe from parents, teachers, friends, or other people.

Very soon you would find that the opinions of others make no difference regarding the possibility of your success. It means nothing. Zero.

A great exercise: Write down all the things your parents, family members, and other people have said that you now think are wrong. What did they say about money? About love, relationships, and trust? What did they say about your creativity and your biggest strengths? What did they say about your weakest points? What did they say about your body?

Take your time. You will realize that you're now experiencing different feelings. Be aware of those feelings. Know that you now have the list of all beliefs that are making you "not good enough." Your job is to remove these false opinions from your mind.

Two things we need to take from this exercise: Don't blame your parents, your teachers, friends or family for where you are now. Love them for your reaching this very moment of self-awareness and growth. They have done the best they can with the best of intentions most of the time. But know you can change things now.

Also, think about the wild and unreasonable dreams you had as a child. You owe that child more one-on-one meetings. You can't afford to disappoint the five-year-old YOU anymore.

Think about it. How could you possibly love who you are if you've been pretending to be someone else until now? How could you love yourself if, until today, it was more important to protect your reputation than your integrity? You will always be "not good enough" if other people's opinion is more important than your own. Loving yourself is the first thing you must establish firmly on your road to success.

As you're exploring your real self, you can get caught up in endless searching for the next thing. Don't get stuck, if you do, you're not 100% honest with yourself. You might be good at many things, but you're a genius in only one. Two at the most.

The real trick is to locate those one or two things, after successfully establishing your strong belief system and core values. You must LOVE what you do . . . Every second of it.

Very few will reach the moment of finding their exact purpose. It is necessary to realize now what the process involves and to go through the steps to start living your life with your real purpose. It's your mission. Your very own journey. That's where everyone has to start. Who are you? Have you gone through with your "search for your true identity?" Do it now. Don't wait!

Finding yourself is critical. When you are not 100% genuine, you always pretend to be somebody else, someone that society would accept better and give more credit to faster. It's easy to think that way, but in reality, you can get much more if you're truly genuine and 100% your real self.

When you reach the moment of accepting who you are - you are going to stop being so worried about the results. The reason is very simple. The results are not the biggest challenge. The results are guaranteed. When you love your organization, your product, and the people who surround you, you possess the power of great attitude. Great Attitude is necessary and is a must for each and every day we live. Great attitude makes ALL the difference. And only with the enormous help of the broad view of life do we have the choice and readiness to take on a massive amount of action.

With our strong belief system, our great attitude and massive action, our results are always guaranteed. When you're not worried about the results, you can be 100% present in every moment and perform at the highest level.

Success is INEVITABLE! Wow, that sounds great, doesn't it? Do you believe it's possible? Great! Now that your belief system is in the right place I can start with revealing what makes success inevitable.

Well, it's simple! It's because you design it. You are the BOSS, the Captain, the King/Queen! You're calling all the shots, whether or not you are aware of it. . . Whether you like it or not. Until you realize you have the ultimate power to design your future and co-create everything you visualize, someone else will be planning the future for you, and I guarantee you're not going to like it. Do you know why? Simple again. It wouldn't be YOU!

If you can't say that you're free and you have total control in making the choices on how to spend your TIME (which is the largest and most valuable asset available to us), your project is missing something crucial.

If you're indifferent toward life and feel you have no control, it's only because of lack of understanding, knowledge, and beliefs. There is nothing embarrassing about this. People will get to this knowledge at different ages of their life or different moments of their life. It is fixable. When you understand your identity, and you know who you are, you know what your real purpose is and what is your pure genius.

When you clearly define yourself and your purpose, it's time to visualize and plan. Plan everything in detail. What do you want and why? What do you want to change? What do you want to achieve? And finally, what are you going to give in return for all this?

Here is the secret. You write it down to make it real and repeat writing it daily until you learn it. Keep writing it until you start meditating and praying over it. Keep writing it daily until you can accept it and feel that you fully deserve it. Then it becomes part of you. It finally looks logical and achievable! It's who you truly are. It is inevitable. You have found success; you can define it, and it's clear!

You know the algorithm now. You're free. You can now do anything you want. You don't need anyone else to define success because you have found your definition. What other people think is completely irrelevant at this point. You have moved to a state of confidence. You have a mission. You have many interesting and great things to complete. Some will criticize you. That's OK. It doesn't matter what they think because you are sure of who you are. And It feels good.

But to get to that level, you will need daily motivation.

What is motivation? What is your motivation? Is it an individual "aha moment," an eye opener. But you can't possibly have these big aha moments daily. So where does motivation come from? Is it external or internal?

Let's go over a few sources of pure, powerful motivation: The most common and the one that almost every human has experienced is "Fear of loss." Decisions are usually made fast to protect something or to prevent something from happening.

Another powerful motivator is "Hope of reward." When you're in a competitive environment, the only thing that drives you is promotions and getting ahead.
It gets real when you gain momentum, knowledge, and experience. Your primary motivation now is: you MUST do it, it's not a matter of choice, it's your obligation to do it. You simply have to do it.

Even when you're excellent at doing something, and you're very successful when you put yourself in that situation, when your motivation is "I have no choice but to do it," the magic fades a little bit. Something big is missing. The passion is not there anymore, and it becomes a daily must thing, and you might not love it fully because of the "I have to do it" factor. Some find that overwhelming and give up, but I believe this is just the hardest step of the process.

Don't get me wrong. Many great business people think this is the best source of motivation. Taking pride in the fact that "They MUST do it!" There is no other way - no plan B. It gives them a tremendous feeling of accomplishment. They don't even think about giving up. But if something unpredictable happens – these people will blame themselves first, take full responsibility for the losses, and experience a sense of guilt, which is a self-destructive feeling.

Taking responsibility is a necessary step to get to the ultimate motivation for real success. *The most powerful source of motivation comes after you connect who you truly are with what you do.*

Pure LOVE is driving you forward now. That is the ultimate source of motivation. You won't find a more powerful one. At this moment, when you're truly happy with everything, and you feel complete for the first time in your life, you will realize that you are part of something HUGE. . . something much bigger than you and your vision. Your focus will change, making a more significant difference will be your primary goal – helping as many others as possible. The time of your life will be dedicated to something bigger, much greater than yourself and what you can imagine. In helping others, you will find yourself doing things outside of your nature, things considered crazy by some. But you'll have the strongest power behind you – the power of love. You have this burning passion, and you're ready to pass it on.

All this is impossible without one primary ingredient. I'm talking about commitment. Commitment means 100%, not 99%. When you play at 100%, you make mistakes, but you learn from them. Because of these errors, you create your principles – your policies will build you up to a person of integrity.

Many people choose the path of loyalty, and they feel that loyalty is the guaranteed path to success. The last recession showed us with a bitter reminder that's not always the case. Many CEO's of companies were let go after 30 years of loyal service.

Integrity is the key. You can break some of your principles in the name of loyalty, but that will immediately hurt your integrity.

When you only follow your core values and your fundamental principles, every decision becomes automatic. You don't have to debate with yourself or struggle with decisions. Integrity is a characteristic that every great person who ever lived possesses. Your rules, your principles are your huge advantage.

You know who you are. You don't need to question it anymore. When you plan and visualize, it seems more realistic. The anxiety from the possible chance of failure disappears from your thoughts. You have found the right direction, and you're moving towards it. You constantly get confirmations and manifestations that you're on the right path, and you believe now. You believe in yourself, what you do, your product and the people who work with you.

But it wasn't always like that. At first, when you reach your major milestone, you feel it was a great luck. But the more and more you follow your principles, luck becomes a regular thing. As you keep going, you get used to success; you start to demand luck. It happened before, you know it's real, and you have a great feeling of gratitude.

You start to believe that you can have luck on your own. Your knowledge and experience allow you to predict and see the outcome of almost every situation and enable you to turn it into a great opportunity.

And the final stage of growth is when you realize that not only do you control your destiny and your path, but also your full potential. You understand that you set the limits – everything is real – this is your reality now.

Yes, success is a high. Success is sweet. Success makes you feel good and accomplished. But there is one necessary, inevitable thing you must be aware of before you take on that incredible journey.

You must get out of your comfort zone and do the things that are necessary to maintain your success. Committing to doing whatever it takes becomes natural. Staying in your comfort zone is the biggest enemy of success. You must be aware of that.

I want to end this with one of my favorite quotes from a relatively successful person, and I will add my conclusion under the quote.

> *Success is a lousy teacher; it seduces smart people*
> *into thinking they can't lose.*
> ~ Bill Gates, Microsoft

So always stay out of your comfort zone and keep learning. Never rely solely on your past achievements, success is something that happens in the present moment, not in the past.

- Don't get satisfied.
- Stay hungry.
- You can always do more.
- You are limitless.
- Protect your integrity at any cost.
- Stay in the right direction.

SUCCESS WILL BE INEVITABLE. YOU DESERVE SUCCESS.

About Velko

Velko Tuhchiev is a nationally-recognized sales teacher, a top producer in the automotive industry, a leader, a motivator, father and entrepreneur. Immersed in the sales industry, he has an intimate knowledge of the world of sales because he has sold and delivered nearly 3,000 automobiles, in his career as an automotive sales consultant, and has been able to achieve that success working only four days per week thanks to his repeat and referral clients.

Velko has been so successful with his methods that he has been able to shift his business to being appointment-only, all while building, sustaining, and growing a clientele list that is 95% comprised of repeats and referrals.

If you ask some of his clients, they all know him as the #ProfessionalProblemSolver. He is results-oriented with a vigorous and consistent record of achievements. He has keen insight into the needs and views of others, and is able to listen and identify issues or problem areas and form innovative solutions for individuals and business organizations.

Velko is known for his high level of self-confidence and outgoing personality.

His incredible success at the dealership was the reason he was invited to speak at several national sales conferences and share some of his innovative techniques and practical strategies for loyalty, retention, prospecting, and branding. Many of the teachers in the sales training world encouraged him to get out there and help the industry that needed a new and more relevant way of delivering world class customer service while increasing profit and productivity.

His teaching method is "Educational Selling" and he firmly believes in offering tremendous value to his clients by describing and demonstrating logical solutions to their problems.

Velko is always providing relevant information because he is still working with dealerships and businesses all over the USA and still actively selling. He believes the best method to teach is to SHOW, not just tell. Working with hundreds of companies and thousands of sales people, his goal is to help businesses to design easy-to-learn and to follow, reliable and efficient processes that guarantee the customer's remarkable experience.

Velko Tuhchiev, the Founder of Velko Sales Training, is focused on developing top producers in the Sales World. Interested in furthering his clients' sales goals and passing on the knowledge and techniques that will design the way to becoming a master at sales and an actual top producer. Championing a "pay-it-forward attitude" that's supported by unwavering gratitude, Velko will inspire any sales force onto incredible accomplishments. Velko's mastery of sales fundamentals, people skills, and drive to help others will empower any team to grow, produce higher gross profit, and attain new personal and professional achievements.

His courses are designed to focus on building enormous value. They will empower one to recognize buying styles, all while executing a high closing rate.

Contact information:
- Velko@VelkoSalesTraining.com
- VelkoSalesTraining.com
- VelkoAcademy.com
- VelkoUniversity.com
- Velko.co
- VelkoSoutions.com
- Facebook.com/VelkoSalesTraining
- Facebook.com/VelkoSuccess
- Twitter-@VelkoTuhchiev
- YouTube: Search for:
  - Velko Sales Training
  - Velko Testimonials
  - Velko Success
- Linkedin.com/in/VelkoTuhchiev
- Instagram:VELKOProfessionalProblemSolver

CHAPTER 45

millionairZ.club®
IT'S NOT WHAT YOU THINK

BY LARRY KOZIN

*The club that guides you to wealth through a spiritual journey
that leads to your personal and professional success.*

For many years my spiritual reservoir was tapped. I had more issues to sort out than what I thought was possible to address: PTSD from child abuse, depression, addiction, bankruptcy, failed marriages, jail and homelessness. I looked out at the world around me and felt that I was drowning in the depths of these tough obstacles. However, I did always understand that I wasn't the only one, and still had a seed of hope implanted within me that things could be different.

**There are so many people out there hurting and
looking for solutions.**

Something about the place known as "desolation" can lead many to be reckless and irresponsible. We try to find solutions in temporary stimulations or a quick fix that get us through the moment, but prove to be even more detrimental in the long run.

A lingering question remains... How do we get past the obstacles and onto the pathway of prosperity and freedom?

Where do we connect with the ideal mentors, who know exactly what we need to do to get on that path?

It's easy to make excuses and blame others, but the truth is:

There is no good or bad luck; it's our thoughts and actions that determine our outcome.

My journey has been tough at times and I've struggled because of the situations I created for myself. Therein lies the answer! It's the situations that we create for ourselves that take us to where we want to be. Why go down, when we are capable of going up? That is the inspiration that moves the millionairZ.club® forward and this is what I'm so excited to share with you. And regardless of where you are right now, I truly believe you'll be excited about where you have the potential to go!

GOING FROM "DOWN-AND-OUT" TO "UP-AND-IN-THE-KNOW"

In the grand scheme of things, what we may first view as a disaster or tragedy transforms into the best thing that could ever happen to us.

As a student of Kabbalah, I was asked by my Rabbi, "Larry, what was the worst thing that ever happened to you, and how did it turn out that it was the best thing?" A tough question that demanded serious contemplation. This is what I did know: the biggest tragedy in my life was the dysfunction that came from being abused as a child, which led to addiction and alcoholism. What I wondered was, with all those scars, *how could anything remotely positive stem from that?* After much thought, I came to this conclusion:

Instead of living as a victim, I looked at my childhood as the best thing that happened to me, since the pain and anguish I suffered set me on this spiritual path of healing, joy, and financial freedom.

Today, I have gone a great distance on, and continue to be on, this spiritual journey and living a way of life that is beyond my wildest dreams. How can this be? The answer is simple: through all the miserable times, I finally reached out for help and was blessed with mentors who had previously learned the Universal Principles to transform themselves and make it to the other side. Not only did they share this wisdom with me, but they lived their lives accordingly; and I wanted what they had, so I did what they did. The millionairZ.club® exemplifies and lays out the actions needed that will allow us to realize our dreams.

428

As we reach higher levels in the spiritual world, material things tend to flow freely toward us. It's hard to grasp this as a concept until it actually happens. It stems from us no longer being attached to them. Material items are not us, they are nice but they cannot define us—just accompany us.

In my life, I was broke for decades and didn't pay attention to the spiritual side of wealth at all. Once I began to focus on living spiritually, the rest began arriving. I didn't have to run toward it, because riches gravitated to me. It is a fascinating and wonderful journey and when it really hit home was when a huge goal that my wife and I had was realized: we were able to relocate and live in our dream villa in San Jose del Cabo, Mexico, located at the southernmost tip of the Baja Peninsula. Wow! And the best part:

> **Within six weeks of our move, we recognized that we could be happy with a taco, a toilet, a bed, and an appreciation for all that God blesses us with each day.**

In addition, we:
- Work less
- Relax more
- Enjoy life and family
- Create wealth for ourselves and other millionairZ.club members

When we attempt to force success through actions that are focused on money and results, we make things so much more challenging than they need to be. However, by investing our energy and thoughts into spiritual practices, in other words, what we can do for others, the Universe rewards us hundredfold.

PAY ATTENTION, OR YOU WILL MISS THE SIGNS.

Pray with your eyes open so you know what may be coming your way.

It was a hot day in Del Mar that summer of 1997. Sweltering, in fact, unless you were by the ocean—the breezes made it bearable then. Internally, I was experiencing so many ups and downs in business that my family was very concerned. My sons were even encouraging me to get a "real job." They just wanted me to be stable, and so did I, but I had no idea what stable was.

**Little did I know that I was on a road that would
change my entire thinking process, shifting from egoistic
materialism to a spiritual craving for enlightenment.**

Just a few years prior I was doing really well—not broke and feeling like I was finally achieving that place of wealth that I'd wanted so badly. I started a health insurance lead business that was flourishing and thought that I finally found my way. I didn't anticipate the sink hole that would appear before me, as the Clintons began to campaign about socialized medicine. What they promised (but never delivered) took everything away from me. My clients vanished, leaving me high and dry, and in need of a new source of income. Why didn't I have multiple sources of income, as I was previously taught?

I'd figured out how to make money from my health insurance business, and had a phone room setup and employees also counting on me to make money. So, I got back to research and development, keeping in mind the wise words that one of my mentors had shared with me:

> *Money is not the most important thing, but it is
> right up there with oxygen.*
> ~ Buck Steffens

I made some attempts at selling investment leads, alarm leads, and even carpet cleaning leads—with no success.

Eventually, through persistence, along with a new business partner and mentor, Arnie Katz, I found an opportunity that had phenomenal potential. Essentially, it was an Advanced Marketing System, specifically for the MLM Industry, an industry that had millions of potential clients operating home-based businesses. We had invented a way to produce higher quality prospects at a fraction of the cost of the competition. Instead of just leads we were now producing relationships!

The invention that we now call the millionairZ.club®

Wanting to go "bigger" with this great concept, I began making calls to corporate headquarters of Network Marketing companies, knowing that lead generation was fundamental to their businesses. The response was terrible at first, but finally, on the umpteenth call, I hit the jackpot and was immediately connected with the President of FutureNet, a new company that distributed WebTV (a new technology and hardware that Bill Gates had recently purchased). He saw the potential in what I was offering and invited me to their global headquarters in Valencia, California—right across the street from Magic Mountain. Could I find some magic there?

I prepared a powerful PowerPoint presentation and headed out on the four hour drive to their headquarters. When I finally arrived and walked into the office, I found that the tables were turned, as my prospect asked me, "If you will let me teach you the inner workings of Network Marketing and how to be a top earner, working part-time, and if it works, I only ask that you pass the knowledge back to as many people as possible, would you be interested?"

How could I refuse an offer that I could not refuse? "Yes, I am interested." and immediately signed up as a distributor. Instead of selling the leads/relationships, we were sharing them with our Team and became the Top Earners in the Company.

A NEW VISION . . . A NEW APPROACH

It should always be about helping others first, remembering that when you help others get what they want, you will get what you desire!

My new mentor opened my mind up to a way of marketing that was so different that it almost seemed impossible. I saw all these directions that it could go, mostly favorable. He gained an attentive audience in me and I was eager to learn more. In summary, I was at a crossroads and had two options:

- Creating never-ending streams of income from each and every relationship.

  Or

- Make a buck off each sale, and then repeat to make just another buck.

It was easy to see why I'd want my work to begin duplicating itself. *The Power of Leverage* was in play. That's where the gift of more free time and less effort to produce more comes in, keeping in mind that quality is never sacrificed throughout the process. My mentor really gave me some insight that I'd never received from other teachers in the past. This is the very reason that the most successful people have multiple mentors with different skills and abilities, in my opinion. He also left me with some golden wisdom:

Tell the truth 100% of the time and have a heart to help people.

My guru had been instrumental in changing hundreds of people's lives, and as a result he was well blessed. And through following his suggestions and working hard to implement what he taught me, success came my way, too. Instead of the peaks and valleys that had defined my life for decades, the chaos disappeared, replaced with serenity and peace of mind. I felt great, appreciated what I had, and saw life as the wonderful gift it was—something meant to be loved and enjoyed with people we care about. Now, I was ready to pass this wisdom on to others. The model I was taught, and that I now have and have used to create the lifestyle that is better than any dream I'd previously had, is now called the millionairZ.club®. It is a life changer, a mindset—a way to revolutionize your personal existence in this world through spiritual practices and a high level of commitment to everyone's success.

THE FIVE TENETS OF THE millionairZ.club®

Membership is open to any race, color, creed, sexual orientation, education, or bank account balance. Maximum benefits will be awarded to individuals pursuing life with honesty and goodwill to all.

With the millionairZ.club®, you don't focus on having a million-dollar net worth (although its practitioners certainly can—and do—have one). It is about creating a lifestyle beyond our wildest dreams!

As our minds evolve spiritually, we begin realizing that life can change instantly for anybody that makes the conscious choice to live and think differently than the masses.

The main thing that you should understand about the millionairZ.club®, is that it is not a traditional organization. You won't find rules, fees, or hierarchal structures. It is simply a lifestyle and marketing system that helps you build teams of people who want more from their lives, following the Universal Principles.

The five basic tenets that, when practiced, are your pathway to prosperity and include:

I. The purpose of our existence on this planet is to experience all of the blessings bestowed upon us from a Higher Power and share with others these Principles that lead to happiness, joy, serenity, and wealth.

II. We will use our worst life experiences as a ladder to gain higher levels of spiritual growth, never stopping the fight or succumbing to the urge to quit. We are never victims, but control our destiny through thought and action.

III. Continually practicing generosity, loyalty, kindness, and honesty, and maintaining a millionairZ.club mindset.

IV. Having 100% faith that everything works out EXACTLY as it is supposed to, even though it may seem harsh at times or is not what we outwardly desire.

V. Embracing that our lifetime goal is to learn and grow every day, staying open-minded and being dedicated to concern for others' well-being, while also being grateful and appreciative to a Higher Power for all that has been bestowed upon us.

Without a doubt, rejection and failure are challenging to overcome, and the golden roads of success are littered with people that suffered adversity and surrendered to working for others. But is this rewarding? Does this offer opportunity to give back? Those are the questions you must ponder. In the millionairZ.club®, it is the encompassing of more than just money, because the quality of life, peace of mind and freedom is really what we are seeking.

About Larry

Larry Kozin is passionate about his love of family, business and helping others succeed. He is the Founder and CEO of NewEconomyMarketingGroup, Inc., a holding company that is devoted to practicing the principles of the millionairZ.club®. Holdings include many other companies he founded, including iDealFurniture, with over 100 locations, PerfectDreamer SleepShops, BigTicketBroker, KozyFurniture, BTBfurniture.com, MemoryZzz.com and many others in different stages of development. Through these involvements and putting his life experiences and skills into practical application, Larry has built sales teams in the thousands in multiple organizations. He also currently serves as CEO of the Furniture Chamber of Commerce.

Previously, Larry founded the National Chamber of Commerce and Federal Chamber of Commerce. He also founded the MainStreetChamber of Commerce in 2006, serving as CEO until its sale in 2014, after establishing over 150 chapters. He also has owned and/or operated over 250 mattress and furniture stores, while his ex-wife and son continue to operate the original furniture business out of the same residence in San Juan Capistrano, California since 1982.

Today, Larry is excited to keep broadening his horizons and growing through helping others. Showing individuals how you can blend spirituality with business ownership and create multiple streams of income with better results in less time is the foundation of much of his work—as well as what allows him to be involved in so many opportunities. He is also a co-author for the upcoming book, *Cracking the Code to Success*, with renowned author and sales expert Brian Tracy.

Due to the circumstances in his childhood, one cause that Larry is very active in promoting and supporting is Prevent Child Abuse (PreventChildAbuse.org), an organization that helps individuals look for the signs of child abuse and then learn how to speak out. Spreading awareness about this important topic is necessary, and lessening the taboos of discussing and acknowledging its existence is fundamental for helping children today...and in the future.

Larry lives in Los Cabos, Mexico, with his amazing wife Angie and their beloved gato, Kozy! He's eternally grateful for his family, including his father, Dr. Frank Kozin, who taught him to "work hard every day and your problems will all work out." At this time, Dr. Kozin is still practicing Optometry at the age of 81! Larry's mother, Suzanne, is actively living life to its fullest in Las Vegas. Larry is both proud and inspired by his sons David and Daniel, who are both successful entrepreneurs on their own, and he's looking forward to a brand new chapter in life as a brand new grandparent to Stella Kozin.

Contact Larry at:

- LK@millionairZclub.com or call him at: (702) 622-7051
- LinkedIn: https://www.linkedin.com/in/LarryKozin
- Twitter: https://twitter.com/millionairZclub
- www.millionairZ.club

CHAPTER 46

CREATING GOOD HABITS
KEYS TO SUCCESS

BY MATT DANE

Picture this. It's Friday afternoon. You've been super busy with work but you have to get ready to go to the airport. You're going to visit your in-laws for the weekend and to attend a big, fancy event on the scale of a wedding. You don't have a ton of time to pack so you quickly throw a bunch of stuff into the suit case at the last minute and head out. An easy flight later, and you're there, and now it's non-stop family time from that second on. Next thing you know, it's Saturday afternoon and everyone is getting ready for the event. You start to change into your suit (or maybe it's a dress in your case) and suddenly your heart is in your throat - you can't even button it. It just doesn't fit! And it's the only dressy outfit you brought. You know that you haven't been working out as much as you should, you've been loose on your diet, but for crying out loud, this IS your fat suit!

I still remember starting to sweat. How frustrated, embarrassed, and just deeply uncomfortable I felt. That's when I reached my breaking point – for the second time in my life.

Oh yeah, and get this – I own a personal training company. In fact, it's one of the biggest in the U.S. So I know perfectly well how to work out and I know how to eat correctly… But still, I wasn't.

Ok, let's take a step back. I'm not your average fitness guy who was born with abs. I was overweight as a kid, (in fact, I weighed 227 lbs. at age

15), and I just wasn't comfortable in my own skin. I HATED having to take my shirt off in public so much that I even wore it in the swimming pool – like THAT hid my belly... Anyway, over the next several years of hard work and discipline (and countless hours reading magazines and books about working out and nutrition), I had built a habit of working out and eating correctly. I went from a soft 227 lbs. to a strong, fit 168 at my peak in college.

But there I was, nonetheless standing in that bathroom sweating bullets...

"How did I get here?" I wondered. Well, when I got started working out originally, I had massive motivation to get into shape. Specifically, I was a teenage boy that wanted the attention of teenage girls – I wanted to look good. I realized that people out there had learned how to change their body so I decided that if they could do it, why couldn't I? At first my focus on the pain of not feeling good about the way I looked and the expected pleasure of getting into shape got me into the gym day after day, but eventually I actually really enjoyed the feeling I got from working out – the stress release, the runners high, "the pump," the endorphins, etc. It became addicting, in a good way. I would actually crave it. And every day that went by I felt that I gained a little more momentum. After a few months of work, I got to the point where I didn't want to miss a day because I didn't want to waste all of the time and effort that I'd put in already. Eventually it just became a central piece of my life, and I loved it.

Flash forward 15 years and life had moved on. Priorities shifted. I was now in a serious relationship, so my previous motivation was no longer really driving me as my girlfriend became my wife. I had started a business which had taken the primary focus in my life. I was setting up training departments in gyms across the country which required extensive travel and very long hours. I wasn't able to be in any single location for too long, so I had to make sure I maximized my time at each gym, hence sacrificing my daily exercise program. I also wanted to lead by example. Our business mission was to change people's lives – not to workout ourselves. That was my misguided mindset at that time at least. "If my team is working so hard to build the business right now, I should be too and not take personal time away from the business to work out." As the business grew, the more I had on my plate and the more my stress increased. Since I wasn't working out anymore, I didn't really have a release valve, so as an escape I started eating worse and worse and enjoying the craft beer scene in my Chicago neighborhood. Days turned into months and the next thing I know, I'm at the doctor's office weighing in at 43 pounds over my comfortable max weight of 185 wondering – "How did I get here…"

I wish I could tell you that since I know so much about working out and eating well that I lost all the weight super-fast and lived happily ever after. The reality was that for months and months I struggled to get started again. I kept telling myself, "look, next Monday it's on! Super low carb diet, workout two times a day…" And there were a number of Mondays that I did exactly that. And a few less Tuesdays and not quite as many Wednesdays. Then I was back to putting it off another week, and so on… Why so many false starts? Why couldn't I just flip that switch again and get back into the routine?

Before we can answer that fully, let's look at the anatomy of a habit (which I didn't yet fully understand while I was trying to button that suit…). Here's a summary of the 4 key points:

1. Cue/trigger - This is the birth of every habit, and typically starts with an internal itch that needs to be scratched. For this to turn from a one-time event into a habit however, we need to find a reminder of some kind that can occur regularly enough to trigger the craving for the below reward.
2. Action/routine. This is the habit itself that you are trying to create. It always starts as a singular action, and the goal is to turn it into a routine. What does that action look like? In my case it was working out consistently. Two key details about success on this point:
   a) Motivation must be high enough to take the action, and
   b) Action must be easy enough to be willing to do.
3. Reward. This is the payoff for the action that we took that reinforces the behavior and help it turn into a habit. *Note: Immediate rewards are best.*
4. Investment. The more time, money, etc. that we have invested in something the harder it is to walk away from.

Ok, now let's dissect how I originally built the habit:

1. My initial trigger was pretty simple—look good/feel good to get attention from girls. But over time, since I was working out after school everyday, when the school day ended I started to picture and crave that good post workout feeling.
2. My motivation was high enough to easily push me through the difficulty of learning how to work out and eat correctly as well as actually following through and doing it.
3. The reward here started off by focusing on the "some day" of achieving my results, but quickly turned into the actual short term feeling you get from working out.
4. The investment of my time and effort helped me to build momentum that worked for me – "I've worked my butt off all week, I'm not going to blow it by over-indulging in junk food tonight!"

Ok, now how did it fail?

1. Both of my triggers started to change. I was no longer driven by "being single" and I started to make myself feel guilty for working out, so it was no longer a "feel good" reward in the short term.
2. Action – my motivation had waned. I mainly kept working out as long as I did because it was a habit.
3. Reward – I used to feel good afterwards, but now I had some new associations to work out such as not being a good leader and not maximizing my time. This led to anxiety and inner conflict which now caused pain.
4. Investment – the shift in trigger and reward was enough to undermine all the investment that I had made. Habit broken.

How did I finally re-establish the habit?

Well, I actually stumbled onto the solution by accident. I have since studied the psychology behind it, but I didn't understand this then. While my priorities had indeed shifted, I realized that I still really didn't like being overweight. I knew I wanted to make a change and what I was doing wasn't working. I eventually shifted my perspective from jumping right back in at 100 miles an hour and working out like a man possessed, to taking baby steps. I simply made the following commitment: I will show up and walk on a treadmill for 8-10 minutes no less than 4 days per week. That was it. If I felt good and wanted to workout after that then great, but no promises.

I proceeded to lose 30 of the 40 lbs. in the next 9 months.

Wait, what's going on here?

First off, admittedly, I didn't stop at walking on the treadmill very often. But that small, easy commitment finally got me in the door day-after-day again, and gave me something to build on.

Let's break it down:

1) What was my trigger? Similar to the original one, I admitted to myself that I still want to be in shape and hated feeling overweight. Plus, the stress and anxiety from work was a new trigger to workout. These emotions may not always be at the forefront of our thought however, so it is best to create some additional triggers to make sure that the behavior is done regularly. For me in this case, I worked out at the same time every day. Wakeup, coffee, workout. The routine became unconscious and I began to crave the reward of feeling good after a workout again.

2) Action – Since this was still not the number 1 priority in my life, it's safe to say that my motivation wasn't as high as it was the first time. The key here was that I finally figured out how to lower the difficulty of the action. The motivation only needs to be high enough to generate the action – and my motivation was plenty high enough to walk on a treadmill. Also, I had to change my associations and admit to myself that I SHOULD be working out and had no reason to feel guilty about it.

3) Reward – I feel that the reward structure most people use for working out doesn't help them make it a habit. Remember, short term rewards are best. The best way to make this a habit is to find a way to enjoy the process so that it becomes a reward in itself. The second-best way is to find something else that you can reward yourself with after taking the action that doesn't hinder your goals. For example, letting yourself binge on ice-cream after your workout (called morale licensing), while common, is very counterproductive to your goals. A better choice may be rewarding yourself by having movie night, or a social gathering with friends (that isn't calorie

related). Personally, I feel better after working out and that is the short term reward I need to keep doing it. . . and eventually the long-term rewards.

4) Investment – It's taken months and months of my life to get back to where I am. I never want to have to start over again.

From my experience, you will be most effective at building new habits when focusing on just one at a time. More than one will test your will power and motivation and the goal is to put success on auto-pilot. So join me in accepting the challenge of never-ending improvement. What habit are you going to start with?

You will never change your life until you change something you do daily. The secret of your success is found in your daily routine.
~ John C. Maxwell

About Matt

Matt Dane is the Founder of Compel Fitness and one of the nation's leading experts in the business of fitness. Despite graduating college with tens of thousands of dollars in student loan and credit card debt and no money in the bank, he was able to build a multi-million-dollar national fitness empire without taking a dime from outside investors. He has directly and indirectly touched the lives of hundreds of thousands of people. His businesses have gotten dramatic results for their clients and built "dream" career opportunities for his team members where the right people get to make life-changing money while actually "doing good" in their communities.

Matt feels that it is truly his calling in life to help people change their lives for the better, and he has an uncanny knack for being able to do so. He helps people to see what is truly possible for themselves by helping them to see past their "stories" as to why they can't accomplish something. Then he is able to break down the situation, create an appropriate strategy and then deliver it in a way so that people feel compelled to take action.

Matt graduated from Ohio State University with a B.S. in Psychology. He has since started, built and manages three companies that work with some of the largest gym chains in the world and currently employ over 120 people. His goal in the coming years is to help develop more entrepreneurs than anyone in the fitness industry.

Matt was recently featured in *USA Today* as one of their "GameChangers."

Matt was born and raised in Cincinnati, Ohio and now lives with his wife and son in Cleveland, Ohio. He is a rabid sports fan and roots for the Ohio State Buckeyes, the Cincinnati Bengals, the Cincinnati Reds and the Cleveland Cavaliers.

You can connect with Matt at:
- mdane@compelfitness.com
- www.compelfitness.com
- www.facebook.com/compelfitness

CHAPTER 47

THE MAKING OF A SUCCESSFUL VENTURE
EFFECTIVELY MARKETING CIGARS IN ASIA

BY HANS RIJFKOGEL

How we choose to focus our efforts will create a
direct correlation to the results we receive.

My journey to end up being one of a few qualified marketers for premium cigars in the Asian market has been filled with adventure, opportunity, and the ability to see the rewards that come along with serving people products they seek. Back when I went to university to focus on economics and marketing, I didn't have the cigar market in mind, but after graduation and through the course of my career, that is what I decided to do and it was meant to be. Starting out working in the export department of a food company, I got my first taste of international business and living in another European country. After working in exports for a period of time, I became responsible for the UK sales and lived in Southport, England for five years. Eventually, work took me back home to the Netherlands and I found a new opportunity awaiting for me to work in exports, in a fascinating market with a unique culture—the luxury cigar market.

Before long, I was visiting customers in many amazing places throughout the world, including Asia. I found a culture and a way of life that deeply resonated with me. The company I worked at that time, Agio Cigars, was wonderful, and they gave me the opportunity to live in Singapore for four years. When my job called for me to move back to the Netherlands, I did, but my heart never really left Asia. That's when I knew that it was time to take the expertise I had in cigars and start my own business in Taiwan. My business, Asia Marketing Services (AMS) gave me an opportunity to return to Asia and market and promote cigars in one of the most beautiful places in the world. By putting my thoughts into actions, I created an opportunity where I don't look back, because every day has an opportunity to move forward.

Some people ask me why I chose the cigar industry. After all, the tobacco industry is a challenging one worldwide, with plenty of opinions about it, which means you need to have a healthy amount of resilience and sometimes you need a thick skin. Yet, it is also a thriving industry, and that is because people are drawn to luxury brands for their social settings and indulgent moments. The cigars that I market and promote fall into that category.

Cigars are a wonderful product to work with and they give you access to some of the nicest people in the industry who, in turn, create a genuinely great environment to be a part of. I am someone who finds joy and inspiration in the moments where I get to see someone enjoying a fine cigar. They appreciate it and it's a moment that is as wonderful as it often is anticipated. However, it takes more than enjoyment to succeed. A great deal goes into understanding the products in my market, as well as selecting the best channels of distribution that are effective for clients and developing an effective promotional plan.

FINDING THE RIGHT BRANDS TO MARKET

Successful marketing is targeted and specific;
you don't try to be all things to all people.

Not everyone who has a product should feel they need to market it everywhere. Likewise, not everyone who knows how to market should take on all products that fit into their specific niche. In my case, cigars. I'm one of a small number of businesses in my position in Asia, and it takes some insight into what products fit into a market. Based on these insights and a thorough market analysis, we determine what is necessary to market these products effectively.

Here are three criteria that I have established to help create the partnerships that will allow me to have what is necessary to market a cigar brand:

1. The company must be well-established.

Established companies with an international audience have the experience and resources to keep up with the demands that will take place after a company such as mine markets their product. This is why AMS doesn't work with brands just entering the market. If demand for the product rises quickly, or regulations change, there may not be a way to keep up with that demand. Increasing output or developing country specific packaging takes time and when distributors and duty-free operators are ready to market a product, they expect quick response times and need products that are ready to go to market on a larger scale.

2. The brand should be well known.

A well known brand of cigars is likely to already have a positive reputation in place. Marketing cigars properly doesn't evolve around rebranding the product. For example, if you already have a wide audience of aficionados in North America or Europe, it will lift your chance of success in the Asian market. If the product is not well known it needs to start with a focus on selected target markets. From there, with the right plan in place, the brand's popularity can grow internationally.

3. Cigar businesses must have a desire to invest in the Asian market.

The brands that I market for are involved in promoting their business to existing and potential clients. This means investing in marketing and making trips to Asia to attend events that are targeted toward their brand's increased recognition as premium cigars. Through participating in exhibitions and visiting customers on a regular basis, we keep our market information up-to-date and create a better understanding of customer and market needs.

AMS is not meant to be the resource for all cigar brands who want to expand their markets. I've been able to focus on offering premier services to elite brands, which include: Royal Agio Cigars, Swisher, and Drew Estate. All three companies meet the above criteria. My future goals with AMS are to work with world-class brands that can benefit from my passion and expertise of the Asian market.

REMAINING AT PEAK PERFORMANCE FOR THE CLIENTS I SERVE

Investing in personal growth will always be necessary to better serve clients, not to mention enjoy life more fully, as well.

Our lives are the sum of the choices we have made. When you invest in personal development, you take responsibility for your life, your circumstances, and your happiness. A great step can be as simple as reading ten pages of a good personal development or business book each day. It would take you ten to fifteen minutes per day and by the end of the year you would have read fifteen to twenty books. Reading just a little bit, on a regular basis, can change your life.

There are five guidelines that I always keep in mind in my life and business and I hope that they are evident in my work and in the decisions I make every day:

1. **You must be passionate about what you do.**
   When we have a choice on what to do, we should choose to give our energy to something that inspires us in some way and gives us the drive for enjoying the hard work that leads to success. I think that it is important to take on challenges that you are passionate about and really believe in. For me, having the pleasure of meeting so many diverse and interesting people from around the world that all have a passion for cigars is very enjoyable and exciting.

2. **Create a plan and follow it.**
   Focusing our efforts on specific tasks and steps that will take us toward the success we've targeted is important. Through planning your work and working your plan, you will boost your chances of success in life and business.

3. **Be a person of action.**
   It's through action that we can find and create our recipe for success. Practice doing things rather than thinking about them. Ideas alone don't bring success. Yes, they are important, but they are only

valuable after they've been implemented. One average idea that's been put into action is more valuable than a dozen brilliant ideas that you're saving for "some other day" or the "right opportunity." If you have an idea you really believe in, do something about it. Unless you take action it will never go anywhere.

4. Be honest and show integrity.

I feel that honesty and integrity should always be two important pillars in life and business. There should be no exceptions to honesty and integrity, either. It is a state of mind and does not depend on the situation. If you compromise your integrity in certain small situations with little consequence, then it becomes very easy to compromise in other situations. In my life and in my work, this means taking things one-step at the time and doing the right thing because it is the right thing to do.

5. Never stop learning.

When you enjoy something, learning more about it is almost like a thirst that cannot be satisfied. It's fun and exciting and you can take pieces of what you've learned to make your life better, or to serve others better as the professional in your field that you strive to be noted as. It's great, and when you are a business owner you have to invest in business development, whether it's training, reading, seminars, etc. For me, embracing this part of my life gives me the fuel and determination to give each day my best.

TODAY'S ACTIVITIES BUILD TOMORROW'S BUSINESS

All of our actions do matter in our pursuit of the success we envision.

Through focusing on what we are meant to do and then doing it the best we can, we will create a process that gives us both professional success and personal fulfillment. Growth that falls within the parameters you've set for success feels great and knowing that you understand how your business should be run saves many mistakes and unnecessary problems. That's why it's exciting for me to connect with cigar producers who truly can benefit from the marketing services that AMS specializes in. They know that once we begin working together that they have a partner who is committed to their success. Through this, a partnership is established, which is the basis of a great co-operation.

About Hans

As an expert and enthusiast in Asia's cigar market, Hans Rijfkogel founded Asia Marketing Services (AMS) in 2013. AMS is a premium services company that markets and promotes tobacco products in Asia. Through Hans' involvement directly with duty-free operators and reputable distributors throughout Asia, he currently handles the sales and marketing in Asia for Agio Cigars, Swisher Cigars, and Drew Estate Cigars. The markets that he serves include China, Hong Kong, Macau, Taiwan, Japan, Korea, Singapore, Malaysia, Thailand, Cambodia, Indonesia, Philippines, Vietnam, India, Sri Lanka, Australia, and New Zealand.

Prior to founding AMS, Hans worked as an Export Manager for Royal Agio Cigars for seventeen years. Due to his knowledge of the products and his network in Asia, Agio Cigars became the first company he represented after he started this company. In 2015, Hans added Swisher and Drew Estate to his portfolio of quality products.

After obtaining his degree in Marketing and Economics, Hans was immediately drawn to international business. He also has a keen interest in other cultures and languages.

With a thriving life that is constantly adjusting to keep up with economic changes and regulations of the industry he is so passionate about, Hans continues to create excellence in his business through his own reputation in the industry, as well as that of the products he offers. He can also add Best Selling Author to his credentials, as he is a co-author with renowned sales expert and author Brian Tracy in the book *Cracking the Code to Success*.

Hans was born in The Netherlands and makes his home in Taiwan today, where he likes to play golf when not traveling for work, as it is another passion of his. He also is a football fanatic whose favorite team is Ajax.

You can connect with Hans via:
- WEBSITE: http://asiamarketingservices.com
- FACEBOOK: https://www.facebook.com/hans.rijfkogel.1
- LINKEDIN: https://www.linkedin.com/in/rijfkogel